The Polish Underground
1939–1947

———◦((•))◦———

Campaign Chronicles

Campaign Chronicles

The Polish Underground
1939–1947

David G. Williamson

Campaign Chronicles
Series Editor
Christopher Summerville

Pen & Sword
MILITARY

To Antonia and Sam

First published in Great Britain in 2012 by
Pen & Sword Military
an imprint of
Pen & Sword Books Ltd
47 Church Street
Barnsley
South Yorkshire S70 2AS

ISBN 978-1-84884-281-6

A CIP catalogue record for this book is
available from the British Library.

Typeset in Sabon 10.5/12.5pt by
Concept, Huddersfield

Printed and bound in England by
CPI Group (UK) Ltd, Croydon, CRO 4YY

Pen & Sword Books Ltd incorporates the Imprints of Pen & Sword Aviation,
Pen & Sword Family History, Pen & Sword Maritime, Pen & Sword
Military, Pen & Sword Discovery, Wharncliffe Local History, Wharncliffe
True Crime, Wharncliffe Transport, Pen & Sword Select, Pen & Sword
Military Classics, Leo Cooper, The Praetorian Press, Remember When,
Seaforth Publishing and Frontline Publishing.

For a complete list of Pen & Sword titles please contact
PEN & SWORD BOOKS LIMITED
47 Church Street, Barnsley, South Yorkshire, S70 2AS, England
E-mail: enquiries@pen-and-sword.co.uk
Website: www.pen-and-sword.co.uk

Contents

The Polish Underground 1939–1947

Contents

The Polish Underground 1939–1947

Maps and Plates

Maps

Plates

The Polish Underground 1939–1947

Maps

MAP 1: PRE-WAR POLAND AND ITS PROVINCES

BALTIC SEA

LITHUANIA

Kowno ⊚

⊚ Słupsk GDAŃSK ⊚ Królewiec/Königsberg/ Kaliningrad/

⊚ WILNO VILNIUS

⊛Koszalin

⊚Elbląg EAST

Suwałki ○

WEST POMORZE PRUSSIA

Lida ⊚ Niemen ⊚ Mińsk

PRUSSIA ○Chojnice

⊚ Olsztyn Ełk ○ Grodno⊚

NOWOGRÓDEK ⊚

Grudziądz ⊚

U
S
S
R

Piła ⊛ ○Chełmno TORUŃ

Narew

Bydgoszcz ⊚

Ciechanów ○ Łomża ⊚ BIAŁYSTOK Baranowicze ⊚

Inowrocław ⊚

Gniezno ⊚ Płock ○ Bug

POLESIE

Włocławek ⊚ Wisła

POZNAŃ Kutno ⊚

BRZEŚĆ ⊚LITEWSKI ⊚ Pinsk

WARSZAWA ⊚ Siedlce

○Leszno Kalisz ⊚

Grójec○

ŁÓDŹ

WROCŁAW Piotrków Tryb. ○Radom LUBLIN Kowel ⊚

KIELCE Wisła

Chełm WOŁYŃ

SILESIA Sandomierz⊚ Zamość ŁUCK⊚ Równe ⊚

ŚLĄSK KATOWICE Wisła

Brody○

KRAKÓW Tarnów ⊚ Rzeszów ⊚ ⊚ Jarosław LWÓW⊚

TARNOPOL

Cieszyn ⊚ Jasło○ Przemyśl ○

Nowy Sącz ○ Dniestr

Stryj ○

STANISŁAWÓW ⊚

CZECHOSLOVAKIA

—— National boundary

------ Provincial boundary

⊚ Provincial capital

xi

The Polish Underground 1939–1947

MAP 2: OCCUPIED POLAND

Maps

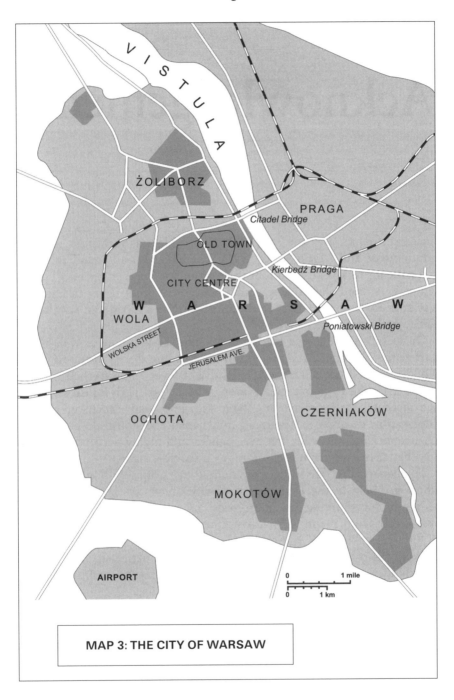

MAP 3: THE CITY OF WARSAW

Acknowledgements

Sincerest thanks are due to Jan Brodzki, Hanna Skrzyńska, Halina Serafinowicz and Maria Karczewska-Schejbal, who all found the time and patience to talk to me about their traumatic experiences in occupied Warsaw. At the Polish Underground Movement Study Trust in Ealing, I was treated with the greatest of consideration and offered invaluable advice and assistance.

Dr Suchitz at the Polish Institute and Sikorski Museum, as well as the staff at the National Archives and in the Reading Room of the Imperial War Museum were unfailingly helpful whenever I approached them. I would also like to thank Ewa Haren, who helped with Polish spellings and accents, and Sebastian Bojemski, who had much invaluable information to impart. Above all my thanks and gratitude are due to Christopher Summerville, my ever patient and highly perceptive editor, who has saved me from making many a careless error.

Thanks are also due to the copyright owners of the following papers, which are held in the Department of Documents in the Imperial War Museum, for granting me permission to quote in some cases quite extensively from them: S.H. Lloyd-Lyne, G. Manners, Z.R. Pomorski, R. Smorczewski and R.K. Stankiewicz.

Every effort has been made to trace and obtain permission from copyright holders of material quoted or illustrations reproduced.

Background

⊸•《(•)》•⊸

In December 1942 Lord Selborne (Minister for Economic Warfare with responsibility for special operations in German-occupied Europe) observed that the Poles alone, amongst the subjugated European nations, had the 'glory' of never producing a 'Quisling'. This was partly because the Germans made no secret of their ultimate intention to eliminate Poland from the map of Europe and to condemn the Poles to perpetual slavery. There was, therefore, little room for political collaboration. But in Poland there was also a powerful and romantic tradition of revolt, which particularly inspired the intellectuals and officer class. For some 200 years, from the 16th to 18th century, Poland had been a great power but then, as a result of internal political instability, she had been partitioned between Austria, Russia and Prussia in 1795, and then again in 1815, at the end of the Napoleonic Wars. The history of the various revolts and conspiracies (1794, 1830 and 1863) against the occupying powers was well known to every Polish school child. Collectively, these uprisings contributed to a heroic interpretation of the martyrdom of Poland – the Christ among nations – destined to rise again and liberate the European peoples from bondage.

In 1918 – with the simultaneous disintegration of the Austro-Hungarian Empire, the defeat of Germany and paralysis of Russia caused by the Bolshevik revolution and subsequent civil war – the Polish state re-emerged. In the west, her frontiers were fixed by the Treaty of Versailles but in the east, due to the absence of Russia from the peace conference, there was no accepted settlement. It was only the defeat of the Red Army by Polish troops in September 1920 that led to the Treaty of Riga, which awarded Poland considerable territory in Byelorussia and the Ukraine. Poland was indeed resurrected but her very existence depended on the continuing weakness of her two great neighbours, Germany and the USSR. Once these states recovered their economic and military power, unless backed decisively by the Western powers, Poland faced the threat of yet another partition.

Poland: a Fragile State

The new Poland was essentially a fragile structure. It was largely a peasant state with only a small industrial base. It was divided ethnically and thus politically unstable. According to the census of 1931, the Poles composed only 69% of the population while, in the eastern territories, they were in a minority compared to the Ukrainians and Byelorussians. There were also 3 million Jews, many of whom were unassimilated.

Political crisis followed political crisis until Józef Piłsudski – the first Polish head of state and hero of the Polish–Russian war of 1919–1920 – seized power in the coup of May 1926. While he managed to stabilize the situation and build up Poland's armed forces, the coup was deeply resented by the democratic parties. On his death in 1935, power passed to the Colonels, who increasingly ruled in a more authoritarian manner, and politics degenerated into a cycle of protest and repression.

Hitler's seizure of power in 1933 dramatically changed the European balance of power. Piłsudski – who believed that Poland had to pursue a policy of equilibrium between the USSR and Germany – signed a non-aggression pact with Nazi Germany in 1934. Initially, the Polish Government attempted to exploit the growing tension between Germany and the former Entente powers, Britain and France, to strengthen Poland's position in Eastern Europe; but by the early spring of 1939 it was clear that, without agreeing to the return of Danzig (Gdańsk) to the German Reich and becoming, in effect, a German satellite, there was little prospect of a German-Polish détente.

After Hitler's annexation of Moravia and Bohemia in March 1939, Poland's position was, on paper at least, enormously strengthened by the British guarantee, which was underwritten by the French: in the event of a German attack, both states would come to Poland's rescue. To make this guarantee effective, Soviet assistance was needed, but Poland's objection to the passage of Russian troops across its territory rendered any military pact between the USSR and the Western powers hard to achieve. Ultimately, however, Stalin's decision to sign a non-aggression pact with Germany on 24 August, which contained a secret protocol outlining the division of Poland between the USSR and Germany, cleared the

Background

way for the German invasion of 1 September and the Soviet invasion of 17 September.

In the event of war with Germany, the Poles decided that the bulk of their forces should be positioned along the western frontier, so that the ensuing fighting would trigger the Anglo-French guarantee. The Polish General Staff hoped to delay Hitler's advance long enough for the mobilization of Polish reserves, and for the French to launch a full-scale attack in the west.

Planning Guerrilla Warfare

To the Polish General Staff it was inevitable that a large part of Poland would, at least temporarily, be occupied by the Germans. Consequently with encouragement from London, plans had been drawn up for partisan activity behind German lines. The Poles had a formidable number of paramilitary leagues operating throughout Poland. Altogether there were some thirty-six of these leagues, which consisted of such diverse groups as the League of Reserve Officers, the League of Young Pioneers, the League of Blind ex-Servicemen, and the Participators in National Rebellions. Added to these were numerous regional groups, such as the League of Upper Silesian Rebels and the League of Rebels and Warriors in Poznań. All these were united in their passionate desire to defend Poland.

In April 1939, in great secrecy and urgency, Major Charasjkiewicz [spelling as per contemporary British report], of the II Bureau of the Polish General Staff, which dealt with Intelligence, began to plan organizations for partisan and guerrilla warfare. He took the decision to set up, on a regional basis, a number of small groups consisting of three to seven people, which were to become the typical Underground 'cell' of the future. As he explained to the War Office in July, the personnel would come from five different groups:

1. Men from fifty to seventy years old.
2. Invalids and cripples and such like, unfit for military service.
3. Women.
4. Youths and children.
5. Certain men of military service who are specially selected for their duties.

[NA, HS4/195]

Each patrol would have a commander, who 'does not, in peace time, know the other people in it, but by certain code words and by symbols the

3

personnel make themselves known to each other on the outbreak of war . . .' In each region, the number of patrols was to vary from between a minimum of seven and a maximum of twenty-five. The key, however, was that the organization was 'elastic' and capable of changing to meet varying circumstances. Seven schools had been set up to train saboteurs. Six of them trained ten men a week in methods and tactics, while the central school, which changed its location frequently, was able to train as many as thirty a week. A recruiting bureau was set up, composed of men 'of outstanding personality', whose duty it was to find suitable personnel for the patrols. These men had been prominent in fermenting various anti-German activities in Silesia, Danzig, the Corridor and elsewhere; in the event of a German occupation, they would be withdrawn behind Polish lines. By July, about 800 men had been recruited and trained.

In each sector, several camouflaged dumps of explosives, arms and devices were set up. An important component was the 'defensive grenade', which broke into small particles with a 'very short range so that the thrower himself is not in danger'. Each patrol was to have access to several dumps: in that way, discovery of one would not lead to the patrol being deprived of equipment. The organizations were primarily designed for sabotage work and the personnel would operate from their home districts in the event of a German occupation. The assumption was that they would be 'constantly in action every day of the week of the year. For example, on 30 km of railway, there should be an act of sabotage at least once a day, and on shorter sectors possibly fifteen a month'. Charasjkiewicz was also planning to form larger sectors (*Okręg*) under a responsible leader, whose duties would cover not only guerrilla activities but also the dissemination of propaganda, incitement to strikes etc., amongst the large Polish population living behind German lines.

Plans were also in existence for partisan groups in Southern Poland. Drawing on their experience of clandestine warfare in Ruthenia in 1938, where some 3,000 irregular Polish troops had been active, the Poles decided that the best size for a unit in partisan warfare along the Carpathian frontier was about fifteen men. The aim of these groups would be to carry out raids across the German–Slovakian frontiers and behind the German lines, targeting the main lateral railway of Žilina–Košice, just south of the Polish border.

In Western Poland, the countryside was quite unsuitable for guerrilla warfare as it was flat, open, agricultural land; but the great forests on the East Prussian border were more suitable. Here the Poles planned a one-off operation. Two bands of guerrillas, one of thirty men and the other of

Background

sixty, were to invade East Prussia immediately on German mobilization, in order to cause 'every inconvenience possible' by attacking railways, bridges and electrical installations. Once this had been achieved, the bands would withdraw and deploy elsewhere. Stores and equipment for these operations were, by July 1939, already in place.

Crucial to these plans for guerrilla warfare was the need for communication between leaders and sub-leaders. For this the Poles were dependent on special messengers and patrols of runners, but in mid-August a Polish General Staff officer visited the War Office to consider the purchase of British wireless transmitters, in order to improve control and communication between the bands and their leaders. He also sought guidance in London about the maintenance of partisan bands behind German lines. Tentatively it was suggested they should rely on pack horses or ponies for carrying rations for fourteen days, that caches of arms and munitions should be prepared in peace time, and that the partisans should be sent home at regular intervals for rest and replenishment of supplies.

How far had these plans developed by mid-August 1939? The British were assured by the Polish General Staff that the allotment of initial tasks to the individual bands had already been completed, as had been the necessary reconnaissance of targets. Sufficient explosive with '100% reserve' had already been 'cached'. The Poles, however, had not yet decided whether the bands were to be controlled by the local army commander or remain centralized under the II Bureau of the General Staff.

Invasion and Partition

The sheer weight and speed of the German attack on Poland forced the Polish armies to retreat rapidly and on 7 September the Government evacuated Warsaw for Brześć. However, by 16 September, Marshal Rydz-Śmigły and his chief of staff, General Stachiewicz, were optimistically convinced that the momentum of the German advance was slowing and the remnants of the Polish Army would be able hold out for several more weeks in the Dniester–Stryj bridgehead (along the Romanian frontier), thereby giving the French more time to launch their offensive across the Rhine. But the Soviet invasion on the 17th rendered this plan impossible to realize and the Polish Government fled over the frontier to Romania, leaving Poland leaderless.

On 27 September – the day that Warsaw fell – the German Foreign Minister, von Ribbentrop, flew to Moscow to agree the new frontier

The Polish Underground 1939–1947

between the USSR and German-controlled Poland. This was to lie along the East Prussian border to the River Narew and then down the Bug to the Ruthenian border, leaving Drohobycz and Lwów on the Soviet side of the frontier. Altogether, this left 4½ million Poles east of the new frontier. The following week witnessed the surrender of the remaining pockets of Polish resistance in Modlin and the Hel Peninsula. With the surrender to the Germans of the Polesie Group under General Kleeberg on 6 October, all large-scale fighting ceased.

Although, by the time war broke out, plans for partisan and guerrilla warfare were still in their formative stage, the Germans – despite their victorious *Blitzkrieg* – had met considerable opposition from the civil population in the newly occupied areas. The great mass of the opposition was spontaneous or else conducted by the various leagues of defenders of the Fatherland, initially in response to the fifth column activities carried out by 'Die Volksdeutschen' – the ethnic Germans resident in Poland. In Bydgoszcz for example, after the withdrawal of the Polish troops, a civilian defence committee was set up, which managed to form a militia of over 2,000 workers, students, civil servants and boy scouts. Arms were distributed from the deserted military arsenals. By 5 September it surrendered but further isolated attacks on German troops and head-quarters goaded the Germans into launching a full-scale pacification of the city and arresting several thousand Poles.

Both Polish and German sources are full of examples of civilian participation in the defence of Poland. A young German gunner, Willy Krey, wrote in his diary on 3 September:

> The war is terrible, one sees for the whole day nothing but burnt-out houses. Every house has to be smoked out. There is no other way when dealing with the Poles. The inhabitants who remain behind are the worst. Yesterday a German officer talked to a few women from the village, and then when he turned round to go to the well to drink some water, he was stabbed in the back by one of the women. He died shortly after that.
>
> [W. Krey, IWM, K94/26/1 (Translated by the author)]

A young Polish cavalry officer, Wiktor Jackiewicz, and his reconnaissance party, managed to escape the Germans near Piotrków, thanks to the efforts of a twelve-year-old boy, who led them to a ford over the River Luciąża. Jackiewicz remembered well how the boy's eyes 'glittered with rage at the Germans and pride that he was helping us'. Multiplied several thousands over, it was from such seeds that the Polish resistance grew.

Siege of Warsaw, 7–27 September 1939

It was the Siege of Warsaw that was to prove formative for the Polish resistance and provide a focus for the whole country. When the Government fled Warsaw on 7 September, the Lord Mayor, Stefan Starzyński, was appointed Civilian Commissar by General Czuma, Commander of the garrison. During the defence of the city Starzyński had to rely on the local population to do work normally done by Government agencies. Thus, each block of flats had to organize its own anti-aircraft defence unit and distribute food rations. Starzyński also had to re-establish a police force and set up special committees to help the homeless, the destitute, and the refugees, who had flooded into Warsaw. In that way, as Jan Gross put it, 'almost the whole population of Warsaw was drawn together to accomplish collective tasks'.

Another focus of opposition in Warsaw was the Citizens' Committee, established on 15 September. This comprised virtually all prominent politicians, representing the whole spectrum of political opinion. Politicians who had been bitter rivals now met in an advisory body, united by the desire to help their country. The emergency also forced soldiers and politicians to confer regularly, thereby establishing a precedent for the deliberations of military authorities and citizens' representatives, which continued throughout the years of the resistance. This went some way towards restoring the trust between the military and civilians, which had been badly damaged during the Piłsudski era.

The formation of volunteer detachments also helped mobilize the citizens of Warsaw. The Polish Socialist Party, despite the reservations of many conservative army officers, formed the Workers' Volunteer Brigade, while Starzyński set up the 'Battalion of the Defenders of Warsaw'. Within half an hour of his broadcast appeal to form the battalion, several thousand volunteers came forward. Poles of all political persuasions flocked to join the Volunteer Brigade, and *Ozon* – the Nationalist movement set up to back Piłsudski's successors – gave all its funds to it. The Brigade fought with fanatical fury against the Germans. When at last the decision was taken to capitulate, its members initially refused to accept it and threatened to shoot the officers who had told them. Only with great difficulty was their commander, Captain Kenig, able to calm them down.

The Polish Underground 1939–1947

Formation of the Polish Government-in-Exile

When the Polish Cabinet fled across the border to Romania on 17 September, it had hoped to be recognized as the legal government of Poland and be allowed to move on to France, but its members were interned by the Romanians as a result of German pressure. Consequently, for several crucial weeks, Poland was without a legal government and there was a real danger the Germans would try to set up a puppet regime in Warsaw. Amongst many of the Poles who had managed to evade the German and Russian armies and escape across the Hungarian and Romanian borders, there was a feeling of intense anger against the Colonels' regime, which had led Poland to its humiliating defeat, and a longing for a new government not composed of the old elites – a revulsion that was also felt deeply within Poland.

It was only on 30 September that President Mościcki resigned in favour of Władysław Raczkiewicz, and a new Polish Government of National Unity was appointed. The Prime Minister was General Sikorski, a long-term critic of the Colonels. He called his first Cabinet meeting in Paris on 2 October, and on 23 November the government moved to Angers. As a coalition between the Right and Left, it marked a radical change in Polish politics. The initial reaction to it was favourable, especially as it was not backward in criticizing not only the *ancien régime* ('Sanacja') but also the French and British Governments for their lack of assistance during the September campaign. Until 1944 it had the support of the majority of Poles in occupied Poland.

'Post-September' Resistance

Although the surrender of General Kleeberg's Special Operational Polesie Group on 6 October marked the end of the brief September campaign, this did not bring to an end all hostilities. Some Polish units attempted to fight their way to the Hungarian, Romanian or Lithuanian borders, and limited actions against the Germans and Russians occurred on a considerable scale well into 1940. The best example is the unit led by Henryk Dobrzański, alias 'Hubal'. He was Deputy Commander of a second-line formation, the 110th Reserve Cavalry Regiment, and was initially trapped between the German and Russian forces near Grodno and the Augustów Forest. He took part in the defence of Grodno against the Red Army. When it fell, the Polish forces were ordered to escape over the Lithuanian border, but Hubal's colonel disobeyed and attempted to head for Warsaw. After being mauled by Russian troops near the Biebrza area, what was left of the regiment was disbanded, but Hubal

Background

and a group of some 180 men continued to make for Warsaw, where they hoped to join its defenders.

After Warsaw's capitulation on 27 September, Hubal decided to head south with about fifty men and cross the Hungarian frontier, from where it was hoped to reach France. When they reached the Holy Cross Mountains near Kielce in November, however, Hubal decided the best option was to stay put and await what he hoped would be the big Allied offensive in the spring. His group initially managed to avoid capture, thanks to the assistance of the local population. The commander of the newly formed Polish Underground organization, the SVP (*see below*), wanted to disband Hubal's unit, for fear that open partisan warfare might provoke savage German reprisals against the civil population. Hubal resolutely refused and insisted his force was a 'separated unit of the Polish Army'.

Hubal was the most famous of the 'post-September' resisters, but in the Russian-occupied provinces, with their impenetrable marshes and forests, the historian Tomasz Strzembosz has shown that many more groups managed to continue the struggle against the Red Army until the early months of 1940, when 'post-September' resistance merged into the broader Underground movement (*see page 59*).

In Wilno (Vilnius) there were two partisan groups led by officers with the same surname (Lieutenant Colonel Józef Dąbrowski and Cavalry Captain Dąbrowski), which led to considerable confusion and contributed to the legend of the 'Dąbrowski Partisans', news of which even reached London, appearing in an article in the London *Times*. This referred to a Polish Colonel 'Dombrowski', whose men 'are burning telegraph wires, raiding provincial centres of the local Russian administration, harassing the new police and their officials, skirmishing with the Red Army outposts, but eluding pitched engagement'.

The remote marshlands in the Białystok Province, along the valleys of the Biebrza and Narew, were an ideal hideout for the 'post-September' resistance groups. For instance, the 'Kobielne' forest range – a few kilometres distant from the River Biebrza – was an isolated area of tall pines surrounded by miles of fields and marshes. Already in late September, Polish soldiers began to seek refuge there. They were joined by a former army chaplain and a parish priest, who began to create an Underground network in the neighbouring villages (*see below*). Similarly, the Red Marsh region in the south of the Augustów Forest provided excellent protection for troops on the run. In October there were reports of a partisan detachment there of several hundred soldiers and civilians.

The Polish Underground 1939–1947

Creation of the Polish Underground

The isolated groups of fugitive soldiers who decided to seek refuge in the forests, marshlands and mountains of Poland provided a link between the September War and the emergence of an organized resistance movement. It was in Warsaw that the foundations of what was later to be called the Home Army and the Underground State were laid. After the decision had been taken to surrender to the Germans, General Tokarzewski, a former corps commander, approached General Juliusz Rómmel, who had just been appointed to succeed Marshal Rydz-Śmigły as supreme military commander in Poland, with a plan for organizing armed resistance against the Germans. Shortly afterwards, Rydz-Śmigły sent a Major Galinat from Romania with the suggestion that he should be given responsibility for organizing Underground operations in Poland. Rómmel ignored this recommendation, and Galinat was sent instead to Pomorze (where, in the summer of 1939, he had been responsible for drawing up plans for diversionary action), to locate his pre-war contacts and re-establish the organizational network, but this had not survived the September campaign, so he was sent back to Romania.

On 27 September Rómmel handed over formal authority to Tokarzewski to command 'Polish military forces on all Polish territories in the war against the aggressor'. He had above all to 'maintain Poland's independence and the integrity of Poland's frontiers'. Tokarzewski rapidly set up a skeleton Underground organization with the nucleus of a general staff of fifteen officers, amongst whom he allotted the commands of the central districts. To finance operations he had received 750,000 złoty from Rómmel, and from the Mayor of Warsaw a further 350,000. The most immediate tasks were to collect weapons, ammunition and explosives and hide them in safe places, establish rudimentary lines of communication, and issue false identity cards.

Before any further organizational progress could be made, Hitler's planned arrival in Warsaw to review the victory parade of German forces through the city on 5 October presented the Underground with a unique chance to strike at the head of their enemy. In great secrecy, explosives were concealed in ruins at the crossing of two of Warsaw's main arteries: Nowy Świat and Avenue Jerozolimskie. They were to be detonated at the very moment Hitler's car crossed this junction. Unfortunately, the Germans took the precaution of clearing the streets of bystanders, which ensured that the observers, who were to signal Hitler's imminent arrival to the conspirator hidden in a nearby bombed-out house, were unable to take up their positions before the parade began. Consequently, the

Background

would-be assassin, who himself could not see Hitler pass by, did not detonate the charge. It is conceivable that, had Hitler been killed, history would have taken a different course!

In the autumn, Tokarzewski toured the country, making contacts with the pre-war opposition parties. He took the decision not to include the political groups who had supported the government before the war, as these were held responsible for the defeat and humiliation of Poland in the September campaign. He managed to gain the support of key figures in the Peasants' Party (which was the largest party in Poland), the Polish Socialist Party, the National Party, and the Democratic Party. The ex-speaker of the *Sejm* (Parliament), Maciej Rattaj, who was the effective leader of the Peasant's Party, was ready to support Tokarzewski, but he was adamant that 'the Underground movement, like the Government-in-Exile, must be based on democratic ideals'.

In the course of several meetings between Tokarzewski and the political leaders – whose parties, of course, were illegal in both German- and Soviet-occupied Poland – the formation of a secret Underground resistance organization was approved. It was named the Service for Poland's Victory (SZP) and was to be a single, unified, political-military organization, whose aims were:

1. To wage war against the Germans until Poland was restored within her pre-war boundaries.
2. To reform and reorganize the armed forces within Poland.
3. To establish an emergency government structure which would be replaced once victory was assured.

While Tokarzewski was the Commander-in-Chief, the political leadership of the organization lay in the hands of the Central Council for National Defence. The Commander could, however, if circumstances required, chair the Council, initiate and veto resolutions. The country was divided into districts and counties, each with its own commander. Again, each region had a national defence council of its own. The smallest district unit (called 'the post') was headed by a 'post' commander, whose second deputy would be responsible for propaganda and financial matters. Around the posts were grouped combat and special units of twenty-five men each. Detailed instructions were also given about the creation of conspiracy cells. These were supposed to consist of five people each, with only one of those in contact with their immediate superior. Further instructions stressed the need for secrecy, the absolute minimum of written records, the constant changing of meeting places, the importance of propaganda and communication, which, if at all possible, should only be by word of mouth.

At the end of October, Tokarzewski, who was travelling with forged documents that identified him as a doctor, made a tour of German-occupied Poland. His aim was to subordinate to his control groups of partisans (such as Hubal's) and establish new commands on the district and council levels. He visited the cities of Radom, Lublin, Kielce, Kraków, Tarnów, Częstochowa and the mining districts of Zagłębie Dąbrowskie, to meet local Underground leaders.

Many democratic politicians, both in Poland and Angers, were highly critical of the powers Tokarzewski had amassed. He also fatally alienated Sikorski, when his first report – addressed to the Commander-in-Chief of all Polish forces – was delivered in error to Marshal Rydz-Śmigły. To Sikorski, this merely confirmed Tokarzewski's loyalty to the *Sanacja*, and he was now determined to get rid of him. Consequently, when Sikorski dispatched his first emissary to Poland from the government in Angers (in November), he was instructed to ignore Tokarzewski and talk only with his Chief of Staff.

On 4 December the SZP was replaced by the Union of Armed Struggle, (ZWZ), and in January the unfortunate Tokarzewski was transferred to Lwów, in the Soviet Zone, to take control of what was designated as VI Corps District, while General Rowecki was put in overall charge of operations in German-occupied Poland. The dispatch of Tokarzewski to Lwów was, as one Warsaw politician put it, tantamount to a 'sentence of death or imprisonment', since he had been commander of the local corps district before the war and would therefore be well known to the Russians. He was arrested as soon as he crossed the border on the night of 6 March 1940 and imprisoned in the Soviet Union until 1941.

The aim of the ZWZ was to prepare 'behind the lines of the occupying powers an armed uprising that will go into effect at the moment when regular Armed Forces will enter the country'. An oath was also brought from France, which all who joined had to take:

Before God the Almighty, before the Holy Virgin Mary, Queen of the Crown of Poland, I put my hand on this Holy Cross, the symbol of martyrdom and salvation, and I swear that I will defend the honour of Poland with all my might, that I will fight with arms in

Background

hand to liberate her from slavery, notwithstanding the sacrifice of my own life, that I will be absolutely obedient to my superiors, that I will keep the secret whatever the cost will be.

[T. Bór-Komorowski, *The Secret Army*,
London, Gollancz, 1950, pp. 28–9]

The organization of the ZWZ was essentially motivated by Sikorski's determination to get rid of the generals closely associated with the *Sanacja*, and to subordinate the resistance movement in Poland to his own government. Thus it was not headed by someone within Poland but by General Sosnkowski in Angers. Six regional commands were set up, covering Warsaw, Białystok, Lwów, Kraków, Poznań and Toruń.

Tokarzewski had urged that the initial network of civil councils be transferred to the new structure, but a series of German arrests in the course of the winter of 1939/40 had effectively liquidated the Central Council of National Defence. Despite the fact that Sikorski had set up the Ministers' Committee for Homeland Affairs to watch over 'all matters pertaining to the Homeland' in February, representatives of the Underground political parties in Poland agreed, quite independently of Angers, to set up the Political Coordinating Committee of the ZWZ, which had the task of coordinating civil and military preparations for eventual victory. The representative of each main party would take it in turns to chair the Committee's meetings. The parties would also undertake to subordinate all their paramilitary groups to the ZWZ by 23 March 1940, and attempt to persuade other groups, which were not represented on the Committee, to do the same. The Committee asserted its claim to be the supreme political institution throughout the whole period of its existence, frequently clashing with General Rowecki and the military, as well as with the Polish Government-in-Exile. At district level there were also coordinating committees, the most active being in Kraków. In an attempt to improve coordination, the office of the Government Delegation for Poland, with Cyryl Ratajski as the Chief Delegate, was created in December 1940. Ratajski's task was to liaise between the Government-in-Exile and the Underground in all political matters, and also to collaborate with the political parties. He was also authorized to give political – as opposed to military – instructions to the command of the ZWZ, to control its budget, comment on military appointments in the Underground Army, and receive periodic reports on its activities.

13

The Polish Underground 1939–1947

Within this context, Ratajski began the task of creating an Underground Polish Government within the occupied Polish state. Various departments were set up, each with its own responsibilities:

1. The Presidium Office attempted to ensure the Delegate's personal safety by protecting him and his staff from sudden swoops by the *Gestapo*, providing a network of secure flats or bases and the necessary forged identity papers, work permits etc. The financial section of the Underground State also cooperated very closely with this section, although ultimate control over the finances, which were dependent on smuggled funds from abroad and small local contributions, lay with the central Auditing Office.
2. The Department of Internal Affairs, headed by Leopold Rutkowski, was responsible for setting up the fifteen local delegacies throughout the country, which were to carry out instructions from the centre and, of course, to cope with local affairs. One of their main tasks was to look forward and prepare for the eventual transition from enemy occupation to full Polish sovereignty.
3. The Department of Information and Press, headed by the Labour Party member Stanisław Kauzik, was to provide the Poles with reliable information about the progress of the war and to counter German propaganda. This involved monitoring the BBC's broadcasts to Poland and producing illegal newspapers.
4. The Department of Education and Culture, directed by Czesław Wycech, had the task of ensuring that culture survived all German attempts to eradicate it and reduce Poland to a nation of slaves. One of its key activities was to organize secret school and university courses.
5. The Department of Labour and Social Welfare, which was initially headed by Jan Stanisław Jankowski, was primarily concerned with providing assistance and welfare to the families of political prisoners. It also assisted various scholars, professors, writers and artists, whose survival was considered essential for national life.
6. The Department of Agriculture and State Forests, headed by Teofil Lorkiewicz, scrutinized German agricultural and resettlement policy and was responsible for planning the re-establishment of the post-war Ministry of Agriculture and for future agrarian reforms.

Background

7. The Department of Justice, initially under Leon Nowodzki, kept a close eye on the German courts and also on the activities of the Polish lower courts, which were still allowed to function by the Germans. The Underground courts, which dealt with traitors, members of the *Gestapo* and collaborators, were left to the Directorate of Civil Resistance.
8. The Department of Liquidating the Effects of the War, initially under Antoni Olszewski, assisted by the Department of Public Works, registered the destruction and losses inflicted by the occupation with a view to demanding post-war reparations from Germany.
9. The Directorate of Civil Resistance, whose head, Stefan Korboński, had been appointed jointly by the Government Delegate and the Commander of the Home Army (ZWZ), controlled a number of departments: the Underground Courts of Justice, Sabotage and Diversion, Radio Information, Armaments, Chemicals, Legislation and Registration of German war crimes.

Enemy-Occupied Poland

The Russians and Germans partitioned Poland on 28 September 1939. There was never any question that Germany would not take back the territory lost in 1919, but initially Hitler toyed with the idea of creating a small rump Polish satellite state, which might just give Britain and France an excuse to make peace. However, when the Allies rejected Hitler's offer of peace on 6 October, he announced in two decrees of 8 and 12 October the annexation of a large area of the west and north-west of Poland, which included the Pomeranian and Poznań *voivodships* (provinces) and the five northern counties of the Warsaw *voivodship*. This amounted to some 94,000 square kilometres with a population of about 10 million, and was a quarter of the territory of the pre-war state. Five weeks later these areas were absorbed into the German customs and currency area. On 26 October the fate of the remaining German-occupied territories was decided. Dr Hans Frank, the chief administrator attached to the Eastern Command of the German Army, announced the creation of the General Government with its capital at Kraków, under his new role as governor general. It was subdivided into four districts: Warsaw, Lublin, Radom and Kraków, and had an initial population of about 12 million.

In the annexed areas Hitler immediately gave orders for carrying out a massive resettlement policy. On 7 October he had appointed Heinrich

The Polish Underground 1939–1947

Himmler 'Reich Commissioner for the Strengthening of the German Race', whose task was, on the one hand, 'to bring back those German citizens and ethnic Germans abroad who are eligible for a permanent return to the Reich', and on the other, to 'eliminate influence of such alien parts of the population as constitute a danger to the Reich and the German community'. During the winter of 1939/1940 a full-scale Germanization policy was launched in Posnań and Pomorze (Pomerania). In the first half of December, nearly 90,000 Poles and Jews were arrested in the Posnań area, forced into cattle trucks and dumped over the frontier in the General Government area. The fit and able-bodied men amongst them were conscripted for labour inside the Reich. Once in the General Government area, the deportees had to be found shelter and food. The director of Szczebrzeszyn hospital, Doctor Zygmunt Klukowski, regularly noted in his diary the arrivals of transports of expellees. On 26 July 1940, for instance, he mentions the arrival of a train at midnight. The evacuees had to be temporarily settled in an unfinished block of flats and the town hall.

The resettlement policy was accompanied by a ruthless attempt to eliminate Polish culture and to suppress the Poles' own feelings of national identity. For instance, Polish schools, museums, libraries, etc., were all closed and the use of the Polish language banned. The names of Polish streets, towns and villages were Germanized. The Roman Catholic Church, which in the past had been crucial in sustaining Polish national identity, was the subject of a particularly bitter assault. A report by Cardinal Hłond, the Primate of Poland, observed that:

> the German authorities, and especially the *Gestapo*, rage against the Catholic clergy. The Church has been forced to withdraw to the catacombs. Priests are beginning to say mass and to administer the sacraments secretly in private houses. The zeal of the priests is astonishing, the piety of the faithful is as great ever, the devotion to the Church is heroic.

[NA, FO371/2470]

General Government

Essentially, the Germans adopted the same policy in the General Government. Frank made it clear to his department managers in December 1939 that 'it was [. . .] the will of the Führer that this area was the first colonial region of the German nation. The interests of German culture must prevail here.' As in the annexed areas, the elite was targeted. In Warsaw,

Background

Mayor Starzyński was seized on 27 September. A few weeks later, in Kraków, 183 professors and lecturers of the teaching staff of the Jagiellonian University were arrested. A similar pattern occurred throughout the General Government. At the end of October, in Lublin, Arthur Seyss-Inquart (Frank's deputy), explained to German occupation personnel and local *Volksdeutsche* that the Polish intelligentsia and elite were, like the Jews, to be destroyed. Events occurring shortly after this speech in Lublin showed that Seyss-Inquart was not making empty threats. From the end of October until early February, the population was terrorized by a series of manhunts, and hundreds of prisoners were delivered daily to the state prison in the castle. Grammar school teachers were seized after they had been summoned to a meeting with the German authorities. On 11 November the professors of the Catholic University were also arrested and just before Christmas were shot, together with several senior municipal administrators. On 12 February a further 180 people were executed. One priest, who escaped to Rome, observed in January 1940 that 'The Germans systematically destroyed Catholicism and Polish traditions with atheistic hatred.'

While the Germans waged an implacable war against the officer class and elites, Hans Frank did not lose sight of the fact that Polish industry was important to the German war effort. Consequently, the mass of Polish people would have to be fed, clothed and 'given the hope that when they are well behaved, they have nothing to fear'. As the war went on, German economic demands on the Poles intensified. Above all it was labour conscription that bore most heavily on the population. As early as December 1939 Frank agreed to extend labour conscription to fourteen-year-olds. In May 1940, to avoid provoking undue 'panic amongst the Poles', Frank came up with the cynical ploy of using police swoops to net unfortunate Poles for labour within the Reich.

The General Government was, like the rest of the Nazi regime, riddled with corruption, inefficiency and inter-departmental rivalries, especially between the SS and the army. The British Legation in Berne, for instance, informed London on 19 January 1940 of 'the venality of the new (German) officialdom', which the Polish Ambassador described as being one of the things that made conditions tolerable – at least for those who had any means of bribery. A Jewish Rabbi from Łódź, who had recently arrived in Switzerland, had told him that there were 'eight different bureaus, at any one of which permission might be obtained after it had been refused at all the others'. A further report from the same source bore this out. A friend of the Polish Ambassador found it impossible to

17

get away from Poznań with the official permission of the competing authorities, but he 'eventually fixed matters up with one of the *Gauleiter*'s chauffeurs for 500 *złoty*'. For this sum the chauffeur actually drove him in one of the *Gauleiter*'s official cars the whole way from Poznań to Warsaw, where the fortunate man was able to arrange his departure to Switzerland!

Hans Frank was described by the Italian journalist Curzio Malaparte as having a complex mixture of 'intelligence, cruelty, sophistication and vulgarity'. He held court as if he were a Renaissance prince at the Wawel in Kraków, the historic castle where the Polish monarch had lived in the days of the Polish-Lithuanian empire. Frank was at pains to stress that he wielded supreme authority in the General Government, but the SS in Poland, as in Germany, formed a state-within-a-state. SS-Obergruppen-führer Friederich Wilhelm Krüger, who was responsible for the police and security within the General Government, created an empire that Frank could not touch.

Terror played a key role in policing the General Government. In November 1939 special courts were set up, usually composed of officials from the security offices, to try 'terrorists'. It was assumed that experienced German judges would be too lenient. The number of crimes punished with the death penalty steadily grew over the period 1940–44. For instance, a person passing on to a German a sexually transmitted disease could be executed, as could Polish officers who had not reported for registration and young men who evaded work conscription. Those involved in the black market, charging extortionate prices or sheltering Jews, could also be executed. The Germans exploited on a large scale the principle of collective responsibility. For instance, in the Lublin area, for every German killed by the Underground or a sabotage action carried out by partisans, at least twenty Poles were murdered.

With the establishment of the General Government, security was no longer the responsibility of the army but of the Security Police, which was composed of the *Gestapo*, the Kripo (Criminal Police) and the SD (the Security Service). The *Ordnungspolizei* (responsible for everyday policing in the cities), the transport police, forestry police and factory police all cooperated closely with the SD. In each district there was also stationed an SS regiment, which possessed a whole range of weapons including artillery and tanks. The SS was used for fighting partisans or carrying out large-scale executions, such as the murder of over 3,000 of the Polish intellectual elite in the Kampinos Forest near Palmiry in June 1940. The Polish police and later, after the conquest of Poland's former eastern territories in 1941, the Ukrainian police, as well as the Jewish security forces in the ghettos, were all subordinated closely to the Germans.

To combat the Underground, the German police relied mainly on informers, agents, and above all on *Die Volksdeutschen*, who had a good knowledge both of their local communities and of who might be working for the Resistance. Sometimes, in order to find a clue or a pointer to Underground activity, the *Gestapo* would arrest literally thousands of people, amongst whom a certain percentage would almost certainly be working for the Underground. The Polish historian Czesław Madajczyk calculated, for instance, that some 6 per cent of the population in Warsaw were active in the Underground. To extract information violence was used. Routine treatment consisted of beating with whips, knouts or rifle butts. Amongst the most painful tortures were the application of electrodes to the sex organs or the head, or a roasting before an open fire. One member of the German occupation authorities observed in 1943 that:

The methods [...] used by the police authorities are ruthless, cruel and humiliating. They involve arresting people in their houses, on the streets, the squares, in pubs, shooting or hanging, without any discrimination or evidence of guilt (collective responsibility), use of tortures to extract confessions [...] It seems that any means and any excuse is valid if it is to make a Pole a cripple or eliminate him from this world.

[Madajczyk, p. 205 (translated by author)]

German Army of Occupation

German-controlled Poland was first placed under martial law and then handed over to the General Government, although in the final resort, a military occupation force of never less than 300,000 men remained. In the autumn of 1939, the mass of the German Army was moved westwards in preparation for the advance into France. The men left behind were, for the most part, comparatively elderly reservists, often sickened by the atrocities they witnessed on a daily basis. They were ordered not to talk about such incidents, but as a Swedish journalist wrote in the *Politiken* on 4 February 1940: 'they do so all the same, and when one hears what these soldiers have to report [...] one well understands that they feel the urge to confess, to shake free from the impressions they carry about with them.' The Polish Father General of the Jesuits, Father Ledóchowski, confirmed this when he told the British Ambassador to the Vatican in January that 'he had heard of German soldiers who had returned from Poland and expressed their horror of what they had perpetrated'.

Bavarian, Sudeten and Austrian troops were more sympathetic to the Poles than the North Germans and Prussians. The desertion rate amongst the Sudetens and Austrians was also higher. Possibly in view of this, the German authorities put up notices threatening with the death penalty anybody selling civilian clothes to German military personnel. The Vatican received reports at Christmas of Bavarian troops going to Confession conducted by Polish priests, who were themselves being persecuted by the *Gestapo*. Dr Klukowski also recorded in his diary a German company rioting in Zwierzyniec because of bad food. The most important incident, however, was reported on 3 May by General Sikorski to Neville Chamberlain. Apparently, Bavarian troops stationed near Radom mutinied and were reinforced by workers from the city and Polish partisan forces in the Świętokrzyskie Mountains. Two hundred Bavarians were shot, 'a large number of villages were burnt and some 1,500 inhabitants, including women and children, were massacred'. In light of such information there was some rather wishful thinking that the German Army was in the throes of decomposition but that was, in reality, very wide of the mark.

With the defeat of France, the bulk of the *Wehrmacht* was then transferred back to Poland. Dr Klukowski commented in his diary as early as 16 July 1940 on the movement of German troops and the belief that war against Russia was imminent. The role of the *Wehrmacht* in occupied Poland fluctuated according to the fortunes of war. Between April 1940 and spring 1942 it played little part in security operations. Only with the retreat of the German Army from Russia and the rise of the partisan movement in Eastern Poland did the army resume its high profile in security operations.

Soviet Zone

It was a moot point in occupied Poland in the period 1939–1941 whether the Russians or the Germans were the main enemy. The British and French, for obvious reasons, tried to persuade the Poles that Germany was 'Enemy No. 1' but until the German invasion of Russia, they had mixed success. While Sikorski agreed with this assessment, and as early as the summer of 1940 perceived Soviet Russia to be a potential ally, the

Background

Polish Foreign Ministry vehemently disagreed. Stanisław Balinsky, the First Secretary of the Polish Embassy in London, for instance, observed that 'the greatest number of Poles would choose Germany as being the lesser evil'. In March 1941, according to the Foreign Office, there was some evidence that the Poles themselves were critical of the Government-in-Exile for overlooking 'the plight of the Poles under Soviet rule'.

The Russian occupation of 1939–1941 was every bit as ruthless as the German occupation. Initial Soviet domination of the eastern provinces was helped by playing off the various ethnic groups against the Poles, and by using local Communists as informers against the 'common enemy'. On 22 October a plebiscite was held under the watchful eyes of the NKVD, the Soviet secret police, to endorse the integration of the eastern provinces into the USSR. Eastern Poland was now subjected to the full force of the Russian revolution and its Stalinist mutations. Private industry was nationalized, the big landed estates collectivized and, above all, terror was unleashed by the NKVD, schooled in the Stalinist purges. The unemployed and refugees were registered for work in the Soviet interior and young men of military age were called up to serve in the Red Army. When the civilian government was set up in early 1940, Soviet officials, together with their families, descended like a plague of locusts on the Zone. This intensified the pressure on local housing, which led to the accelerated eviction of those deemed bourgeois or anti-social from houses and flats in the towns and cities. The local shops and factories were stripped of all clothing, pharmaceutical products, food stuffs and consumer goods. The introduction of the *rouble* on 23 December caused particular problems for the population, as the Polish *złoty* could only be exchanged at one-tenth of its value for the new currency. Prices also rocketed during the winter.

In schools, universities and public life a re-education programme was introduced. Russian and Ukrainian became the main languages and Polish children had no option but to learn them. Communist ideology inspired the new teaching. Stefan Kurylak, a schoolboy at the time, remembered that, in order to emphasize the 'bogus' nature of God, the children in his school were told to ask God for sweets. When nothing happened 'a teacher put on a Stalin mask and entered with sweets after the children had asked our great leader'. Lwów university was organized according to the principles of Soviet higher education with a special chair in Marxism-Leninism.

The new regime was determined to purge the Polish landowners or 'Pans', the officer class, the clergy and the intellectuals. Both Germany and the USSR followed similar deportation policies. Between October and

The Polish Underground 1939–1947

the end of December 1939, the Germans had forcibly deported nearly 150,000 from the areas annexed to the Reich, while the Soviets deported some 1.7 million people to Siberia and Kazakhstan. Stefan Kurylak recalled how the 'Siberian holiday specials' carrying whole families to Siberia or Kazakhstan steamed past the bottom of his garden:

> The nights were made unbearable not only by the racket of the trains themselves but by the piteous cries of adults and children begging to be [...] let out of locked compartments. Sometimes in the winter the villagers would discover a frozen body beside the tracks.
>
> [Stefan Kurylak, IWM, 78/52/1]

As part of this policy, all Polish officer POWs in the Soviet annexed territory were sent to camps at Kozielsk, Ostashkov and Starobielsk, where they were subjected to intensive interrogation in an attempt to find men who were sympathetic to Communism, and who might be useful in eventually setting up a Communist regime in Poland. Only a handful were found suitable and in April and May the great majority were shot by NKVD guards in the Katyń Forest and the prisons of Kalinin and Kharkov.

Collectivization, the closing down of Polish and Ukrainian cultural societies, and persecution of the Orthodox and Catholic Churches effectively alienated most of the population by the spring of 1940. As one British diplomat in the Moscow Embassy observed after visiting Lwów in January 1940, 'the Russians have only one achievement to their credit: they have united Poles and Ukrainians in hatred of a common enemy.'

Terror, the NKVD and the Red Army managed to keep the lid on the simmering discontent. The initial occupying force was withdrawn when Soviet troops invaded Finland, and was replaced by second line units, which were almost entirely composed of poorly equipped infantry suffering low morale. A Swedish paper described them in March 1940 as predominantly 'undersized Circassians or Kazbeks newly arrived and recruited from Mongolia'. In Lwów, the inhabitants were openly scornful of the Red Army. A British diplomat reported a story to the Foreign Office in February that was going the rounds of the city:

> A detachment of Red Army men [...] were drilling in one of the public parks at the foot of a hill on which a number of children were skiing. A man in the rear rank, happening to turn round, saw to his

horror a group of skiers advancing rapidly downhill in line abreast; with the cry of 'My God, the Finns!' he broke and ran, followed by the remainder of the detachment.

[NA, FO24471]

In January 1940 the British Legation in Kovno reported that four divisions of troops from Moscow had to be sent in to bolster morale.

The Polish police force was disbanded and replaced with a new militia force composed mainly of Ukrainians and Byelorussians strengthened with some Russian personnel from Kiev. Crucial, however, to Soviet control of Eastern Poland was the NKVD, which was staffed entirely by experienced officials from Russia, well used to rooting out 'enemies of the people'. In the early spring, reports smuggled out of the Soviet-occupied area gave a chilling picture:

Arrests are so common that men from the intellectual class do not sleep at home, but every night in a different friend's house. Ogpu (NKVD) always comes during the night. One never knows what is the cause of the arrest. Anyone can denounce whom he likes by writing his name and leaving the card in a box at the Ogpu's office. He receives 120 *roubles* reward for every denunciation of Polish and Ukrainian patriots or social workers [...] not only intellectuals are executed, but workmen and villagers too. Not long ago all Polish Communists were arrested. The reason was unknown [...] To see Russian Communism in practice even for a few weeks is enough to be utterly cured of all sympathies for it.

[NA, FO889/223]

This process was highly visible and therefore all the more frightening. Irena Haniewicz, who had just started school in Dubno, boarded with a family who lived next door to the local prison. She remembers distinctly the chilling sound of people being tortured by the NKVD.

Poles and the Occupation

The destruction of the legitimate Polish Government and the partition of the Polish state between Germany and the USSR created what sociologists call a 'normative void'. Unlike Denmark, Norway or Vichy France, there was no government put in place to which the Poles could look for

The Polish Underground 1939–1947

guidance as to how to cope with the occupying power. Initially, the Poles best placed to survive the occupation were the peasantry in the General Government area. War or no war, land still had to be tilled, and there was the added bonus that any debts owed to Jewish money lenders or agricultural merchants were nullified. Initially, no taxes were levied and thefts of timber from the state forests were overlooked. By the spring of 1940, however, labour conscription and high grain and food delivery quotas put an end to the peasant honeymoon with the Germans. For the urban population, already suffering food shortages, lack of heating, and often poor housing, and living in daily terror of the *Gestapo* or of being caught up in sudden swoops to provide forced labour, life was much more difficult.

The German and Soviet occupations effectively atomized Polish society by removing not only the legitimate government but also by destroying the Polish state itself and all the organizations that helped knit society together. It was thus hardly surprising that corruption – which might also involve denouncing either Jews or Poles for money – alcoholism and crime were widespread. The sudden catastrophic collapse of Poland and the horrors of the occupation inevitably left the population bewildered and ready to clutch at straws. Rumours that 'Marshal Rydz-Śmigły has occupied Kraków' or that 'British aviators are bombing German aerodromes' abounded; while elsewhere credence was given to a story that, on the sacred icon of the Black Madonna at Częstochowa, the date '12 December 1939' had appeared, signifying that the occupation would end on that day. Clearly, as one Polish officer in January told Sir Howard Kennard, the British Ambassador to the Polish Government-in-Exile, these rumours might be 'untrue and sometimes even fantastic but the population needs them to keep up its spirits'.

Increasingly, the 'Underground State' began to fill the disorientating void created by the occupation. In March 1941 the Government Delegate reported back to London that different social groups, artists, doctors, workers, etc., were asking his opinion on the admissible limits of their cooperation with the occupier. Summing up the significance of the Underground state for the Poles in occupied Poland, the historian Jan Tomasz Gross wrote:

> Psychological comfort derived from acquiring a sense of guidance in the morally disturbing social environment of an occupied country; the sense of belonging, and a positive bond with a group at a time

Background

when isolation from other people and suspicion of their hostility was
a prevalent experience; the support of a group of people who were
prepared to do anything in their power to help one another in danger,
if for no other reason than the imperative calling for the preservation
of the organization ...

[Gross, pp. 280–1]

Campaign
Chronicle

—▷—◁(○)▷—◁—

Resistance, September 1939–June 1940

General Tadeusz Komorowski (or 'Bór', to use his Underground alias), who was later the Commander-in-Chief of the Home Army, observed in his autobiography that:

> I don't think it has often happened in history that the leaders of the people could be so very certain of fulfilling the will of the nation. This time a country completely overrun by two invaders and torn in half had decided to fight. No dictator, no leader, no party and no class had inspired this decision. The nation had made it spontaneously and unanimously.
>
> [T. Bór-Komorowski, *The Secret Army*, p. 22]

By and large this was true, even if, in the immediate term, overwhelming German and Soviet strength had left the Poles with little option except sullen acceptance of their fate; but inevitably there were collaborators, denunciations and plenty of crooks posing as Underground members. Jewish reminiscences of the time are full of stories of Polish betrayal and how some Poles were willing to accept bounties from the Germans for denouncing Jews and to lay claim to their businesses. Klukowski's diaries show how rife denunciations were. For instance, in May 1941, he complained of the difficulty of hiding anyone due to a growing wave of denunciations. 'The meanness of people has no limits.' To a young Jewish girl in the resistance, Miriam Peleg-Marianski, the whole of Warsaw was 'contaminated by a plague of informers and *"szmalcownicy"* – the blackmailers and extortionists.'

Of course it would be wrong to put too much emphasis on betrayal and denunciation, which occurred in all occupied countries. Inevitably, the Poles had, up to a point, to collaborate with the Germans. In the final analysis, the German administrative system in the General Government relied on Poles in the lower and middle echelons to function. Such employment shielded an employee from forced labour in the Reich and offered a degree of protection from the *Gestapo*. It did, too, at times, enable officials to bend the rules to help their fellow Poles, but some Polish officials also collaborated to save their own skins. Cheating the Germans was refined to an art and became a way of life. Consequently, it is hard for the historian to assess whether a particular official cheated the Nazis for personal gain or to assist the Resistance.

Resistance has gradations all the way from armed opposition to minor acts of civil disobedience. The German historian Martin Broszat made a useful distinction in his work on Nazi Germany between the few resisters ready to use violence and a larger number who kept a low profile. The latter defied the Nazis in a relatively unprovocative way, such as, for example, attending church services rather than Nazi rallies. The former activity he called 'resistance', the latter (to use the German word) *'Resistanz'* – a medical term meaning immunity to a disease or epidemic. If this analysis is applied to Poland, there was a whole host of actions that were caused by individual defiance, compassion, or the desire to defend Polish culture and civilization from the Germans. They usually occurred spontaneously: it might be the refusal of a girl to dance with a German officer, the offer of food to POWs or Jews in a ghetto, or the singing of forbidden hymns in church.

In the six months following the September defeat, numerous small resistance groups sprang to life. The Underground in Poland was in fact a mosaic of movements, varying in size and aims. For many officers the first reaction to defeat – particularly when it became clear that they would be unable to escape across the Hungarian or Romanian frontiers – was to retreat to the forests and continue resistance; while others sought to set up Underground movements with a view to gathering information, distributing anti-German propaganda, and performing acts of sabotage.

By November two main organizations had been formed in the General Government area: in Warsaw, the Service for Poland's Victory (SZP), under General Tokarzewski (*see page 11*); and in Kraków, an organization

The Polish Underground 1939–1947

under Bór-Komorowski and Klemens Rudnicki. Rudnicki and Bór recruited a small group of staff officers, who met secretly at regular intervals. To avoid the *Gestapo*, code names such as 'Monastery, 'Dining Room', etc., were given to the various addresses where they met. Nothing was committed to paper. They were constantly visited by a stream of officers and civilians, including a monk 'from a remote monastery', who reported the numbers and details of their local organizations, and asked for instructions and orders. All volunteers formed groups of five. As Bór later explained:

> Each member of the group was allowed to know only his four fellow members, each one of them in his turn creating a new group of five. In this way a pyramid with me at the top was constantly growing. The use of real names was forbidden and pseudonyms were introduced.
>
> [Bór-Komorowski, p. 22]

Similarly, officers who had escaped the clutches of the Germans and Russians, as well as students, intellectuals and members of the professions, sought to contact the Underground in Warsaw. Let us take the example of Major Alojzy Dziura-Dziurski, a native of Silesia and half German. He had managed to escape from a transport bound for the prison camps in the USSR and, hiding in a freight train, returned to Poland. After crossing the frontier into the General Government he met 'a haggard old man', his former CO, who recruited him into the resistance. He was given a forged *Luftwaffe* pass and travelled to Warsaw, where he met a Captain Kłosiński, and was sworn into the SZP. He was given the job of armaments officer. His task was to find the locations of arms caches in the Częstochowa district, which had been hidden by Polish troops in September. These caches were then reported to local community leaders, who were usually already members of the Underground. Years later, he recalled that 'with two professional NCO gunsmiths and six special guards to protect us at our work we descended on farms, churchyards, estates and forest hiding places.' Although many weapons had already rusted beyond repair, over the course of three months they recovered two serviceable heavy MGs, eight light MGs, plus dozens of rifles and pistols with ammunition. One peasant even showed them a 15.5mm howitzer with an ammunition carrier, but it was not until the spring that they were able to tow it away to a safe place. At one stage, Dziura-Dziurski's search party was surprised by German troops and he had to fob them off with a story that they were *Gestapo* officers digging graves for Polish bandits!

Campaign Chronicle

Dziura-Dziurski's bilingual abilities made him a valuable asset to the Underground. In March 1940 he was sent to Kielce to spy on the activities of the *Reichsumsiedlungsgesellschaft* (Reich Settlement Company), which was evicting peasants to make way for the construction of new military installations. He was given the papers of a German-speaking Ukrainian and told to apply for the post of interpreter. A few months later he actually became the manager responsible for assembling fifty barrack sheds for SS troops, as the Underground needed to see plans of the buildings for a possible later operation. Dziura-Dziurski was expected to eat in the SS canteen and was terrified that a fellow Silesian conscripted into the SS might recognize him. Consequently, he became more German than the Germans and would condemn the slightest criticism of Hitler, Germany or the *Wehrmacht*, which might be made by his colleagues. Unsurprisingly, he was left alone to read the Nazi Party newspaper, the *Völkischer Beobachter* or the SS paper, *Der Stürmer*!

The ZWZ – the SZP's successor (*see page 12*) – and the many small resistance groups which functioned independently of it, financed themselves partly through black market profits and contributions from a wide range of people. At times the difference between extortion and voluntary gifts could become rather academic! One young Jewish member of the Underground, Szamuel Goldberg, who was a comedian by trade and joined the Underground in late 1939, wrote years later that

> Most of my time was spent collecting money from merchants in the market place. I would be given the name of the merchant who was sympathetic to the resistance. I then approached him and requested money. The merchant would give me anywhere from 50 to 100 *złoty* and often inform me of another merchant who was sympathetic to the cause. I wondered where the partisans were in this story [...] [there were rumours of an army in the forests] but the whole thing continued to look unorganized.

> [S. Goldberg, Vol. 2, IWM, 06/521]

There are frequent references in Dr Klukowski's diary to armed robberies, some of which were undoubtedly carried out by Underground groups. For instance, on 22 January 1941, he noted that 'around 6 p.m. an employee from a local factory, who had been sent to Zamość to bring back 15,000 *złoty* in cash, was robbed of all of it.' Apparently, a young man had asked for a lift and then, a few minutes later, pointed a gun at the driver and seized his briefcase, containing the cash. Later, Klukowski learnt that this whole action was carried out by the Underground.

The formation of five-man Underground cells led intentionally to the 'atomization' or isolation of members. An individual or small group would receive instruction to carry out certain tasks but had no idea of the overall context. Szamuel Goldberg was always being told that he 'was one of us' but, as he remarked later, 'who "us" meant was still a mystery . . .' He was only aware of four other people besides himself in his particular cell. To escape forced labour, Szamuel had fled Piotrków for Warsaw, where he got in touch with the Underground via 'somebody by the name of "Czarniecki" in the inner yard of an apartment block'. For the next few months, Goldberg acted as a clandestine messenger, black market agent and arms deliverer. He was taught how to watch out for German patrols when travelling on trains and to dispose of whatever he was carrying before they boarded at the station. His first job was to deliver pistols to a bakery in Falenice. After that he was ordered to Minsk, together with his friend Zelig; but while staying the night in the predominantly Jewish village of Dubra, they were given fresh instructions, which involved taking weapons and ammunition buried in grain on a horse-drawn sleigh. At one point, owing to the thin covering of snow on the road, the sleigh became grounded just as they noticed the lights of a German army lorry approaching, but fortunately it turned off the road before reaching them. Szamuel was then ordered back to Warsaw, where he was billeted in a brothel. As a Jew, he was arguably in greater danger there than in the ghetto, as its madame was a fanatical anti-Semite. In the end, disillusioned with the Underground, Szamuel decided to seek security in the Warsaw Ghetto. He brushed aside attempts by his friend Zelig to dissuade him:

'What Underground movement?' I snapped, 'The Underground that robs stores, executes people [...] This organization is nothing more than organized crime. They do no harm whatsoever to the Nazis and their actions bring only increased persecution upon the Polish people.'

[S. Goldberg, Vol. 2, IWM, 06/521]

In the early months of the occupation there was considerable illegal traffic in refugees, particularly Jews, fleeing German persecution by trying to cross the frontier into the Soviet Zone. A student, Z.R. Pomorski, for instance, was approached 'by some person' one Sunday after he had been to Mass, and asked to take a group over to the Russian Zone. If he were stopped by the Russians his excuse would be that he was escaping from the Germans to continue his studies, and if caught by the Germans he was to say that he was working on the farmland near the border. Several crossings were successful and increasingly he became a 'nocturnal animal'. In the end he ran into a Russian patrol. He managed to ensure a safe escape for his charges by distracting the Russians with his own flight, which he described later in his memoirs:

At present all that you care is to lead the hunters away – that extra energy you were hoping for is suddenly here [...] You behave more like a fox. The instinct now takes over. You keep going as long as your body can manage, and a glimpse of hope begins to creep [*sic*], giving you that extra spurt. At once the voice of the chase seems to be all around you – then some blundering flashes and some more shots. The next thing you know you are lying on the ground and you couldn't care less. You are so tired, too tired even to think.

[Pomorski, IWM, 96/55/1]

He was caught, sent to Siberia, and escaped in 1941 to join the Polish Army in the Middle East.

There were numerous gradations in the Polish resistance. Pomorski described his activities as being part of the 'proto-Underground'. There were also many spontaneous acts of defiance. When British prisoners of war passed through the countryside near Poznań in July 1940, the women working in the fields waved at them, and once they had started working in the fields, gave them food where possible. Gordon Manners, who was in a camp near Thorn (Toruń) witnessed the guards firing at a Polish woman visiting a nearby cemetery who had tried to slip some bread through the wire. Fortunately she managed to escape. Two months later, in September, he wrote in his diary that children were lobbing apples over the wall:

One girl borrowed a baby and dropped a bag of buns out of its long clothes as she passed. We all crowded round and by the time the guard had got amongst us, there was no sign of any buns.

[IWM, 05/64/1]

The Polish Underground 1939–1947

The desperate shortage of food left little alternative for many individuals but to defy the Germans if they were to survive. This was the dilemma that confronted the Ślązak family, who ran a draper's business in Łódź. As early as October 1939 the fourteen-year-old George Ślązak [spelling as per IWM records] and his mother went out into the country by train once a week to buy black market food, thereby running the risk of German police checks. Several times they were nearly caught. George and his friends also got drawn in to a more high-risk activity by passing loaves of bread to Jews in Łódź Ghetto. Disembarking from the tram at the terminus on a visit to his uncle, George noticed children peering through a hole in the ghetto wall, begging for food. From that point on, until the hole was filled in, George and his friends regularly brought them bread. As he was later to observe:

> We did these things without contemplating the danger and the likely consequences for us and our families if we had been caught.

> [Ślązak, IWM, 95/13/1]

The Catholic Church, as well as the Ukrainian Orthodox Church in the Russian Zone, were a source both of reassurance to the population and often of opposition to the occupying powers. At the highest level, Prince Bishop Sapiecha of Kraków appealed personally to Hitler to stop the forced deportation of Poles from the annexed areas in November 1940, albeit without any success. In the General Government, the Churches were bastions of Polonism. There were frequent reports of priests and nuns discreetly assisting the Underground. Even British POWs received their portion of encouragement. Gordon Manners, for instance, records that a Sister of Mary deliberately dropped a mark note as she passed him and his fellow POWs. In Kraków, the Underground was able to arrange financial help for Jews through the Ursuline Convent, while elsewhere individual priests or nuns hid Jews or arranged for false Aryan documentation to be provided. In the Russian Zone many priests – both Polish and Ukrainian – were arrested, and the Churches forced to pay heavy taxes, but the Russians found the actual closure of the Churches no easy task. One report on the Russian Zone, reaching the Foreign Office in London, observed that: 'The women especially were ready to fight for their churches, even if it cost them their life.'

In both zones, just under the surface, there was bitter resentment and anger. At times this boiled over into open confrontation. One British diplomat observed an incident in Lwów in January 1940:

Campaign Chronicle

Four of the local militiamen were trying to control an extremely disorderly queue. Their methods of doing so were rough in the extreme, one militiaman in particular distinguishing himself with sadistic brutality [...] As I was going by he had just knocked an elderly peasant woman down and was beating her with the butt of his rifle as she lay on the ground. Eventually she struggled to her feet, drew a large bottle of vodka out of her string bag and with it struck the militiaman a resounding blow square between the eyes. The bottle burst into a thousand pieces, the militiaman went down like a log and his three colleagues, who sprang to his rescue, were brought to a sudden stop by the old lady's evident determination to use the jagged neck of the bottle as a Venetian dagger upon whoever attempted to arrest her. The crowd cheered. The three militiamen pretended not to have noticed the incident and the old lady held the field.

[NA, FO371/24471]

One of the catalysts for the formation of Underground groups was the need to obtain accurate news about was happening to Poland, as this affected almost every family. The official newspapers contained only propaganda and announcements, although occasionally even here the Polish editors were able to slip in some guarded criticism of their German masters. In October 1939 a small paper called *Poland is Alive* started to be published in Warsaw, and by May appeared five days each month. The top of the front page bore the following inscription:

It is forbidden to accept any payment for this bulletin. It must not be allowed to pass into the hands of the enemy. Do not throw it away. Do not destroy it. Read it through and pass it on only to someone you can trust.

[NA, FO24476]

It was reckoned that something like 150,000 people were able to read the paper. It contained articles, official statements from the Sikorski Government, and much material taken from British and French radio broadcasts. There were several other similar papers, such as the *Polish News* and the *Voice of Poland*, both of which supported the Sikorski Government. The latter was really an official bulletin of the government in Angers. There were also roneographed sheets, much of the content of which was taken from leaflets dropped by Allied planes.

To avoid capture by the *Gestapo*, the printing presses were moved from place to place. It was often the work of the girls who joined the Underground to deliver the papers to various clandestine distribution points, often at great risk. In Kraków, for instance, the newspaper *Wolność* (*Freedom*) was edited by a young Jewish Socialist, Miriam Peleg-Marianski, who had been given 'Aryan' papers by the Underground. She was assisted by Bronisława Langrod, wife of Poland's former envoy to the League of Nations. The danger was that Bronisława had been forced to accept a German lodger. One day, Miriam remembers that he passed through their sitting room and a copy of the paper was lying on the table straight from the press. Miriam nearly panicked but Bronisława calmly remarked: 'Why are you in such a state? After all, he cannot read Polish!'

Attempts to Centralize Armed Resistance and Avoidance of Premature Action

The key to effective resistance was somehow to centralize the myriad of resistance groups in Poland. In October 1939, General Tokarzewski undertook a dangerous tour of the main centres in German-occupied Poland in an initial, but not very successful, attempt to subordinate to his command the numerous resistance groups that had already sprung up. He reckoned there were at least 100 of them. Sikorski, too, had only partial success in centralizing and consolidating the resistance when he set up the ZWZ in January 1940.

In January 1940 the message from the Polish GHQ in France was that, for the next few months, the Home Army (ZWZ) should remain inactive and devote its efforts to stock-taking and consolidating supplies. In the meantime, units should obey orders of the central command and only conduct minor sabotage operations. GHQ feared that anything on a greater scale would provoke savage reprisals from both the Russians and the Germans. Indeed, there were suspicions that the Germans were actually trying to provoke a revolt. In Warsaw, for instance, there were several organizations of an 'allegedly patriotic nature', such as the Union for Active Struggle (ZWC), which in fact worked as *agents provocateurs* for the Germans. This line was echoed by all who managed to leave Poland and report to Angers or meet Allied officials. The Master of the Rolls, Sir Wilfrid Greene, was told in no uncertain tones when he met Madame Potowska (niece of Prince Radziwiłł) in Rome that Allied broadcasts should in no way encourage the Poles to take premature action, as this would only lead to savage reprisals: 'Our theme should be: Be patient and wait.'

In practice this advice was often ignored, both in the mountainous areas in the Kielce region by Hubal (*see page 9*) and in the great forests and marshes of the Soviet Zone. Reports and rumours of what may have been Hubal's activities in the Holy Cross Mountains trickled out of Poland. In December news reached Paris of a Polish group that had been operating in the district of Kielce. It consisted of

> about 250 men, and these have been divided up into ten small groups. These are armed with rifles and with some light and heavy machine guns. The detachment also possess some field guns, radio sets and anti-tank guns. They have all been buried to prevent their discovery, but the danger of rust and damp and general deterioration is very great, and in fact there is great difficulty in preserving these materials from damage. Each small detachment requires twelve hours to assemble, and if ordered to move out of their own area, three days would be required.
>
> [NA, HS4/163]

The same sources also reported that, in the same area, there were 'other detachments', not yet properly organized, while in the town of Opoczno a 'political organization' of some 500 men existed.

In March 1940 Hubal's unit managed to destroy a whole battalion of German infantry near the village of Huciska. The Germans countered by forming a special anti-partisan unit made up of SS and *Wehrmacht* troops, as well as a Panzer unit. A grim catalogue of their revenge reached Paris in June 1940: fourteen villages were burnt to the ground and 1,200 people murdered. At Szałasy, 'all the men over fifteen were arrested, some of whom were shot, the others were locked up in the school and burnt'. On 30 April Hubal was ambushed in a ravine near Opoczno and killed. His body was mutilated, exhibited in the local villages, and then taken to Tomaszów Mazowiecki, where it was either burnt or buried to prevent it becoming a shrine for the resistance.

In the winter of 1939/40 there were also frequent reports of Polish partisan groups in Russian Poland. Prince Charles Radziwiłł told the British minister to the Vatican in January 1940 that there were 'thousands of men' gone to ground in the Pripet Marshes, having hidden away large

The Polish Underground 1939-1947

quantities of arms. He believed that once the Russians and Germans were engaged on other fronts these men would rise up. Similarly, in November the Polish Consul in Cernauti (Romania) sent some interesting reports to his Government-in-Exile to the effect that '*franc-tireurs*' were continuing to fight against Bolshevik troops in Polesie and Volhynia, and that in Eastern Galicia a Ukrainian organization 'with about 10,000 members and a considerable stock of arms' was preparing itself under the leadership of Polish officers for the struggle against the Russians.

Potentially, Soviet-occupied Poland, in the continued absence of Allied action in France, was the more vulnerable to partisan action by the Poles. The remote northern provinces had taken longer to pacify, and the outbreak of the Russo-Finnish war in November had led to the withdrawal of the best Soviet units and, briefly, to the real prospect of a decisive Russian defeat by the Finns. One report coming from 'an intelligent Polish lady', who left Lwów around the New Year, informed Ambassador Kennard that:

> The results of four months of occupation had been [...] to unite Poles, Ukrainians and, at any rate, the middle-class Jews to a degree which few would have believed possible. No one felt any respect for the Russian occupants and it would not be difficult to organize risings, provided it was done soon, before starvation and imprisonment had sapped the vitality of the inhabitants [...] As it was, Russian officers were frequently killed even in Lwów itself and in consequence, most of them barricaded themselves into their houses at night. In the countryside, bands of young men and lads formed, were broken up, and were formed again. There were, no doubt, considerable stores of arms well hidden in the forests and even perhaps in the towns.
>
> [NA, FO371/24470]

Yet she doubted whether such an uprising would be successful unless 'a serious attack' was made in some other quarter on the 'feeble colossus of Russia'.

Colonel Gubbins, an expert on guerrilla warfare in the MI (R) Department in the War Office, who was later to be Director of Operations in the SOE for Western and Central Europe, foresaw the possibility that the Estonians, Latvians and Lithuanians might use the war to eject Soviet troops from their territory. In that situation, the interned Polish troops in those territories would enthusiastically join in and trigger a large-scale revolt in Eastern Poland, but the collapse of Finland in March 1940 reduced such plans to mere pipedreams.

Sabotage Operations in Romania and Hungary

While large-scale resistance within Poland was in reality, despite the illusions of some hot heads, out of the question, a more modest campaign of sabotage was possible. Within Poland there was an abundance of targets but there were also tempting targets outside Poland, particularly in Romania and Hungary, where oil and other raw materials passed through by rail and Danube-barge bound for Germany. However, to destroy these supply lines the necessary equipment and explosives had to be sent.

By mid-October 1939 the Poles already had agents active in Hungary and Romania. In Budapest the contact man was a certain Polish major, who worked in the Legation, but the real leader was the mysterious Mr 'A', who headed a group of nine officers now working in Hungary, each of whom had his own agents in Poland. The major was just a go-between, who was not even allowed to open letters addressed to Mr 'A'. This group had already notched up successes by attacking cargoes of wheat and oil on the Danube. They had ruined the wheat by ensuring that the holds of the barges sprang leaks, which led to the grain rotting, and the oil by boring holes in the tankers so that it drained out into the river.

There was a similar set-up in Romania, where Mr 'B' was looking around the Polish internment camps for suitable volunteers. There were also embryonic groups in Northern and Western Europe. At Stockholm there was a Polish officer trying to recruit suitable Polish personnel who had escaped from the Baltic States. In Western Europe an officer had been sent to the Hague to assess whether there was scope to get in touch with 'local people'. In Switzerland a Polish officer had contact with diamond smugglers who were able to get into Germany. The purpose of the agents in Holland and Belgium was initially to infiltrate propaganda materials into Germany, and to see whether it was 'possible to pass men through these channels' to get in touch with Polish agents in Germany, with whom contact had been broken off in September. Ultimately, they hoped 'to establish a line up the Rhine, which would take hardware'.

The British were well placed to help the Poles with their sabotage plans. In mid-October the War Office, through MI (R), began to liaise with the Poles. In discussions that took place 'with the utmost frankness on both sides' it was agreed that both armies would have a plenipotentiary in London, who would have direct access to their respective commanders-in-chief; and that they would be charged with preparing a plan of operations and the creation of an effective sabotage organization. This was to include:

- Selection and detailing of personnel for all types of work.
- The training of these people.
- The provision of explosives, devices, etc.
- Provision of wireless.
- Arrangements for delivery of equipment.
- The passing of men when trained to the areas where they were to operate.
- The preparation of a general plan of campaign.
- The transmission of orders.

[NA, HS4/193]

In the short term, MI (R) and the specially appointed Polish staff officer had to find out what was really going on in the countries concerned, 'as regards existing organizations, their state of preparedness, their aims and equipment, their means of communication, etc.', and also to establish effective means of communication so that arms, money and men could be safely dispatched. Finally, a general plan of operations was to be drawn up, but here it was emphasized, as it was on all sides throughout the winter months of 1939/40, that 'for the moment resistance must be passive in character, so that the enemy is unaware that an organization is being built up'.

In November Colonel Gubbins was sent to Paris to work with Lieutenant Colonel Gaino of the Polish II Bureau. Gaino went off on a fact-finding mission to Budapest, Belgrade and Bucharest. He urged his agents to extend lines of communication into Poland and the USSR and build up their supplies of weapons. First of all, these were to be cached in secure dumps near the frontier and then moved north into Poland 'as chance offers'. They had already hidden in Hungary some 'hundreds of pistols and revolvers' brought out by refugees, and were in the middle of taking an inventory of these weapons. They did, however, have a formidable shopping list of weapons required from Britain: hand grenades, gelignite and wirelesses, which would be worked by dry batteries, were high on the agenda.

Campaign Chronicle

Gaino also discussed future sabotage plans with Gubbins in Paris. While stressing that all sabotage and guerrilla activities in Poland had to cease for the moment, he suggested that sabotage against the Germans should begin in neutral countries in ways that could not be traced back to the Poles. He believed that the best prospect for action was on the Danube, where, in December 1939, there were between 150 and 200 barges lying empty at Bratislava. The Poles had sufficient agents to undertake such an operation and were already working on a plan. Gubbins reported that 'as a general line of attack, they suggest the placing of delayed-action bombs in every second boat'. This would be effective because the barges are made of wood and were 'more or less moored together'.

For future plans, agents within Poland were sending reports on the machinery in German armament factories in Upper Silesia, so that the best way for sabotaging them could be worked out. They also received reports from contacts within Germany via what Gaino called the 'letter box system'. As an example, Gaino referred to the recent arrival in Bucharest of a letter and sketch from a dissident German workman, recently employed on the Siegfried Line. He had posted this letter to an address in Hungary, and it had successfully passed the censor because the authorities failed to discover the overlay in secret ink, which he had used to convey the information. From Hungary it was then sent to a Polish agent in Romania.

There were considerable problems involved in the supply of sabotage materials from London to Romania and Hungary. In Romania, the British Legation feared that dispatch could only be achieved by bribery, which, in turn, would lead to the risk of blackmail. To avoid this, it suggested the goods be consigned to some agent in Belgrade or Budapest, and categorized as 'transit goods', which could then be unloaded at 'some quiet spot up the river'. The Poles managed to set up depots in Budapest and Bucharest and, theoretically, were able to receive some 1,000 kilos a month; but Britain, with its existing lines of communication, could only send material at the rate of 250 kilos a month. At the end of January, a small number of wireless sets was dispatched and plans were drawn up for further deliveries in February.

By February 1940 Polish plans for sabotage were still in a formative stage. Groups of 'keen and well-qualified individuals' had already been formed to plan the sabotage of rail transport. It was decided to inject a small amount of emery into the openings used on the Knorrbrakes of the rolling stock for oiling, which would result during the journey in the axles overheating and the malfunctioning of the brakes. As the lines to

The Polish Underground 1939–1947

Germany ran mainly along winding tracks with steep gradients, faulty brakes would rapidly cause long delays.

Another target was the German barge traffic on the Danube in Hungary. English and French businessmen, with financial assistance from their governments, were already causing considerable delay to river transport to Germany simply by paying above the market rate to hire smaller craft from Hungarian barge firms, which could navigate the full length of the Danube. The scarcity of these barges compelled the Germans to transport their goods by means of Greek 'szlepers', which had such a deep draught that they could not get further up the river than Turnau-Severin, where their cargoes were re-loaded onto the barges of a German-Romanian company. Consequently, there was considerable congestion here, making for a potentially good target. According to Polish sources, these barges were rather laxly guarded by middle-aged men, and so it was possible to sabotage them. Groups had already been set up for this purpose in Turnau-Severin in November, and, in order to deflect suspicion, Hungarian artefacts – such as matches, buttons, cigarettes, books, and newspapers recently published in Hungary – were also being collected, so that the sabotage might be attributed to local Hungarian residents and not to Poles.

Plans were also in hand for sabotaging the oil pipelines running to the Giurgiu area in Romania, where the oil was loaded onto tanker barges on the Danube. The British were assured that the necessary groups could be mobilized in a period of three weeks, once consent was given from London. However, the realization of these plans was not so easy. Romanian agents were judged to be potentially unreliable, as their aims often diverged from the Allies'. Consequently, it was decided to recruit 'Polish patriots', who also had Romanian citizenship, but by March 1940 only six operatives had actually been selected, although the records of over 100 possible candidates were being examined.

In Budapest, the Polish ring of agents had been penetrated by the Germans and, as Captain Peter Wilkinson who had been sent to Hungary from Paris to report on the situation recalled years later in 1974, 'the whole place was in turmoil'. There were a small number of Poles who, encouraged by the British SIS, regularly crossed the frontier (on foot or on skis) to deliver explosives to resistance groups. Their guides were often peacetime smugglers. One of the most dramatic of these figures was the Countess Skarbek, whose codename in 1941 was 'Christine Granville'. She was the prototype James Bond girl – both promiscuous and very brave. She inspired such passions that one Polish agent, Józef Radzimski, whose advances had been rejected by her, attempted to shoot himself in the genitals and, when he missed, threw himself off a bridge into the Danube, only to survive as it was frozen over! Inevitably, such a drama contributed to the 'turmoil' described by Wilkinson.

Organization, Supply and Sabotage in Poland

By early 1940, the nucleus of an organization to carry out sabotage on selected targets was already in place in South East Poland. In January, an oil well near Borysław was fired by 'Polish youths', although this was just an isolated incident. Two possible sabotage points on the Lwów–Przemyśl and Lwów–Podwoloczysk lines had been identified and explosives, which were already in Poland, earmarked. Efforts were also being made to contact railwaymen with expert knowledge of the Polish rail network.

By spring 1940, however, operations in Poland were made increasingly difficult due to a general tightening-up of frontier security by the Germans and Russians, making the passage of couriers and the smuggling of weapons and ammunition increasingly difficult. In June, Wilkinson reported that the Russians had fortified the Polish–Romanian frontier so strongly that every courier party had to be covered by a 'company of the Polish Free Corps in Romania'. The company would storm one of the Russian frontier posts and, in the resulting mêlée, the couriers would attempt to slip over the frontier, but losses were running as high as 50 per cent. Consequently, the Poles became increasingly reluctant to waste manpower crossing frontiers, and advised that weapons and explosives should be stored in Turkey or Egypt, from where they could be drawn when opportunities arose.

It was not only explosives, small arms and radios that needed to be taken across the frontier. The Polish Underground also needed money. On 15 March the Germans issued new 100, 500, and 1,000 *złoty* notes, leaving the smaller denominations still in circulation. Theoretically, those smaller notes could still be smuggled across the frontier but only in large unwieldy sacks, making their agents all the more vulnerable. The Polish Foreign Minister therefore approached the British Government to ask permission to give a contract to a British firm to print exact replicas of the new currency. His government promised to redeem all the notes for which they had been responsible after the war. Despite Treasury reluctance, this was agreed upon.

In February 1941, General Sosnkowski was able to give a report on some of the sabotage achieved within both zones of occupation up to the beginning of June 1940. The most common forms were:

The Polish Underground 1939–1947

Letting the petrol out of cisterns while the trains are running, rendering petrol useless by adding sugar, setting fire to [the petrol] by means of time fuses, which only act after the train has gone a considerable distance and is already on Reich territory, cleverly concealed damage done to machinery and tools in use in factories, derailing of trains, employment of substances to contaminate foodstuffs and cause sickness amongst human beings and animals.

[NA, FO371/26723]

Sosnkowski then gave a few precise examples of sabotage in both zones, but these were not accompanied by dates:

- Two trains were derailed near Łódź, one carrying soldiers and the other oil. Several German soldiers were killed and wounded and petrol was burnt. The Germans shot several of their own transport staff as a punishment for their laxness.
- Regular sabotage in the factories, such as Starachowice, which were engaged in war production, by spoiling machine tools and making machines unusable by removing vital parts.
- Contamination of railway carriages on express trains going to the Reich by means of germs, which caused serious kidney troubles.

In the Soviet Zone, sabotage was aimed at the traffic en route for Germany, but a large store of ammunition was also destroyed at Lyczakow in Lwów, and stocks of hay and food were also burnt near the railway station. [Source: NA, FO371/26723]

Fall of France
In the spring of 1940 the Polish Government-in-Exile was delighted to receive an invitation for General Sikorski to attend the Supreme Allied War Council. Sikorski argued that this showed that Poland was 'completely equal with the Allies' and refuted once and for all the German 'myth' that Poland was the drudge of the other powers. The Poles fully lived up to their status as active allies of Britain and France. By the spring of 1940 they had a force of two divisions plus one cavalry and one light mechanized brigade in France. They sent a brigade to Norway in April 1940 and, in the brief French campaign that ended in the fall of France, the Polish Legion fought tenaciously. Pétain told General Sikorski that he had witnessed the 1st Polish Division drive back four German divisions and added: 'if there had only been ten Polish divisions, victory would

have been certain'. With the fall of Paris on 19 June 1940, the Polish Government was determined to evacuate as many of its own troops as possible to Britain. British ships managed to carry some 22,500 men from the Channel ports. On the evening of 21 June, the Polish President was met at Paddington station by King George VI.

Sikorski was determined to continue the fight against Germany, both by re-equipping Polish forces that had escaped from France, and by continuing to direct the activities of the Underground resistance in Poland; but he had first to reassert control over his government in London. The fall of France, the chaotic evacuation of the Polish Government, and the plight of the Polish troops in Britain had reawakened the slumbering resentment between the *Sanacja* and members of the pre-war opposition. Sikorski's willingness to explore the possibilities of improving relations with the USSR and of the creation of a Polish legion in Russia to fight Germany – if Russia came into the war against Hitler – had also caused intense resentment amongst Polish Conservatives. At one stage, Sikorski even feared for his safety. He managed to defeat an attempt to set up a new government under Foreign Minister Załęski, thanks to the mediation of General Sosnkowski. On 19 July Sikorski was asked by President Raczkiewicz to form a new Government of National Unity, supported by 'harmonious cooperation between the parties'. In reality, it had become clear, to quote Sir Howard Kennard, that 'there is in fact no alternative to him [...] As a man and a public figure, the Poles cannot easily do without him.'

Now, with France beaten and British troops ignominiously ejected from the continent, Sikorski faced a Herculean task to maintain an effective resistance campaign within Poland.

Impact of the Fall of France on the Polish Underground

Dr Klukowski wrote in his diary on 16 June 1940 that 'the news from France is terrible. People are emotionally broken. Some have lost all hope.' There is no doubt that the appalling news of the French collapse stunned the Poles. Major Alojzy Dziura-Dziurski, for instance, was so depressed that he temporarily resigned from the ZWZ. He confessed years later that, momentarily, he considered joining the victorious Germans, who were now the masters of Europe; but realized that, in reality, no Pole could commit to such a course, as 'the vicious Nazi persecutions in Poland bred resentment and opposition, which when multiplied, would destroy Germany'.

The Polish Underground 1939–1947

For the Underground, the totally unexpected defeat of France and the repulse of British troops from the continent created a new situation. The original plans drawn up by Sikorski and Sosnkowski assumed that Polish resistance would strengthen in proportion to a German weakening in the west. In fact they envisaged a virtual replay of the First World War: only when the German military machine was sufficiently weakened to allow the entry of Polish armies into Poland would a general insurrection take place, aimed at both the Russians and Germans. Clearly this now seemed unrealistic. As General Bór observed, 'all logical hopes of a German defeat had now gone'.

Three days after the fall of Paris, Bór travelled by train to Warsaw to confer with General Rowecki. On the way he observed the Germans delirious with victory. Once in Warsaw, he and Rowecki began to reconsider the situation. The consequences were indeed dire. The defeat of France had driven a coach and horses right through the ZWZ's organization. The liaison network, the courier routes to and from France, which were the means for sending messages and instructions from the Government-in-Exile, had now virtually collapsed. It looked, too, as if the Underground would be without funds. All thought of a general uprising had now evaporated. The two generals came to the conclusion that 'our work must be switched over to long term policy'. Primarily this involved, in the short term, intensifying intelligence work and producing clandestine newspapers and propaganda, in an attempt to maintain the morale of the Polish people. The Underground was also able to provide Britain with valuable Intelligence from within Germany, as large areas of Western Poland had become Reich territory. Given the increased German police surveillance that was now possible, both generals came to the conclusion that, for the time being, the Underground needed to go deeper and restrict the number of new members.

The next six months were to be a most critical period for the Underground, but still no Quisling or Vichy-style government emerged in Poland. The prominent pre-war conservative Władysław Studnicki, for example, attempted in vain to persuade the Germans to re-establish a Polish state. In the summer of 1940, Prince Janusz Radziwiłł, who had been released from a Russian prison as a result of Göring's intervention, resolutely refused to cooperate with the Germans. Polish agents crossing the border into Hungary reported a new German propaganda campaign aimed at convincing the Poles that Germany was their sole hope, and that the Nazi Government was ready both to create a new Polish state at the expense of the USSR and to form a Polish legion to fight the Russians.

44

They even reported that maps of the proposed frontiers of the new state had been prepared. Possibly – if combined with magnanimous treatment of the Poles – this might have been effective but, for the Germans, Poland was essentially an area to be ruthlessly exploited. Once victory had been secured in the West, there was little chance of any magnanimity towards Poland. On 6 November 1940 Hans Frank told his lieutenants that the General Government area was destined only to be a massive source of labour for the Reich.

London and the Polish Resistance After the Fall of France

When the Polish Government arrived in London after the fall of France, the bulk of the Polish Army was sent to Scotland, ostensibly to protect the coastline from a German invasion. The Polish political and military head-quarters were set up in the Hotel Rubens in Buckingham Palace Road, London. On 5 August 1940 the Anglo-Polish military agreements were signed, which established the framework of the cooperation between British and Polish Armed Forces. The Polish Council of Ministers announced that 'Poland is allied with Great Britain and in accordance with this the Polish Army will fight arm in arm with the British Army whenever need arises.'

After Dunkirk, Britain's principal weapons against the Germans were sabotage, bombardment and blockade, and it was to the first of these that Poles could make a key contribution. On 22 July the Special Operations Executive (SOE) was created out of a fusion of the Secret Intelligence Service, the Foreign Office propaganda department and the MI (R) section of the War Office that specialized in sabotage. The chiefs of staff directive stressed that 'undermining the strength of the spirit of the enemy forces, especially those in occupied territory, should be the constant aim of our subversive organizations'. In the long term, the SOE was to encourage and plan revolts right across occupied Europe, but in the short to medium term, its priority was to cut enemy communications and subvert enemy morale. In a Europe shell-shocked by the German victories, Poland was undoubtedly one of SOE's most important assets. Dr Dalton, as the Minister of Economic Warfare, was the Cabinet minister in overall charge of the SOE, while the Foreign Office was represented by Gledwyn Jebb. The responsibilities of the Polish section of the SOE were to help the Polish Army's VI Bureau develop contact with the Polish Underground and assist it in every way, especially by sending personnel and equipment.

Although the main body of Polish troops, to quote Jan Gross, remained to 'brood on their fate' in Scotland, a quick start was made to prepare men for special operations in Poland. By August fifty men had been recruited. They were based at a camp on Loch Ailort and trained in a series of special eight-day courses at Inverlochy Castle, Fort William, beginning on 17 September. Besides instruction in grenade throwing, explosives and demolition work, they were also taught unarmed combat, movement and stalking as well as 'killing, butchering, cooking and eating a sheep'. The British officer in charge, Major Stacey, found the Poles as 'keen as mustard'. Essentially, these picked men were to be trained for formidable tasks. In a memorandum drawn up for SOE by the VI Bureau, the skills needed were outlined:

- They were to be practised in handling automatic and machine pistols and trained 'in attempts on the life of single individuals or small enemy groups in houses, streets, railways, etc.'
- They would also become experts in placing mines and 'manage in conditions requiring improvisation where necessary', e.g. improvise a switch, a mine with delayed action, prepare an HE [high explosive] mixture with chemicals, etc.
- The main emphasis was laid upon demolitions and damage to transport. Consequently, operators were to be trained in derailing trains, damaging bridges and junctions, planting AT [anti-tank] mines for use on roads and defiles and also damaging telecommunications.
- All soldiers were to be proficient in driving cars and motorcycles.
- Although there were to be a number of specially trained radio operators, it was imperative that all participants should be familiar with British W/T [wireless transmitter] sets and should be able to 'receive a few simple coded signals'.
- They were to be able to subsist in 'woods and fields without assistance of the local population, changing continuously the place of stay and with great efforts in long marches'.
- Training in parachuting was essential.
- They were also to have a thorough knowledge of the German Army, administration and the Nazi Party, as well as the vehicles and equipment currently in use with the *Wehrmacht*.
- They also needed to have a grasp of basic German and Russian and a certain amount of Ukrainian, White Ruthenian or Lithuanian.
- Finally, 'each one of the operators would have to be capable of training local units in Poland for diversive operations and to lead them himself'.

[NA, HS4/315]

Campaign Chronicle

The other arm of Polish resistance was directed by Professor Kot, who, as a close ally of Sikorski, was appointed Polish Minister of Interior in the Government-in-Exile. Kot saw his work as promoting civil unrest and, ultimately, preparing a revolutionary situation in Poland. At a meeting on 11 October, Kot boasted to Gledwyn Jebb that 'he could, for instance, tell the Polish railway workers, or even the subordinate ranks of the Polish police, what their attitude should be and what they ought to do', and that he was also in touch with the vast army of Poles who had been transported to Germany to work on the land or in the factories'. However, in a conversation with Gubbins and Wilkinson on 6 December 1940, General Sikorski defined Kot's role more as 'keeping up the spirit and morale of the country' through political propaganda, information services and 'charity', which involved subsidising certain collective bodies, such as the Railwaymen's Union. His organization was to be run from Budapest. Kot impressed both Jebb and Dalton, who came to the conclusion that, with some material help as well as money, his organization could do 'real damage' to the Germans. To act as liaison officer between Kot, the Polish VI Bureau, SOE and the War Office, Gubbins was appointed to the SOE as Director of Training and Operations with the rank of brigadier.

To facilitate his work, Kot demanded the use of a wireless transmitter in the United Kingdom and the sum of 20,000,000 *Reichsmarks* and 100,000 US dollars to be placed at the disposal of his organization. These sums were to be paid into the Polish Government's account in a series of small instalments up to July 1941. They were to be used to maintain the morale of the Polish agents and those officials who still remained loyal to the Polish state. Kot recommended to the SOE on 7 November that 'all feasible methods' to get the money into Poland should be attempted: agents due to be dropped by parachute should take some notes with them and, possibly, if sums could be transferred by diplomatic bag to the Vatican City, Polish priests might act as couriers.

In principle, the British Government was ready to find the sums needed, but raising the amount of *Reichsmarks* in Stockholm, Lisbon and Zürich without provoking the suspicions of the Germans would prove difficult. The Bank of England had a comparatively large holding of *franc* notes and a suggestion was made that these could be exchanged in the occupied zone of France for *Reichsmarks* but such transactions would take time to arrange. Kot himself suggested 'discreet' enquiries among Jewish organizations in London.

On 6 December, when Sikorski, Kot, Sosnkowski, Gubbins and Wilkinson met at the Polish headquarters in Hotel Rubens, Sikorski effectively gave them a progress report on the development of the resistance movement in Poland. He described the Underground political organization within Poland and stressed how vital it was that it should receive financial subsidies from Britain to buy food and medicines, which the American Red Cross had delivered free in 1940, but could no longer do in 1941. General Sosnkowski was then asked about the military situation in Poland. He claimed there was already 'a restricted secret organization of 30,000 first-line troops fully armed and equipped', which would only be fully activated when the military situation was favourable. These troops were backed up with first and second reserves. When Gubbins observed that both the military and civil organizations would surely remain passive until it became clear that the Germans were relaxing their grip on Poland, Kot pointed out that the two organizations were not facing quite the same situation, as 'the political organization must be more active the lower morale sank due to setbacks on the other fronts'. As far as resistance in the Russian Zone went, Kot conceded that the recent mass deportations had seriously weakened both the military and political organizations. Summing up, Sikorski stressed that 'both the political and military organizations were now as complete as they could be and it remained for the British Government to decide what assistance they could offer'. Gubbins replied that Britain was ready to help but that funds, communications and military demands were limited and that to make effective use of them, planning and coordination were essential.

Sikorski then raised the vital question of air links with Poland. He noted that four Polish squadrons were being equipped with Wellington bombers, but was highly critical that the Air Ministry 'appeared reluctant to break up existing squadrons in order to release planes for long-distance flights to Poland'. The other problem was the matter of wireless transmitters. There were, at the moment, only three Polish transmitters in England, which were being used by the Army, the Secret Service and VI Bureau. In the end it was conceded that Kot and the VI Bureau would use the same transmitter, although they would use a different cipher and a different frequency.

Communications with Occupied Poland

In March 1941 the Treasury agreed to supply $100,000 and RM 20,000,000 to the Polish Government-in-Exile. This was to be paid monthly and debited to the £5 million credit granted to cover the Polish war effort. The problem, of course, was how to get the money into Poland. Initially, SOE had been very reluctant to back the Poles' requests for money, owing

Campaign Chronicle

to what it regarded as the 'general insecurity and amateur nature of the Kot organization'. Polish Representatives in Lisbon, Istanbul and Budapest were all suspected, in the opinion of the SOE, of 'at the worst treachery and at best incompetence'. The main courier lines in and out of Poland went via Slovakia, Hungary, Yugoslavia and Bulgaria to Turkey and Greece and thence to Cairo. In January 1941, 90 per cent of the money, most of the mail and all the couriers still went through Budapest, which was also an important Polish base for radio communication. In the spring of 1941, with the German advance into Yugoslavia and Greece, these lines became much more difficult to operate. The Polish Legation in Budapest was closed on 11 April and the hurried arrangements made by the Polish agent 'G.N. Norton', whereby messages would be accepted by the Turkish Military Attaché for transmission to Istanbul, were not carried out.

Alarming news was beginning to emerge in December 1940 of German penetration of the Polish courier and spy network in the Balkans, for which Kot was responsible. A Polish agent, A/H2, claimed that one Sameon Mikiciński, alias 'Paluchowicz', was 'the mainspring' of this. Claiming to be a Chilean diplomat, Paluchowicz convinced Kot that he was able to liberate eminent Poles from imprisonment, and he had indeed been instrumental in persuading the Germans to release the wife of General Sikorski. In reality, however, this was a cover for collaboration with the German *Abwehr*. According to A/H2's report of December 1940, Paluchowicz was responsible for 'one heinous act of sabotage' by betraying the recipients of the money being smuggled into Poland, which apparently resulted in the arrest of more than 1,000 Poles. The evidence of his collaboration was so compelling that the British, helped by a Polish agent, ESS, planned to have him kidnapped in Istanbul. After two attempts, when the 'knock-out pills' did not work, despite being given a double dosage both times, Paluchowicz was finally beaten unconscious, chloroformed, and flown to Palestine, where he was imprisoned for six months. Eventually, because the Poles had no jurisdiction to try civilians in British territory, he was taken out into the desert and shot by the Polish agent Edward Szarkiewicz.

Organization and security of the Polish courier networks in both Jerusalem and Cairo were also dangerously lax. In Jerusalem, Colonel Zakazewski (*sic*), the former Military Attaché in Budapest, had created an organization that Wilkinson called the 'Crazy Gang', and had been disowned by the Polish II Bureau. In Cairo, too, security was equally lax, largely because of rivalry between Tadeusz Zasuliński, the Polish chargé

The Polish Underground 1939–1947

d'affaires at the Legation, who was considered to be close to Kot, and Colonel Józef Matecki, alias 'Jacob Alek', of the VI Bureau. Kot's couriers were usually 'very young men', who were often bewildered and, according to Wilkinson, ready to confide in the first stranger who spoke their language. When they arrived they were not given secure accommodation or properly looked after. To illustrate his point, Wilkinson described somewhat cryptically for the benefit of the SOE, the 'case of young W', a Polish courier, who was about to leave Cairo for the overland route to Poland:

> On arrival here, he goes straight to Z [Zasuliński], and the news runs so quickly round the [Polish] Legation that J.A. [Jacob Alek] was asked by the native Kavass [an Egyptian official] whether he wanted to see the courier who was just going to [...] or the one who had just come from [...] Not content with that, Z sends the wretched W to stay at the local 38-land [Polish] hostel, packed with refugees, mainly Jews, all of whom are agog why he is here and what he is doing ...

> [NA, HS4/198]

Given the difficulties of the land route, it was understandable why Polish Headquarters in January 1941 should stress that 'the establishment of a quick and direct liaison with Poland is at the moment a question of utmost importance'. Not only did the Poles want to be able to drop couriers by parachute but also to be to land and pick up personnel and mail. Consequently, the RAF was asked to organize monthly flights to Poland. The Air Ministry was only able to offer one Whitley aircraft, which was adapted for long-range flights. In cooperation with the Polish VI Bureau, cylindrical containers that could be released from its bomb bays were designed. The first flight took place on the night of 15 February 1941 and three agents were dropped. Although they landed in the Cieszyn area in Southern Poland, some 80 miles short of their target, they managed to reach Warsaw safely. One agent, Žukauskas, who managed to return to London in 1943, reported that he made his way on foot to Warsaw without incident, where his duty consisted of organizing reception committees for further parachutists.

That was to be the last flight for over a year. During the summer months, the Air Ministry refused point blank to fly any more sorties to Poland, as the distances were such that an aircraft could not return in the hours of complete darkness. The RAF also rejected requests to hand over three or four long-range aircraft, which would be manned by a Polish crew, on the grounds that the aircraft were needed for bombing operations elsewhere.

Plans for Future Action

The Polish General Staff spent much of the winter of 1940/41 drawing up plans for action in Poland and elsewhere. The Polish Joint Planning Committee produced, in January 1941, a key plan for the final phases of the war. In essence, it envisaged domination of the air and seas by British and Commonwealth forces, the erosion of German strength through fighting on several fronts and then an armed insurrection in Poland that would enable British forces to land in the Baltic, Netherlands or Denmark. It was calculated that about 180,000 men could be mobilized in the General Government, with perhaps another four divisions coming from the areas annexed to the Reich. The 'principal base of the insurrection' would be the General Government and it would be 'developed' in the direction of Pomorze (Pomerania), so as to facilitate outside reinforcements. At the same time, the industrial area Kraków–Lublin–Łódź would be paralysed by insurrection. In the words of the final version of the plan, which was sent to Brigadier Gubbins on 5 May 1941, 'the armed movement would have the character of a big diversion on an operational scale'. Its execution would be based on diversionary action by sabotage, which would be aimed at disorganizing the German occupation forces, both by dislocating their command system and by preventing reserves in the Reich and the Balkans from intervening. Clearly, well before the insurrection began, the insurgent groups would have to be supplied with the necessary equipment, which would include signal units, wireless sets, cadres of instructors, etc. In a paper produced about the same time on the *Characteristics of a Modern Insurrectionary Movement*, the Polish General Staff observed that 'insurrections of popular type feebly armed and without modern weapons are foredoomed to unsuccess [*sic*] ...' For the insurrection to be successful the Poles would have to be supplied with both planes and tanks. Consequently, it was vital to seize areas that could rapidly be set up as air bases, on which supplies of men and equipment could be immediately landed.

In a sense, this plan was simply bringing up to date with greater detail the existing Polish strategy for victory. It would open up Poland to a British invasion, thereby also ensuring that Soviet forces did not exploit

The Polish Underground 1939–1947

the collapse of Germany to invade. It was, of course, in the winter of 1940/41 very much a case of the Polish General Staff whistling in the dark to keep up their spirits. Realistically, all that could be done in Poland was to persevere with a modest sabotage programme.

On 14 February, General Rowecki was instructed by General Sosnkowski to carry out sabotage activities 'within the limits of sporadic action'. This was to involve the sabotage of oil and ammunition transports, machines and production in the war factories, especially in Germany. To avoid reprisals against the civilian population, it was to be 'unobtrusive'. The instructions stressed that the time for large-scale action had not yet arrived, but limited action would be allowed in self-protection and in the pursuit of spies and traitors, as long as the permission of the Government Delegate was obtained.

Polish Resistance Amongst the Diaspora

Another front for sabotage was the harnessing of the Polish Diaspora in the USA, South America, France and Northern Europe, which altogether numbered some 8 million Poles. The idea originated with Kot's assistant, Jan Librach, and was approved by both Sikorski and the British Government, which agreed to fund it. The money would be used to set up groups, which would strike at German citizens and economic interests. To assist with this, the European Polish Minorities Section or EU/P was set up within the SOE. By May 1941 'organizers' were installed in France, North Africa, Denmark and South America.

In France, the Polish community consisted of about 500,000 civilians. Two organizations had been set up to organize resistance amongst this population: 'Angelica', which was responsible to Kot at the Polish Ministry of the Interior and 'Adjudicate' under the II Bureau. The latter was geared to carry out small-scale sabotage operations, while the former had the more ambitious aim of setting up what was in effect a Polish Underground in France, which, like its counter part in Poland, would prepare itself for an eventual uprising against the Germans when the time was ripe. By the summer, some 5,000 French Poles had been enrolled for active anti-German operations. The cell organizations were spread throughout the country in about seventy districts, of which the largest by far was the industrial city of Lille, where the organization totalled some 1,700 men. Other groups were centred around Caen, Grenoble, Montluçon, St Etienne, Toulouse and Perpignan. There were also cells amongst the Polish peasantry settled in the Toulouse–Limoges area. As early as the night of 10/11 April 1941, six Polish parachutists were flown out to execute a mission aimed at destroying the Passac power station near Bordeaux, but as a result of an electrical fault the plane had to return to Manston airfield in Kent and crash-landed, killing two and wounding four of the crew and the six parachutists.

The Poles were also well organized in South America. There were cells in the Polish communities in Brazil, Argentina, Uruguay and Paraguay, which were directed from a chief agent in Buenos Aires. By December 1941 the organization numbered 500 men, and agents were already infiltrated into the Lahti-Condor Air Service offices, the Police, and the port authorities in Buenos Aires. In Denmark a start had also been made in organizing cells in the Polish sports and cultural organizations.

Finally, there were also well over a million Polish men and women working in the labour camps in Germany, who were targeted by both the Kot organization and VI Bureau, as they could provide invaluable Intelligence for planning sabotage within the Reich. A considerable amount of Intelligence already came from these sources, and plans were being drawn up for a more intense propaganda campaign. In July 1941 the SOE and Foreign Office were very surprised, indeed incredulous, to receive information emanating from Polish sources in Budapest that Polish Underground groups in the General Government were receiving 'arms and ammunition, including machine guns, in very substantial quantities', from dissident German organizations 'with the connivance of the Soviet Government' (Foreign Office minute of 30 July 1941).

To keep in touch with this conspiratorial network, radio communications were of vital importance. The II and VI Bureaus shared facilities as far as possible. They had a 100-watt home-made transceiver in Cairo, which could communicate with Poland, Budapest, Belgrade and Bucharest. There was also a 100-watt Hallicrafter transceiver in Istanbul, as well as clandestine transmitters to the north of Bucharest, near Budapest and in Belgrade. The Kot organization was also able to communicate directly with Montenegro. Communications with Lisbon and Stockholm were via the Embassy transmitter, and with France via II Bureau channels to Vichy and Paris. Messages were also sent through the Commander of 'Adjudicate', Lieutenant Teodor Dzierzgowski, whose task was to organize minor sabotage operations and the evacuation of key personnel to Britain.

Growth of Resistance in German-Occupied Poland

The ZWZ, on paper at least, was already a potentially powerful force, although central control over its units was still not very effective, as they often pursued their own agendas and functioned independently of orders from the Home Army Command in Warsaw. General Sosnkowski had initially put the active strength of the Home Army at 30,000 men, but by the end of December 1940 this had been revised upwards to a figure of about 3,500 officers and 48,000 other ranks. This was backed by two reserve forces: the first, numbering some 286 officers and 70,000 other ranks, was composed of men loyal to the cause but lacking the skill and training to carry out conspiratorial as opposed to paramilitary work. Their equipment was made up largely of material hidden in September/October 1939 and consisted mainly of rifles and small arms with a few anti-tank weapons and light mortars. The second reserve, whose members were registered with the ZWZ, would be mobilized as '*franc-tireurs*' as soon as the insurrection began.

Judging by the reports of British POWs who managed to escape from camps in East Germany in the autumn and winter of 1941, the ZWZ already had a network capable of helping fugitives cross the frontier into Russian Poland. In most cases, British personnel reported later that they met nothing but kindness from the local population as they were passed from farm to farm and village to village. Just to take one example: three soldiers, Corporal Bainbridge and Privates Roberts and Waller, who escaped from a POW camp at Konitz (Chojnice) in September 1940, were, after being given maps and directions by the Polish camp doctor, eventually put in touch by the Underground with 'an organization, of which the local leader was an ex-flying officer' and given 'a Mauser pistol for defence'. They were hidden in a village where a German deserter was also concealed and later taken across the frontier by a member of 'the Organization'. He crossed over with them, intending to take them to a hideout 'belonging to the Organization on the Russian side'. They were, however, arrested and imprisoned by the NKVD. The unfortunate Polish guide was 'even worse treated' than the escaped POWs.

One of the key roles the Underground played in Poland was the gathering of Intelligence, both within occupied-Poland and the Reich itself. Wireless reports were made to London weekly and more frequently if warranted. From the winter of 1940/41 onwards, a mass of information flowed into London, detailing the build-up of German forces in Poland. In March 1941 a general appreciation based on 'numerous fragmentary but trustworthy' Intelligence reports, received from Poland from July 1940 to March 1941, enabled SOE and ultimately the British Government to form a picture of German preparations for war against Russia. German road building and aerodrome construction, as well as troop concentrations and the accumulation of large quantities of military supplies in the winter of 1940/41, had all been carefully monitored. However, Polish sources stressed that, given the absence of German mechanized divisions, which were engaged in the Balkans, a May offensive was 'highly improbable'.

Throughout the winter of 1940/41 limited sabotage operations had continued in Poland. ZWZ personnel instructed skilled workers and trade unionists in the intricacies of sabotage, while the Polish Railway Employees Organization was ordered to intensify the wear and tear on locomotives and railway stock both in Poland and, where possible, in Germany. By February 1941 some 43 per cent of the locomotives in the General Government were awaiting repair. Information also reached the SOE that in September and October 1940 mysterious fires had broken out in factories in Mielec, while 'large stores of hay, corn, and food were burnt out on the Praga suburb of Warsaw under the pretext of an accidental fire'. The German press also carried frequent reports of 'unexplained' fires or sabotage. For instance, the *Thorner Freiheit* reported on 14 May 1941 that three large mills had been destroyed by fire in Lubicz, Toruń Mokre and Inowrocław.

In the spring of 1940, General Rowecki had formed the Union for Revenge with a brief to conduct sabotage plus diversionary and reprisal operations against the Germans. Leaders of the Union took a course that involved tactics, communications, mechanics and bacterial, chemical and toxicological warfare. In May 1941 General Sosnkowski informed General Gubbins at the SOE that there was a special laboratory attached to the Underground Headquarters of the ZWZ, where 'the necessary material' for agricultural and forest sabotage was prepared. This involved producing bacilli and breeding insects to infect grain crops and the great timber-producing forests in both Germany and Poland. To carry this out, the ZWZ relied on Polish POWs or conscripted workers. Bacterial sabotage was also directed against German personnel during the spring and early summer of 1941: there were 178 known cases of typhus amongst German soldiers in Poland. One Pole, by the name of Jan,

> delighted in spreading contagious diseases among the Germans. Jan, who spoke German fluently, would visit bars, talk with German soldiers, and at the right time drop from a little box a louse bearing microbes and typhoid-bearing germs behind the collar of his German acquaintance.
>
> [Lukas, *The Forgotten Holocaust*, p. 65]

The Polish Resistance in Auschwitz, 1940–41

The Polish Underground even reached into Auschwitz, which received its first transport of Polish prisoners on 14 June 1940. Three months later, Witold Pilecki, a former officer in the 13th Regiment of the Uhlans [*Ułan*] and a member of one of the many small resistance groups that had sprung up in Poland in 1939, volunteered to go to Auschwitz as a prisoner to organize resistance groups within the camp and smuggle out information, which could be sent to London. Consequently, with the initially reluctant acceptance of his Underground commander, Pilecki deliberately got himself arrested in September. Once inside he began to form opposition cells based on the standard group of five, whose members knew each other but not the other cells. His plan, as he formulated in a report that later reached Warsaw, was to:

- Encourage his fellow prisoners by providing news from outside.
- Provide extra food and clothing for the members of the Underground.
- Send reports outside and 'above all' to prepare 'one's own units to take over the camp, if the moment should come, in the form of an order to drop either weapons or parachutists on the camp'.

[Józef Garliński, *Fighting Auschwitz*, p. 38]

A number of other resistance groups sprang up independently of each other, as indeed they had done throughout Poland. Members of the Polish Socialist Party created their own resistance group, based on units of three, while Jan Mosdorf – a member of the right wing National Radical Movement (ONR) – organized groups based on units of six. In 1941 the ZWZ set up its own network of cells in the camp. As early as October 1940, Pilecki managed to send out oral reports on Auschwitz by means of released prisoners. In March 1941, the wife of Władysław Szpakowski, a member of the Underground in Auschwitz, managed to obtain her husband's release through the aegis of the Swedish Consulate. On his release, he took with him a comprehensive written report on what was happening in Auschwitz, which was then taken to London by courier.

Pilecki escaped from the camp in 1943 and took part in the Warsaw Uprising a year later. He remained loyal to the London-based Polish Government-in-Exile and was executed in 1948 by the NKVD.

Campaign Chronicle

The spreading of propaganda was also an important part of the ZWZ's activities. A key source for this was Polish broadcasts from London, delivered via the BBC. In July 1941 it was decided to give the Poles fifteen minutes a day broadcasting time, but this was subject to vetting and efforts to tone down any attacks on the USSR. Much of this news was immediately incorporated in the Underground Polish press and circulated rapidly within the General Government. For instance, Kennard reported to Anthony Eden on 14 February 1941 a story he had been told by a Polish refugee recently arrived in Britain: as soon as the gist of an important announcement by Churchill was received through the BBC bulletin, the Pole had been immediately sent by 'his political leaders' to a neighbouring town in the General Government to convey the news, but by the time he arrived there a few hours later he found that hastily roneo'ed sheets giving the news were already in circulation. Apparently, according to Kennard, the Jews were amongst the most active disseminators of news, and clandestine periodicals were often printed or roneo'ed 'behind Convent walls'.

Increasingly, from March 1941 onwards propaganda was developed on a grand scale through the distribution of pamphlets and flysheets. Its main areas of attack were:

- Stressing disagreement and friction between the *Gestapo*, the Party and the German Army.
- Exploiting the German soldiers' worry about the home front and their families by stressing financial difficulties and the threat from air raids.
- Stirring up separatism in Austria.
- Exploiting the hardships of *Die Volksdeutschen*, who were awaiting resettlement in German-annexed territory.

[NA, HS4/197]

Parallel to military actions, the Underground State also waged war against collaborators. It kept a close watch on attempts by Władysław Studnicki, a member of the pre-war Polish elite, to negotiate a political settlement with the Germans (*see page 44*), but decided he had acted in good faith, as he was bitterly critical of their atrocities and was eventually incarcerated by the Germans in the dreaded Pawiak prison. The Polish clandestine press began to print 'a roll of dishonour', in which were listed the names of Poles who had cooperated too closely with the German authorities, visited German gambling houses or committed other acts 'not consonant with national dignity'.

The most celebrated case was that of Igo Sym, an Austrian-born film star and actor of German and Ukrainian origin, who, before the war, passed himself off as a Pole. With the German occupation of Warsaw he speedily claimed *Volksdeutsch* status and was made managing director both of a new German theatre and of the *Nur für Deutsche* (Only for Germans) Cinema. Besides producing German drama, he infuriated Polish patriots by staging (under specific German instructions) low-brow, erotic and – in the eyes of the Underground – corrupting productions in Polish, which had the specific aim of undermining Polish self-respect. As Kennard reported on 19 March 1941, 'the theatre [...] together with gambling houses and cheap vodka was to serve as a means to corrupt the Polish nation'. Sym was also a *Gestapo* informer. Consequently, on 7 March 1941 he was shot dead in his own flat by two Polish agents of the ZWZ pretending to be postmen.

A few weeks earlier, on 19 February, there had been another 'judicial killing'. The German newspaper *Krakauer Zeitung* reported the death of a Polish judge, Witold Wasilewski, who had allegedly collaborated with the Germans. The German response to these murders was swift and radical. In Warsaw, the Governor imposed a curfew on the Poles and arrested thirty hostages, who were to be shot if the assassins were not discovered. In London, the Government-in-Exile was disturbed by the news of these assassinations, as they considered the victims not worth the reprisals the German authorities would certainly take. Kot actually advised the Underground to avoid such acts of violence 'for the time being' but, as Ambassador Kennard observed, 'whether Polish society, and especially the young men, many of whom are grouped in secret military organizations, will listen to such counsels from afar, is another matter'.

The mere chronicling of the various acts of the Underground inevitably plays down the ever-present threat of *Gestapo* torture and imprisonment. Polish reports to London painted a bleak picture at the turn of 1940/41. Out in the countryside there were large-scale deportations in connection with the building of aerodromes and other military installations. In some communes in the Radom district, 20 per cent of the population were ejected from their farms and holdings. The collection of grain and foodstuffs was another source of friction. In Lublin it was reported that 2,000 peasants were in prison for not supplying corn. In Warsaw there were repeated mass arrests. Between 10 and 14 January, for instance, at least 1,000 people were arrested, suspected of being involved in the Resistance, some of whom were boy scouts. The intensity of German police measures ensured that the Underground was put under maximum pressure. In the space of two years, five consecutive commanders of the Silesian sector were arrested and in the spring of 1941 seventeen members of Bór's staff were seized in Kraków, after the *Gestapo* found in the diary of his Chief of Staff the address of his headquarters, located in a stationery shop. Miraculously, the *Gestapo* failed to arrest Bór, who had to live in concealment in the countryside and could only visit Kraków disguised as a milkman.

Soviet-Occupied Poland

The Russian grip on Eastern Poland intensified after the defeat of the Finns in March 1940. The frontier was strengthened so that it became increasingly hazardous for the Warsaw-based ZWZ to send in officers to take command of partisan units. Escaped British POWs, who were helped by Poles in 1940 to escape across the frontier to what they hoped was freedom and speedy repatriation, were also quickly seized by the frontier police and thrown into prison. The ruthless deportation to Soviet Russia of the professional elite, small tradesmen, the whole of the forestry service, the more well-to-do peasants, as well as families of POWs and military personnel who had escaped to the West, deprived the Resistance of its natural leaders and made the growth of an 'Underground state' – as had developed in the General Government – much more difficult. The conscription of young Poles into the Red Army, together with the deportation of 180,000 POWs, of whom over 25,000 officers and senior NCOs were murdered at Katyń and elsewhere, also depleted the natural recruiting ground of the Resistance. Altogether, nearly 1,492,000 Poles were deported to the USSR. In their place came a horde of Soviet officials and their families. The Swedish paper *Stockholms-Tidningen* dryly commented on 18 March 1941 that 'countless former inhabitants have disappeared and been replaced by newcomers'. It was no wonder that the Polish population was inclined to criticize the Government-in-Exile for overlooking the plight of Poles under Soviet rule.

Russian-occupied Poland was the Cinderella of the resistance but, according to General Sosnkowski, it did have a 'regular cadre' subordinated to the ZWZ in Warsaw, which was able to undertake limited sabotage activities. By carefully piecing together fragments of oral history, memoirs and personal reminiscences, the historian Tomasz Strzembosz has been able to shed considerable light on the activities of the Resistance in the North East of the Russian Zone. In Wilno province, which was ceded to Lithuania, it had collapsed by the spring of 1940, but in Nowogródek Province the opposition was largely spontaneous and operated outside the control of the ZWZ, and was active until June 1941.

By the spring of 1940, the ZWZ had managed to bring under its command in No. 2 Region, Białystok, 'Major R's' partisan unit, which consisted of three groups. A few months later, in October, General Rowecki was reporting that his regional commander in Białystok had managed to organize 'strong partisan detachments with weapons and ammunition, which could be used at a moment's notice'. The area on the north-east border of German-occupied Poland had a strong network of ZWZ units. In December 1939, Aleksander Burski arrived from Warsaw to take over an Underground network centred on the small town of Jedwabne, and within a few months had expanded the network to embrace some twenty villages. He commanded about 200 men and trained them in Intelligence and sabotage operations but, as a result of betrayal by one of his soldiers, the group was broken up by the NKVD in June and Burski had to escape across the border to the General Government.

Partisan groups fought on against the Russians in the Augustów Forest until the German invasion of 22 June 1941. The majority were peasants, reinforced by people under threat of arrest and deportation by the NKVD. By early 1941 the ZWZ had, at least nominally, brought these disparate groups under its control. The partisans moved about the countryside in small 'fighting squads' with a leader and six men, but could form larger units when a bigger operation was undertaken. Their tasks consisted of executing NKVD agents and collaborators, and at times they fought actions against Red Army border guards and NKVD troops. In March, what Strzembosz calls 'a major skirmish' took place just south of Augustów. When cornered, the partisans were often able to escape across the frontier to the German-annexed Suwałki region. Sometimes, however, they fell into the hands of the German *Abwehr* (German Military Intelligence Organization) official Major Diaczenko, a former Polish officer. They were then usually sent back across the border with orders to carry out various sabotage and espionage missions, although many managed to evade the *Abwehr*'s control by hiding in the forests.

Diplomatic Consequences of *Barbarossa*

The German invasion of the USSR, in Churchill's words, 'altered the values and relationship of the war'. From this point onwards, British policy was

Campaign Chronicle

at all costs not to alienate the USSR, and to avoid any issues that might threaten the Anglo-Soviet Pact of July 1941, and the subsequent alliance of May 1942. To Sikorski, it was clear that if the Poles were to continue to enjoy British support, they had little option but to come to terms with Stalin. Thus, on 30 July 1941, in the British Foreign Office, in the presence of Churchill and Eden, Sikorski and the Soviet Ambassador, Ivan Maisky, signed what became known as the Sikorski-Maisky Pact. The Soviet-German treaties of 1939 were declared void and both countries became allies in the struggle against Nazi Germany. A Polish army was to be set up within the USSR under a commander, 'who would be subordinated in operational matters to the Supreme Command of the USSR'. The future of Poland's eastern frontiers was not discussed, but in the secret protocol it was agreed cryptically that 'Various claims of a public and private nature will be dealt with in the course of further negotiations between the two governments'.

On 11 August General Anders was released from prison and, with Soviet agreement, was appointed by Sikorski as Commander of the Polish forces in Russia. He immediately created assembly points to which the personnel released from the various prisons and *gulags* were to report. His work was complicated by mutual suspicion between the Poles and Russians and the mysterious shortage of officers, who had vanished into Russia in the winter of 1939/40. To iron out these problems, in December Sikorski flew to Moscow to meet Stalin. After difficult negotiations it was finally agreed that six Polish divisions would be formed within Russia and that 20,000 men, mainly technical specialists, would be evacuated. However, Anders rapidly came to the conclusion that it would be impossible to create an effective army on Soviet soil, and advised Sikorski that a total evacuation should take place. While this was not achieved, Stalin accepted the arguments that the formation of a Polish army in the Middle East would assist British efforts to contain a German advance in that theatre, which, if successful, could ultimately bring Turkey into the war on the Axis side and so threaten the oil wells of the Caucasus. By September 1942 General Anders and well over 100,000 Polish troops, women and children, were evacuated from Tashkent to Iran. The thousands left behind were cut off from any links with the London Government and the men eventually enrolled in the Communist-controlled Polish People's Army under General Berling.

During the Kremlin meetings of December, Sikorski did not accept Stalin's offer to discuss the vexed question of Poland's eastern frontier, hoping that, while Russia would emerge from the war victorious, she would be so exhausted that Stalin would be unable, particularly in the face of Anglo-American pressure, to be able to reclaim the Polish territories annexed in 1939 or influence internal Polish politics. Clearly this was a gamble. The emergence of Russia as a belligerent against Germany and ally of Britain was fraught with uncertainty for Poland, as it opened the door to the possibility of liberation from the east. In that case, what sort of Poland would Soviet bayonets create? To what extent would Britain and, after December 1941, America be able and willing to defend Poland's pre-war frontiers? Polish-Russian relations were constantly bedevilled by mutual mistrust. In essence, they were enemies waging a common struggle against Germany.

Conditions in Poland, June 1941–January 1943

The public mood in Poland oscillated between brief moments of optimism and renewed anxiety for the future. The immediate invasion of the USSR was greeted with relief because Poland's two major enemies were now locked in mutual conflict, while the news that Hitler had declared war on America on 11 December was welcomed with profound joy. Dr Klukowski recorded in his diary that 'everyone is happy today. Now we are completely sure that Germany will be defeated.' Yet disillusion quickly set in when the Western Allies suffered defeat after defeat in the first nine months of 1942 and the Germans advanced right up the Caucasus. The news of the victory at El Alamein, on the other hand, was greeted ecstatically.

But the great dramas of the war were overshadowed by the daily struggle to find sufficient food and fuel, to avoid arrest and, if one was eligible, to avoid being press-ganged into the Reich's labour service. Dr Klukowski's diary becomes almost monotonous in its day-by-day chronicling of *Gestapo* raids, murder of the Jews and arrests, so much so that on Christmas Day 1942 he observed: 'More than a week ago I stopped my diary. I am tired of writing the same stories again and again.' In Eastern Poland, particularly in Janów and Zamość counties, the Poles also had to contend with German resettlement policies that threatened their very existence.

The information coming out of Poland from neutral businessmen, the Church and Underground intelligence, continued to paint a bleak picture of arrests, torture, mass round-ups by the *Gestapo* and ever-growing scarcities. During periods of mass arrests, the streets were extremely dangerous places to be. When people left for work in the morning, they had no idea whether they would see their families again. Similarly if, in the evening, any one was late, their absence led to the wildest fears. The

Church continued to be a target for persecution, and in eastern Poland the Theological Faculty of Wilno, which had even managed to survive the Soviet occupation, was closed. In the areas annexed to the Reich young adult males were also eligible for call-up into the *Wehrmacht* on the grounds that they were now German citizens. With the example of the Jews very much in mind, many Poles were beginning to see German policy, in the words of one report in November 1942 to the Government-in-Exile in London,

> as the commencement of an action of annihilation similar to that employed against the Jews, the more so as, in spite of the fact that there are very few Jews left [...] Lithuanian, Latvian and Ukrainian auxiliary police are still quartered in Poland.
>
> [NA, FO371/31098]

In all parts of Poland the picture of repressive German policy was the same. Any voices within the German Foreign Office or *Wehrmacht* urging a more humane strategy and the creation of a semi-independent Polish satellite state were overruled by Hitler, Himmler and Hans Frank. In May 1942, the Polish Government Delegate in German-occupied Poland informed General Sikorski that 'I am receiving alarming news from different parts of the country, which proves that the *furor teutonicus*, reaching a state of murder-paroxysm [*sic*], is spreading death and devastation among innocent Polish people.'

This nightmarish picture was accompanied by acute economic hardship. By November 1941 the Poles only received 175 grams of black bread per day, 100–200 grams of meat a month and only 400 grams of flour a month. There was, too, an almost complete absence of coal. Not surprisingly, the survival of Warsaw and the other big cities was dependent on the black market. In the countryside the quotas imposed on the peasantry were increasingly onerous. For instance, in Janów County between 1939 and 1944 the food quota increased sevenfold in both grain and potatoes. Farmers who could not fulfil their quotas were fined or arrested, and sometimes their farms were burnt down.

Growing Popular Resistance

Paradoxically, the more severe the German reign of terror became, the more it strengthened the desire of the Poles to resist. The actual Underground state and secret army were only the tip of the iceberg as far as resistance to the German occupation went. Without the widespread

The Polish Underground 1939–1947

passive resistance of the population, arguably the Underground itself would not have survived. In the countryside, where, initially, there had been a marked lack of resistance to the Germans, growing interference by the occupiers in everyday rural life began to change attitudes. The arbitrary shifting of Church holidays to Sundays, so as to facilitate un-interrupted work in the fields, the confiscation of church bells and then, increasingly, the insistence that work must continue on Sundays began to alienate the deeply religious rural Poles. This was exacerbated by the bureaucratic police measures introduced to control the population.

Forced food levies, unrealistically high quotas and a massive increase in taxation also led to a pauperization of the population. Food became the chief source of wealth. For peasants with larger farms this opened up considerable opportunities on the black market, while smallholders had to show enormous initiative in cheating the authorities just to survive. The more ruthlessly the Nazis cracked down, the more devious the local peasantry became in resisting their demands and exploiting the black market. In the words of the historian Marek Chodakiewicz:

> This grass-roots conspiracy grew from below by including first family members, next certain neighbours, and finally a few trusted officials. Similar networks sprouted practically everywhere, but they operated largely independently of one another.

> [Chodakiewicz, M.J., *Between the Nazis and the Soviets*, p. 120]

Right across occupied Poland the most successful facet of popular resistance was the black market. Urban dwellers scoured the countryside for food while, in turn, thousands of peasants and middlemen travelled to the towns to sell their products illegally. The trains were full of what Klukowski called 'petty smugglers' out to drive hard bargains. The Nazis attempted in vain to stop this trade. George Ślązak, whose parents originally owned a tailor's shop in Łódź, remembered, for instance, how his mother made a living out of the black market once the shop had been taken over by a *Volksdeutscher*. He and his mother would visit his uncle's farm every week to buy food, which she afterwards sold on the black market. They had frequent escapades. Once, for example, when they returned to Sieradz railway station laden with meat, they realized that a major security operation was being conducted and had no option but to send the meat back in the buggy. Another time they overheard *Gestapo* agents talking in a cafe about raiding the premises of a pig farmer, one Mr Kuza, a neighbour of George's uncle. Immediately, George was dispatched through the woods to warn him of the impending raid. He reached the farm before the police and all evidence was successfully hidden.

Not all were so lucky. Throughout Poland thousands of black marketeers were arrested and sent to concentration camps. Yet the black market continued to flourish. Essentially, food shortages and the Nazi policy of imposed quotas ensured that its services were needed by virtually the whole population just to survive. Unlike the farms, which could be easily raided, the black market was mobile, flexible and decentralized. It was, without any doubt, the most successful form of popular resistance.

Labour conscription also became increasingly hated. In his study of Janów in Eastern Poland, Chodakiewicz has shown that, by 1942, the Germans were only able to fill 8 per cent of the labour quota for the county. All sorts of tricks were used to avoid being caught. Polish bureaucrats, for example, were bribed with money or food to grant exemptions or deferments. Occasionally, girls would offer sexual favours for exemption. Others simply fled and hid in the forests or indeed actually deserted from the *Baudienst* (Building Service) sites. Once again, the Germans had to resort to coercion. Police units and special personnel trained to catch work dodgers, the *łapacze*, traversed the countryside. Sometimes they disguised themselves to make it easier to catch their prey. The police combed through towns and villages, arresting scores of people. Often they did not shrink from entering churches when services were being held. In February 1943 some 500 Poles were caught in Janów County and sent to the Reich. Initially, the only protection against police terror was 'the swiftness of one's feet'. At the mere rumour of a German search expedition, a whole village would run away, but the Germans did not hesitate to shoot any fugitives. Consequently, the peasants began to construct underground shelters, where they could hide both people and animals as well as food produce.

Initially, peasant resentment was caused largely by self interest as, indeed, the earlier collaboration had been, but gradually the sheer brutality and rapaciousness of the occupying authorities strengthened the nationalism of the Polish peasantry. As one peasant from the village of Antolin in Janów County observed:

In 1942 all critical voices concerning Poland ceased. The ruthlessness of the Germans, their impudence and arrogance, which they manifested towards the 'Polish pigs', made for the best school of patriotism. This was a very positive and desirable development! My [pro-German] detractors shut up ...

[Chodakiewicz, p. 120]

The Polish Underground 1939–1947

The Poles lived under such intense strain that, inevitably at times, they felt deserted by their allies. They were highly critical of the Western Allies' refusal to make reprisal raids against the Germans, and disillusioned by their apparent inability – up to El Alamein – to defeat them. So much so that (according to information reaching London from Poland in the autumn of 1942), it produced a 'widespread disinclination to carry on the Underground struggle', making the Russian-backed Communist partisans appear the more effective option in the struggle against Germany. The Russian and Polish Communists, of course, lost little chance to contrast the 'inertia' of the Allies and, indeed, of the London-backed Polish Underground with the 'decision and energy of the Bolsheviks'. In eastern Poland particularly this was to cause a considerable problem. Partly to counter this propaganda, on 14 February 1942 General Rowecki changed the name of the ZWZ to the Home Army (AK), to emphasize that it was the Underground National Army of Poland.

Attempts to Supply the Underground by Air

The German invasion of the USSR enhanced the strategic importance of Poland. It now formed the hinterland of the Eastern front, across which went Germany's vital supply lines. As the Russians reeled back under the hammer blows of the advancing German armies, they sent out urgent messages to the Polish Underground to launch an uprising in the German rear, which would severely disrupt the advance. As early as September 1941, Józef Retinger, a trusted adviser of Sikorski, informed the SOE that the Russians were pushing for an insurrection in Poland, but both the Polish Government-in-Exile, as well as the British Chiefs of Staff, the SOE and Churchill himself, believed that such an uprising would be premature and should be postponed until a 'more opportune time'. The principal role of the Underground was still to carry out sabotage on the German lines of communication and to provide intelligence on troop movements, munitions production, and other matters of interest to both London and Moscow.

To carry this out effectively, the Underground needed to be supplied with more radio sets, explosives, sabotage equipment, money, specialist agents and instructors. The key to achieving this was to establish from Britain effective air contact with Poland, but this was to run into the determined resistance of the Air Ministry, which Lieutenant Colonel Harold Perkins of the SOE described as a 'brick wall of non-cooperation'. The Air Ministry was extremely reluctant to part with aircraft for use in what it saw as fringe operations. Only one flight had taken place in February 1941, which had successfully dropped three agents (*see page 50*). During the summer months all flights had to be suspended as the nights were too short for aircraft to return under the cover of darkness. In the autumn of 1941 there was, briefly, a hope that General Zhukov – whom both the new Polish Ambassador in Moscow, Kot, and General Anders rated highly – might be empowered to fly to London to negotiate an agreement that would provide bases in the USSR for 'a certain number of long-range British planes under British, Polish or joint control'. But in the event, with Zhukov's involvement in the defence of Moscow, little happened and the bases were never established. In October, the Air Ministry at last agreed to allot three Halifaxes to 138 Squadron, based at Tempsford, for 'special duties'. During the winter of 1941/42, eight operations were carried out but only two, code-named *Łąka* and *Ziege*, were completely successful. The remaining six – as a 'Report on air liaison during the season 1941/2' observed – 'had faults caused mainly by the insufficient range of the aircraft or by mistakes in the organization'. In some cases, last-minute changes of codes or instructions resulted in muddling the reception committee, which consequently failed to give effective signals to the incoming plane. On 28 December 1941 two agents were killed in a blind drop.

In February, the Polish General Staff in London were informed by a W/T message that the Home Army (AK) intended to start 'diversion operations against German transports in the rear of the Eastern front', and asked for the despatch of eight instructors, who must be trained in mobile patrol work, four of whom would go to the Ukraine, while the remainder would go to 'White Russia'. Rowecki also requested fuses (time or chemical) that could be set for a period 'ranging from half an hour to several days', as well as concentrated food sufficient for ten days per parachutist. Finally, 'a large sum in gold coins, minimum value of 50,000 gold dollars', was 'absolutely indispensable', as the operations could not be carried out without bribing local Ukrainian peasants and the buying of explosive material from German and Russian soldiers.

Faced with a renewed German offensive against Russia in the spring of 1942, the Defence Committee, chaired by Churchill, approved on 26 March both Polish plans for sabotaging the German lines of communication with Russia and 'for the acceleration and continuance' of flights to Poland to supply the necessary personnel and equipment. Lord Selborne, who had recently replaced Dalton as Minister of Economic Warfare, also managed to obtain Churchill's approval to use Liberators, which had a greater range than Halifaxes. However, the following day he was told by the Air Secretary, Sir Archibald Sinclair, that these were not available. Instead, Sinclair was ready to increase the number of Halifaxes to five. This was certainly better than nothing: between the nights of 27/28 March and 8/9 April, four flights to Poland managed to drop twenty-two agents and a limited amount of material.

Grudgingly, the Air Ministry agreed a few weeks later that one or two flights could continue up to 5 May, but only to the Płock area north-west of Warsaw, as a result of the shortening nights. This area was, however, not acceptable to the Poles, as it was too near the German frontier and large numbers of *Wehrmacht* troops were stationed there. Ground reception teams could therefore only be provided in the area some 60 miles to the south-east of Płock, but the Air Ministry judged that this would put the aircraft at an 'abnormal risk'. In the end, due to a shortage of aircraft and the need to preserve for training purposes the one surviving Polish crew, the SOE decided to recommend no more flights to Poland until the next flight season, beginning in September. It decided quite correctly on 20 April that the Poles would be able to conduct some sort of a campaign as 'half the money and some of the men and materials had been transported in the April flights and [had] arrived safely'.

During the summer, Polish attempts to obtain Liberators promised them from the USA came to nothing. In March, Sikorski had bypassed the British Government and personally persuaded President Roosevelt to supply six Liberators. His request was granted but little, in practice, happened. The RAF's Chief of Air Staff, Air Marshal Portal, advised the Americans against it on the grounds that it was British policy as far as possible not to operate American aircraft from Britain. On the other hand, the RAF did provide Halifaxes, which were fitted with extra fuel tanks and denuded of some of their armaments, to extend their range and increase the number of parachutists they could carry to six.

Operations started again in the moon period on the night of 2/3 September 1942, and were initially a complete success. During these two days it was possible to deliver:

1. 21 fully trained operators
2. 2 political couriers
3. Dollar notes: $600,500
4. Gold dollars: 620,200
5. RMs. in paper: 1,000,000
6. 1 Rebecca (a portable homing beacon for aircraft)

7. 5 wireless sets capable of transmitting to the UK
8. 10 receiving sets capable of receiving BBC messages
9. 15 containers capable of carrying 2 tons of sabotage material

[NA, HS4/149]

Over the period August 1942–April 1943, some 119 agents and 49 tons of supplies were dropped.

The flight to Poland was hazardous in the extreme, as the Halifaxes were operating at the end of their range. The aircrews were presented with the problem, as Wing Commander Corby, the Air Liaison Officer at Tempsford, put it in his memoirs, of 'finding three hand torches in a field up to 600 or 800 miles away, and a drop from 500 feet over it'. To reach the area north of Warsaw they had to avoid the anti-aircraft defences of Kiel and go via Kattegut and Bornholm. Some Polish crews, to shorten the distance, were ready to risk flying over Kiel. Corby later heard that one crew, in such an attempt

> had been fired at by flak and the aircraft hit over Kiel Canal with George, the automatic pilot, damaged and flying the aircraft, and the whole crew playing poker in the fuselage. Such matters were not discovered at debriefing because the Poles always had a very convenient difficulty understanding English!
>
> [J. Corby, IWM, 87/44/1]

Once over Northern Poland, the usual method was to locate and fly over a landmark, normally a distinctive river bend, lake or coastline, made visible by moon reflections. Then, from this fixed point, to proceed to the field where the three torches were displayed. Later, with the introduction of Rebecca/Eureka equipment, crews carried a radio set that would home in on a set on the ground, but this was not infallible, and would only work if the ground set had fully recharged batteries.

Diversionary Activities in Poland

The airlift from Britain could hardly satisfy the Home Army's need for weapons, munitions and equipment, even though what was sent was invaluable. Consequently, the Underground had to improvise much of the time. Initially, much of the work was on a small scale and consisted mostly of transforming and adapting weapons and armaments seized from the Germans; but as the sabotage operations grew in scope by the autumn of 1942, there was little option but to rely on clandestine home production. Up to that date, production had been carried on in several secret workshops, but it was then centralized and put under the overall control of an engineer directly under the command of General Bór, now deputy commander of the AK. Production was divided into two main departments: armaments and weapons. Some of the production was earmarked for the eventual uprising and secretly stockpiled, while the rest was used for current diversionary tactics. After considerable research and experiment, automatic pistols and flamethrowers were made, as well as a whole series of specially devised mines for disrupting rail traffic.

The raw materials came from the German-controlled industrial plants in Poland, which employed native Poles. Scientists working in the Underground devised ways of extracting saltpetre, which is one of the basic elements for the construction of explosives, from artificial fertilizers. Large quantities of this product were consequently stolen from the two German-controlled fertilizer factories at Chorzów and Mościce. The key explosive for sabotage was cheddite, but to make this potassium chlorate was needed. Radocha – the only chemical plant in Poland which produced this – was so tightly guarded by the Germans that any attempts to steal its stock were in vain, but limited stocks were procured by the seizure of two railway wagons in transit, and an attack on a large chemical warehouse outside Warsaw. This only resulted in the acquisition of about 1½ tons but it was supplemented regularly by supplies from the match factory at Błonie.

Thanks to this work, the AK was able to embark on a sabotage programme, which progressively became more effective. Detailed results were hard to come by in London but the VI Bureau did receive news in April 1942 that, in the period 1 July–30 November 1941, about 400 tanker wagons loaded with benzene had been destroyed and three oil wells in the Jasło–Krosno Basin were 'jammed'. Further reports trickled out during 1942, showing that sabotage actions directed against railway traffic were regularly taking place throughout Poland. In March and April 1942, data sent to London claimed that 134 locomotives and 2,262 railway carriages had been damaged. In June, a further 135 locomotives were damaged and 561 wagons. Accumulatively these attacks caused considerable delays in the Reich and forced the Reich Government drastically to cut down on the number of passenger trains and step up the protection of the whole railway system.

By the summer of 1942, in the *Bahndirektionen* (railway regions) of Breslau, Opole, Poznań, Stettin, Danzig and Königsberg, all the important bridges and viaducts had to be protected by police or military units. The further east one went, the tighter the security. In the Lwów region, the lines were patrolled by special armed trains; and on the lines Lwów–Krasne–Tarnopol, Lwów–Brody and Lwów–Rawa Ruska, military posts existed 'every few score metres'; while on the Chełm–Dorohusk stretch two German soldiers were stationed every 200 metres. In areas where guerrilla warfare was rife – such as the districts of Wolkowysk in Białystok Province and Wilno – night traffic was cancelled from 2200 to 0300 hours. According to an SOE report on sabotage activities covering the period January to July 1942, 'Locomotives are detached from the trains, which are left on the stations, [and] patrol the line manned by crews of 6–7 persons [...] with the speed of 10 km per hour'. Even small bridges were protected by sentries. In October 1942, for the first time, instead of a series of piecemeal sabotage actions, a successful coordinated operation took place. The AK's HQ was able to inform London of some interesting news of 'the big scheme'. Using some of the railway specialists trained in Britain, and equipment parachuted in, the Poles had managed to carry out the first large-scale operation against railway communications running east from Warsaw. Six lines were simultaneously attacked on the night of 6 October and put of action for some twelve hours.

These incessant sabotage attacks both interrupted supplies to the Eastern front and added to German manpower difficulties by absorbing a considerable number of troops, who had to be used as guards. Dr Klukowski recorded in his diary a particularly dramatic attack on the station at Szczebrzeszyn at midnight on New Year's Eve 1942. Approximately sixty men surrounded the station. They threw six hand grenades and ordered everybody to lie flat on the ground. Then all the money was removed from the booking office, as well as several cans of gasoline from the store room. Finally, the water tower was set on fire. Simultaneously, the railroad bridge between Izbica and Ruskie Piaski was blown up. A local German official did call the gendarme post at Szczebrzeszyn but the gendarmes were all drunk and ignored the calls!

Operation *Wachlarz*

Part of the 'Great Scheme' was to launch a sabotage campaign behind the German front in Russia. The whole Eastern front, from the Baltic to the Black Sea, was divided into seven sections like a fan (*wachlarz*), which spread out radially from Warsaw. Pretending to be Polish labourers, the AK was able to smuggle its agents into the work forces toiling on the construction of airfields and barracks. These operated in groups of five, which only came together when they were engaged in an act of sabotage or military operation.

According to information that reached London in July 1944, the chief of the *Wachlarz* organization was a Major Łapecki, while the recruiting was carried out by a priest with the pseudonym of 'Mis' ['Bear']. The organization of the first *Wachlarz* group was entrusted to an officer with the codename 'Donat Ponury'. Initially, three groups were formed and were to be based at Lwów, Brześć and Wilno. The detachment based on Brześć consisted of two patrols of ten men and a commanding officer. According to instructions, these men had initially applied to the German authorities in Warsaw to work in local firms and had been given permission to travel eastwards. One patrol was then based in Pinsk, commanded by an officer sent from England and known as 'Little John' or 'Baby'; and the other about 30 km away in the direction of Luminiec. Each patrol was supplied with demolition equipment consisting of 30 to 40 kilos of trotyl, some Bickford fuses, explosives, percussion caps and a light portable apparatus for exploding mines. In addition there were a number of automatic pistols and some hand grenades. Liaison with headquarters at Brześć was carried out by local Poles.

The second patrol based at Pinsk was commanded by a Lieutenant 'without much energy' known as 'Tadeusz'. Its liaison agent was arrested by the *Gestapo* in July and later the whole patrol suffered the same fate, possibly having been betrayed by two prostitutes who enlisted in Pinsk, although some managed to escape to Warsaw. By October, the whole Brześć group had become demoralized and disorganized and drifted back to Warsaw. In November, another group of fifty men was sent to the Minsk area, but was discovered and destroyed before it became active. The Foreign Office in London came to the conclusion that 'the activity of the "Wachlarz" had an experimental character and the organization, after more or less negative results, was dissolved in February 1943.'

At its height, there were about 1,000 members active in the *Wachlarz* organization. What they actually achieved is not clear, but a list of guerrilla activities in the east from January to July 1942, which was supplied to SOE, chronicles a series of attacks, some of which were almost certainly the work of *Wachlarz*. These ranged from an attack on a mill and German military granaries in Chełm on 16 May, to ambushes and thefts of ammunition.

Campaign Chronicle

Intelligence and Liaison, 1941–1942

Arguably, one of the most important contributions to the Allied war effort by the Polish Resistance was the communication of intelligence by both couriers and clandestine radio stations. Couriers continued to use land routes through Hungary, Romania, Sweden, Spain and Portugal to Britain and the Middle East. The Allies were kept informed of preparations for the spring offensive of 1942, which was to take the Germans to the Caucasus. They also received detailed information on German atrocities. In January 1942 negatives showing the appalling conditions in which Soviet POWs were imprisoned were smuggled out of Poland and in November the Allies were given detailed information about the German liquidation of the Jews.

The great strength of the Polish Intelligence service was that its tentacles stretched throughout occupied Europe and into the heart of the German

---

How the News of the 'Final Solution' Reached London

In the spring of 1942 rumours began to reach the Underground state of the gassing of the Jews in Chełmno. In July the liquidation of the Warsaw Ghetto began and reports from railroad workers informed the Underground that transports of Jews were being sent to Treblinka. Information from both Polish and Jewish sources was transmitted to London and Washington but, inexplicably, both maintained complete silence. The decision was then taken to send an eyewitness emissary, Jan Kozielewski, alias 'Karski', who, dressed as an Estonian guard, had managed to infiltrate Belzec concentration camp to gain first-hand experience of what was happening. He was also briefed by leading members of the Jewish *Bund* in Warsaw. He managed to make his way overland and thence to London. In November 1942 he reported to the Polish and British Governments and the American Ambassador on the situation in Poland and the Holocaust of the Jews. To confirm this, he had managed to smuggle out of Poland microfilm, which enabled the Polish Government-in-Exile to provide the Allies with one of the earliest and most accurate accounts of the Holocaust.

Sadly, as Stefan Korbonski, the Chief of the Directorate of Civil Struggle, pointed out, although Karski accomplished his mission, to 'all practical purposes' it achieved no results.

The Polish Underground 1939–1947

Reich. As a consequence of Polish workers being employed in Germany and German-run concerns in the General Government, a stream of information was fed to the AK and thence, by courier or wireless, to London. Within Germany, accurate Underground reports on the damage done by air raids and on the production and conditions in each major factory were invaluable; and were supplied, for the most part, by foreign workers, of whom, by the spring of 1942, some 1,080,000 were Poles. In a report on the damage done in a series of raids on Hamburg in the last two weeks of October 1941, the RAF was requested by its authors 'not to bomb the promontory near the *Stadtpark* in the southern district of Ottensen', as the Poles had an observation post there. The report also gave a detailed analysis of German morale and the deteriorating conditions of everyday life. Conscripted Polish workers had noticed, for instance, that at the Berlin Knorr-Bremse factory there was an acute shortage of turners, who had been called up and replaced by 'young men from technical schools and women'. Poles had also noted that 'the greatest intensity of passengers is always on the lines Hamburg–Berlin, Berlin–Breslau' and that the overcrowding of coaches was 'noticeable, especially in the afternoon. The majority were women in mourning [...] going to deal with inheritance problems and women visiting the wounded'. As far as the Ruhr went, an interesting communication dated 10 November 1941 was sent to London:

> In the Ruhr district, where almost all the men were taken away and where Communist propaganda is strongest, the recent repression of Communists in which several women were arrested, resulted in public meetings, which were dispersed by uniformed Party members. One often sees chalked on the walls 'Heil Stalin!' or the symbol of the Hammer and Sickle.
>
> [NA, HS4/280]

Another report, of 8 November, highlighted the complaints of German troops returning from the Eastern front, about the lack of underclothing and warm winter quarters giving protection from the cold. In Siedlice, for instance:

> the police have for some time been making raids in search of deserters. On 31 October wounded soldiers on a transport beat up an officer and two policemen. Frequent cases are noted of German soldiers offering to sell weapons (pistols).

Campaign Chronicle

That same report also contained detailed observations of rail traffic on the lines passing through Brześć: food, petrol and ammunition trucks were carefully noted, as were the transports of the wounded, POWs and troops heading to or from the front.

The *Gestapo* had a grudging respect for the Polish Intelligence service and attempted to penetrate and paralyze it through arrests, executions, and by persuading – either through torture or bribery – Poles to become double agents. In Korbonski's words 'a fascinating duel of Intelligence services ensued, in which both sides won victories and suffered defeats'. One of the greatest successes of the *Gestapo* was to smash the Polish Intelligence organization in Warsaw in August 1942 and seize a large quantity of Intelligence material and money. In the process, it also discovered crucial material shedding light on the activities of Polish agents throughout Central and Eastern Europe. In due course, its report on this successful operation fell into Allied hands at the end of the war and enables historians to reconstruct the network of Polish Intelligence in Germany. By the summer of 1942 the Polish Intelligence section was divided into four sections:

- Central section, covering the General Government area (code-named 'Strargen').
- Western section covering the whole Reich area (code-named 'Lombard').
- The eastern section which stretched from the Bug to the Front (code-named 'Meerauge').
- A section dealing only with railway transport (code-named 'Witzer').

[NA, HS4/268]

The Reich was covered with a dense network of 'report centres' (*see appendix*), and agents were told by their minders 'to focus particularly' on:

(a) Works and factories producing weapons, gas, aircraft, tanks, warships and synthetic petrol ('important'). They were to find out what quantities were produced and the destinations. Plans and sketches were also to be made of key buildings where products were finished. If an interruption in output occurred, they were to find out why.
(b) All hidden, camouflaged, and heavily defended plants were to be identified.

(c) Aerodromes, camouflaged or underground, and their special object (training, research etc.) and the types of aircraft on them were also of great importance.

(d) Notes were also to be taken of the morale of the population (civil and military) and its reactions to the war and the regime.

(e) Where possible, through casual conversations with men on leave or convalescing from wounds, attempts must be made to extract information about new weapons and particularly where U-boat crews and parachutists are trained.

[NA, HS4/268]

The Intelligence received from these sources was to be carefully collected 'without apparently showing any special interest'. Lengthy conversations, which could cause suspicion, were above all to be avoided. Agents were also told emphatically that sketches of factories, aerodromes, etc. 'were to be made on thin paper' and that their 'exact locality' in relation to the nearest railway stations, bridges, road junctions and crossings must be notified, so that 'targets can be described in words, e.g. munition works 1.5 km south of x railway station [...] camouflaged with artificial shrubs'. All this information was then to be sent to Poland, either by rail passengers or by post, hidden inside such innocuous objects as fountain pens or teddy bears. In letters, the information was to be penned between the lines with lemon juice or milk. Then it was sent on to London.

The courier paths to London could take a number of ways. There were still hazardous routes open through the Balkan States to Turkey, from where it was possible to get to Egypt or Palestine. It was also possible, with forged papers indicating that an agent worked for the *Todt* Organization, to travel through Germany and France to the Spanish border. For example, in September 1943, when a merger was being discussed between the NSZ (National Armed Forces) and the AK in Warsaw, an NSZ officer was sent to London to negotiate directly with the Polish Government-in-Exile. He was given forged papers with the new name of Bartke, which enabled him to travel through Germany and France. Thanks to the French Red Cross, he made contact with the British Consul at San Sebastian and was given a safe conduct to Madrid. He was then put in touch with a Polish lieutenant in charge of the illegal evacuation of Poles from Madrid over the border to Gibraltar.

Žukauskas, one of the first agents to be dropped by plane over Poland in March 1941 (*see page 50*), also travelled through the Reich in

Campaign Chronicle

October 1942 with forged papers, which certified that he was proceeding to Alsace as a voluntary skilled worker. The journey took three days. He was questioned by the police at Katowice and Mühlheim, where the *Gestapo* 'objected to his travelling alone instead of with a party of workers'. Žukauskas replied that he was merely following instructions. Fearing that he might be held at Mühlheim for further checking, 'he slipped away and boarded a different train', which took him close to the Swiss frontier, which he crossed safely. From Switzerland he proceeded to Portugal and the UK as soon as the necessary visas had been obtained.

Polish Legations in all the neutral countries on the Continent were important centres for receiving couriers and news from Poland. In the summer of 1942, seven Swedish citizens were arrested in Warsaw by the Germans on the charge of acting as agents for the transmission of funds between the Polish Government in London and the Underground. It further emerged that both the Swedish and German Governments had been able to read the cypher telegrams sent from London to the Polish Legation in Stockholm. The danger of this development was that the Germans would intensify pressure on Sweden to close the Legation and that the Germans might also be reading the cypher telegrams to the Polish Legations in Switzerland, Portugal and elsewhere.

Development of the Polish Home Army, June 1941–December 1942

In August 1942 Sikorski ordered all military groups in Poland to subordinate themselves to the AK. The Peasant Party's paramilitary force, the Peasants Battalions (BCh), which disagreed with the AK's strategy of delaying a general uprising against the Germans until they were on the point of the collapse, did, in early 1943 (at least theoretically), subordinate itself to the AK. The para-military forces of the National Democratic Party, the National Military Organization (NOW), also agreed to merge but a significant minority split off and formed a new organization, the National Armed Forces (NSZ); while on the left, the People's Guard (GL), supported by the USSR, refused point-blank to recognize the overall control of the AK. In reality, the AK still remained very loosely organized. The Anglo-Polish historian Anita Prazmowska has pointed out that 'agreements forged between the leaders of the Underground organizations were not always respected in the provinces where local commanders had their own way of dealing with friendly and rival organizations.'

The Polish Underground 1939–1947

In the great forests of the east there were an increasing number of partisan groups that were completely independent of the AK (*see page 88*). In the General Government there were also several small resistance groups, like the *Muskieterowie* (the Musketeers) led by Stefan Witkowski, which tried hard to maintain their independence. In May 1942 one of their agents, Countess Mankowska, told MI5 that she had established a very good courier line to Paris and thence a chain of safe houses across unoccupied France, Switzerland and Germany to Warsaw, which were all independent of the AK.

The great plan of an uprising was still the ultimate goal of the AK, but it was constantly under revision. A paper on the *Principles of the Polish Insurrectionist Warfare*, drawn up in March 1943 by the Polish General Staff, observed that:

> Insurrection as a type of armed action takes place midway between the action of regular troops and revolt. For this reason and because of the scarcity of actual experience, we must base our indications of the methods of carrying on a war of insurrection on both these models.
>
> [NA, HS4/191]

In essence, according to an SOE memorandum of 21 August 1942 [NA, HS4/147], there were few changes from the initial plan drawn up in the winter of 1940/41 (*see pages 51–2*). The object was still to attack German forces in Poland when the bulk of the German Army was engaged 'elsewhere', and when the Western Allies had secured a substantial bridgehead in Europe and were about to launch their final attack on Germany. Hopefully, the insurrection in Poland would lead to the liberation of the country and the mobilization of the Polish Home Army, which would then defend Poland's frontiers and possibly even invade Germany. The signal for revolt by the Home Army would be the seizure by airborne forces and Home Army forces of four main centres. These would include airfields, which, once air protection could be provided, would be vital for receiving transport planes loaded with equipment, thereby enabling the Home Army to raise another forty battalions. The Poles laid great emphasis on the fact that the revolt could only be staged once, since, if it failed, the reprisals would be so heavy that any future action would be out of the question.

In principle, the British chiefs of staff agreed with the objects of the Polish plan, and a technical examination of the plan was made by SOE.

Campaign Chronicle

A start was also made with the formation of the Polish Airborne Brigade in Scotland, and a Polish flight was included in 138 Squadron. However, nothing could disguise the fact that in 1942 the pre-conditions for its fulfilment were still a long way away. Its sheer scale was also a problem, given the reluctance of the RAF to divert any of its bombers away from the nightly missions of destruction over Germany. On the Polish 'D-day' alone it was calculated that 249 transport aircraft would be needed, while in the build-up to the revolt approximately 5,000 containers would have to be dropped during the seven months from October to April. Assuming that each aircraft could carry four containers, this would require at least sixty aircraft initially to equip the Home Army for the insurrection.

The 'big bang' of the revolt was, at this stage, a pipedream. For most of the 130,000 people who formed what was called the AK's 'cadre of the Inner Organization', resistance was a lot less dramatic and low key, but always potentially dangerous in that it could end in death or a *Gestapo* cell. The role of a person in the Underground, of course, depended on his or her skills and the needs of local resistance organizations. Volunteers might be allocated to newspaper production, courier work, nursing, Intelligence, assassination or sabotage. Many members of the Underground were recruited through personal contacts. Adam Truszkowski, for example, who enlisted in the Warsaw's Citizen Guard in 1939, managed to scrape a living teaching English illegally, and was recruited in the spring of 1940 to the ZWZ by a Colonel Radwan, one of his language students, possibly with the intention of holding 'staff meetings' at his house. For the majority of Underground members there were long periods where their participation was not required. Truszkowski, for instance, served on Radwan's staff but had no specific activities as he was reserved for the post of English liaison officer in the event of an uprising.

Military training, at least in the cities, often consisted of lectures rather than practical field work. Stanisław Rudzinski, who, on his father's prompting, joined the NSZ in the summer of 1941, went to 'meetings' attended by six and then later eighteen members, which 'consisted', as he told his British interviewer in 1945, 'of theoretical instructions in the use of various weapons and lectures on tactics'. A year later his first, and apparently only, experience of guerrilla activity occurred when he and four others successfully intercepted three German soldiers in a tunnel at night and seized their weapons. He later attended a clandestine NCOs' school and in September 1942 was put in charge of a section of six men, but the activities 'consisted only of lectures as before'.

The Polish Underground 1939–1947

Zbigniew Tabęcki, on the other hand, had a more dramatic story to tell of his Underground activity in Warsaw. Trained as a clerk, he joined the AK in 1943 after being introduced to it by a friend, who was the owner of a greengrocer's shop. Growing bored with the courses on weapons and military tactics and the lack of any real Underground work, he volunteered to be transferred to an 'executive cell', where he was tasked with taking part in the execution of a *Volksdeutscher* in August 1943. This was achieved but on their way back the executioners ran into rather more excitement than Tabęcki had perhaps bargained for. They boarded a tram so full that one colleague, Jan Fabrinski, could only travel by holding on to the rail and standing on the running board. As this was strictly illegal, he was stopped by German gendarmes. Fabrinski, over-excited by his recent adventure, started to shoot with his revolver but unfortunately for him all this occurred outside a café frequented by Germans. Fabrinski was shot in the leg and arrested by a group of SS men. The others managed to disperse and were advised, for the time being, to disappear from Warsaw. Tabęcki himself joined the *Todt* Organization to escape Poland and left to work in Berlin.

The resistance inevitably attracted patriotic but rash young men. This was, perhaps, both its strength and weakness. While its achievements were often great, there were, inevitably, some bungled and at times farcical operations. For instance, Ralph Smorczewski and his brothers – sons of a wealthy landowner near Zamość – joined the Underground through the offices of an old family friend, and at the end of the summer of 1942 were dispatched to Lublin to complete their 'conspiratorial education'. Sometime in the winter, Ralph's brother Mark 'had a brain-wave'. He suggested a raid by the AK to disarm the German officers who were billeted in their family house. Contact was made with the AK command through the taciturn and forbidding farm manager. Basically, the plan was that the raid would appear to be nothing to do with the Smorczewski family, who would be innocently playing bridge when the AK broke in. Mark would show the way to the Germans' room with his hands up to indicate that he, too, was an innocent victim of the AK. After two evenings waiting in vain, the AK group at last arrived and the Germans were duly surprised and relieved of their guns. Mark was rather taken aback when, at the entrance to the library, the AK lieutenant turned to Mark and 'politely asked for instructions on how to work the Spandau machine gun'. It was agreed that the family should call the police twenty minutes after the AK had left. On the way out, the partisans discovered that the administration building where more German soldiers were billeted was empty and unlocked: its occupants were out on a binge but they had left some weapons and maps lying around, which were immediately seized by the partisans. The raid had gone well but Mark could not help shaking his head 'in disbelief at the ignorance of the partisans and slovenliness of the Germans'.

British POWs and the Polish Resistance

Escaped British POWs – captured in France and Belgium in 1940 and incarcerated in camps in East Prussia and the annexed territories – began to arrive in the Kraków and Warsaw districts as early as September 1940. Their numbers had increased so dramatically by August 1941 that it became necessary to formulate some general guidelines for the ZWZ/AK on how to deal with them. An 'Anglo-Polish society' was set up, composed of key figures involved in hiding and protecting the escaped POWs. Unfortunately, in the summer of 1941 two POWs being smuggled through the Balkans by a Polish agent were caught by the *Abwehr* and revealed several key addresses in Warsaw. According to information transmitted to London, this led to the society's penetration, apparently with the help of 'a Mrs. M., a British-born woman', by a *Gestapo* agent impersonating a British Intelligence officer, and the subsequent arrest of twelve of its members on 27 February 1942. It had to be replaced by a special committee of three, which closely cooperated with the Home Army and the Government Delegate.

Organizations were also created to arrange the actual escape of British prisoners from POW camps. Edmund Ziotkowski and Antoni Staruszkiewicz, for example, ran a Polish escape organization based at Bromberg in the German-annexed territory, which consisted of just four men, who had 'full freedom of movement' and permission to drive lorries from the German authorities. Not only were they able to smuggle POWs from Stalag XX aboard ships bound for Sweden, but were also able to supply the camp with wireless receivers, suits of plain clothes and cameras, etc. Initially, they financed their endeavours through the sale on the black market in Warsaw of ladies' stockings manufactured by a firm in Bromberg, but by mid-1943 they were running out of money and escaped to Sweden (in December) in order to raise more funds for their organization.

During the period September 1940–May 1942, help was given to sixty-five British servicemen, fifty-two of whom were smuggled out via Hungary, Romania or 'the East'. The rest remained in Poland. Two of these men, Corporal Ronald Jeffery and Sergeant John Ward, went native and joined the Home Army. Their accounts to the British authorities when repatriated shed a fascinating light on the day-to-day activity of the resistance. With Polish help, Jeffery escaped on 3 January 1942 from a POW camp near Łódź and was hidden in the city until given a forged Lithuanian passport and identity papers. Thanks to a Polish guide, he crossed the frontier into the General Government and was taken to Warsaw, where a Mrs Makoska, the English wife of a Pole who was in charge of about ten escaped POWs, found him a temporary billet. The AK made contributions towards the costs of supporting the POWs. But Jeffery was no parasite. Shortly after his arrival in Warsaw, he started work for an Underground paper, listening to the news on the London radio in 'a secret room in the town' and then writing it down for the Poles to translate. He also worked the Gestetner machine and did the 'donkey work' in producing the paper.

The *Gestapo*'s penetration of the 'Anglo-Polish Society' ensured the arrest of several POWs and their Polish helpers, but Jeffery managed to evade capture. With the collapse of the Society, he liaised with the AK on feeding and hiding British POWs in Warsaw, at one point (in October 1942) travelling to Kraków to bring back four British pilots. He was then recruited by one of the Home Army's Intelligence sections, and, after receiving instruction in cyphers, codes, industrial sabotage and shipping sabotage from one Józef, who had been parachuted into Poland in March 1942, was sent on various courier and intelligence missions to Vienna, Hamburg and Prague.

After his intelligence cell was broken up by the *Gestapo* in May 1943, Jeffery, desperate to support himself and his new Polish wife, agreed to join the execution squads carrying out the sentences of the Underground Courts. He was useful because 'he looked like a German when dressed in breeches and top boots'. He helped execute two couples and rob the house of a wealthy Pole 'who had been making too much money with the Germans'. The potentially thin line between some of the Underground's actions and criminality can be seen by the ruling that the assassins were allowed to take clothes and any small amounts of money from their victims' flats. Jeffery managed to sell a roll of cloth on the black market for 15,000 *złoty*.

By the autumn of 1943, Jeffery decided he wanted to return to England. He approached a Polish Communist group in Warsaw but rejected the proposal that he should go to the USSR. In the end, through a contact with an eccentric White Russian, he managed to reach Sweden by convincing the Germans that he was a reliable Estonian agent. Stefanski, his Polish minder, was clearly uneasy with this, but accepted that it was the best way to get to Britain.

Sergeant Ward's experiences in Poland were less dramatic until the Warsaw Uprising. After his escape from the POW camp in April 1941, he made contact with the ZWZ through a Roman Catholic priest, whom he contacted in a confessional box in a church in Sieradz. He was then taken to a barber's shop, where he was hidden for three days, and passed along a chain, ending up in the home of a former colonel in the Polish Army. Initially, the ZWZ had plans to send him to Russia, but once the Germans invaded this was impossible. Instead, he was given the task by the editor of *Dzień*, Otto Gordziałowsky, of noting down the contents of BBC broadcasts. When the *Gestapo* closed the paper down and arrested all the printers and distributors, Ward set up a news information bureau with the help of multi-lingual Poles, who listened to broadcasts in German, English, Czech and Turkish. He then moved on to constructing wireless receivers and transmitters, which were supplied to 'various Underground political organizations' in Warsaw, and a year later trained five or six Poles as radio operators. In June 1942 he bought a Gestetner duplicator, paper and ink, and using funds from the Underground began to publish the *Echo*, which reached a daily distribution of about 2,000. In February 1943 he handed the paper over to the AK, but continued to run his news agency until October 1944. In June 1943 he had a dangerous brush with the German police when he was stopped while carrying a pistol and various incriminating documents:

> He wanted to search me and examine my identity papers. I knocked his pistol arm down and hit him on the jaw with my fist. He fired his pistol as I hit him and the bullet entered my right thigh. As he fell, I ran off and mingled with the people in the street. I then hired a cab and left the vicinity. I was confined to bed for thee months until the wound healed.
>
> [NA, HS4/256]

Of course, not all escaped POWs were so well received. Sergeant Rofe's experiences in 1943 were far from happy. According to his interrogation report in London, after he was repatriated by the USSR in 1944:

> He first escaped in June 1943 to Poland, with the help of the AK in Jaworzno [near Katowice] and a miner named Kawecki. He was

passed after two weeks to an address in the village of Nowa Góra in the General Government, but the person concerned was unwilling to assist him. He then tried to contact other Poles in the various villages, but they were all afraid to help him. Finally, a Pole whom he approached handed him over to the police on the grounds that he was a Jew, in the village of Sucha, and from there he was returned to Lamsdorf on establishing his identity as an escaped P/W.

[NA, HS4/260]

The Written Word as a Weapon

The Underground press sought to overcome the Poles' sense of isolation by reporting what was happening in both the West and on the Eastern front, while at the same time emphasizing anything that reflected adversely on the German war effort. The Underground press, with its unquenchable hope in final victory, aimed to encourage the Poles to endure. By June 1942 some 150 clandestine Polish periodicals and papers had made their appearance, although, of course, the given number of papers at any one time depended on the success of the *Gestapo*. The format of these journals was tabloid rather than broadsheet, and they usually appeared as a small brochure of anything up to sixteen sides. The majority were weeklies but there were also dailies and monthlies, some of which were specialist publications devoted, say, to agriculture or youth development. The very names of the periodicals, as the *Polish Fortnightly Review*, which was published by the Polish Ministry of Information in London, observed, expressed an 'indomitable will to struggle': *Poland Lives*, *The Struggle Goes On*, *To Arms*, *Free Poland*, etc. Many had patriotic mottos or slogans written prominently on the title page, and their readers were exhorted to pass them on after reading them. The press was financed with funds both from the Underground State and from its readers. On the back pages of the journals there was usually a list of donors' pseudonyms. *The Cause* listed, for example, some 214 gifts, some of which consisted of such contributions as forty *złoty* for dinner for the printers and gifts of butter, eggs and even fifteen cutlets.

The Polish Ministry of Information rightly called the free Polish press 'one of the most outstanding manifestations of the vitality and resolution of the Poles, who refuse to submit to the yoke of the oppressor'. The Germans certainly grasped its significance. To be found reading it or, even worse, distributing it, could lead to imprisonment in Pawiak jail in Warsaw or elsewhere. The free press fulfilled an important function in obtaining news from abroad, mainly from the BBC's daily broadcasts, but it also contained thoughtful yet independent-minded analyses of Allied war policy and military successes – and failures. Considerable coverage was given to Germany – its economic and military problems were particularly concentrated on – and any evidence of poor morale in the army was gleefully pounced upon. For instance, on 26 February 1942, the Press Agency ran a brief report from Jędrzejów 'that German soldiers pay high prices for lice, as the presence of these insects in their clothing postpones their dispatch to the Eastern front'.

The Underground State used the press to warn the public not to patronize cafés popular with the Germans, and to boycott tobacco and spirits produced by German-controlled State monopoly enterprises. People were also told to turn a deaf ear to German demands that skis and skiing boots be handed over to the *Wehrmacht* for use on the Eastern front. The *Jutro* commented that the few skiers who surrendered their equipment to the enemy had cards pinned to their backs with the inscription: 'I am a swine, I help the Germans.' The Underground press also gave considerable thought to the coming post-war order. The war was seen as a revolutionary upheaval, which would lead to greater international integration and, in particular, close cooperation between Poland and the Balkan States.

The Underground press and the 'N' scheme, which was organized by the Home Army, were arguably two sides of the same coin. The 'N' scheme took the fight directly to the Germans through a series of pamphlets, letters and periodicals written in German, and through the use of highly intelligent black propaganda concentrated on shaking the enemy's confidence in ultimate victory. In June 1942 nearly 1,000 people were engaged in the 'N' scheme, and about 25,000–30,000 copies of subversive propaganda were distributed per month. It covered most fully the General Government area, where there were about sixty cells organized in six districts, but there were also cells in the annexed areas in the West, and in Russia behind the German front. To ensure contact between these cells and the Home Army's HQ, four inspectorates were created.

The despatch of 'N' literature was mainly the responsibility of railwaymen, whose job required them, quite legitimately, to travel deep into the Reich or to the German supply bases in the east. Sometimes, however, the literature was simply sent through the post or carried by courier, or even by an ambulance doubling up as a postal van. The pamphlets had a wide circulation. Copies were found on the Channel coast, where they were brought by young recruits from the Lublin area. In the east, copies were also traced as far as Orel and Smolensk, where they had been clandestinely delivered by Polish railwaymen.

The subversive matter was, for the most part, written in German and aimed at German servicemen. In periodicals such as *Der Soldat* and *Der Hammer*, differences between the Army and Party were highlighted and quarrels between leading personalities of the regime reported and exaggerated. *Die Heimat* touched a raw nerve by dealing with the impact on soldiers' families of the British bombing campaign in Germany. A favourite topic frequently explored was sexual relations between German women and POWs and foreign workers. One leaflet contained a bogus appeal by a fictional woman's organization in Cologne, *Die Frauenschaft-Köln*, to the men at the front. It directed the attention of the soldiers, in a highly patriotic and self-righteous tone, to the 'demoralisation spreading among German women, living with alien workers and prisoners of war'.

Another theme explored was the disloyalty and incompetence of the Axis nations, who let the main burden of war fall on the Germans. Japan's successes against Britain and America were played down, while it was pointed out that 'an alliance with [...] Japan [...] is contrary to the basic solidarity of the white race and opposed to the economic interests of Germany'. Playing on the heavy German casualty rate on the Eastern front, one leaflet succinctly gave expert advice for feigning illness, drawn up by a group of specialist doctors and enumerating all practical methods of simulating illness before the recruiting commissions, in hospitals, and at the front (NA, HS4/203).

Humour was also an effective propaganda weapon. Copying the design and format of the popular German periodical *Erika*, cartoons, articles and jokes at the expense of the Nazi regime abounded. According to reports by Polish observers, there were no examples of soldiers destroying the material. Indeed, according to one report:

> The soldiers show great interest in the literature; they pass on copies from hand to hand, they take care that no uncalled person [*sic*] should lay his hands upon it, and even – if possible – try to read it in groups.

> [NA, HS4/203]

German Communists in the *Todt* Organization were also appreciative of the material. Apparently, a drunken group at Puławy station, where leaflets were distributed whenever possible, were inspired to shout such slogans as 'down with Hitler!', 'Poles, start a revolution!', etc.

Another approach pursued by the 'N' scheme aimed at making the Germans quarrel amongst themselves by undermining their confidence in the General Government administration. One example was the dispatch of 164 letters notifying German civilians and wives in Warsaw that gifts for the wounded should be delivered to the *Kreishauptmann*'s [District Head's] office. When they dutifully arrived with them, there was, of course, no provision for the collection of such gifts. Some Germans decided to leave them in the local offices but once they realized that the whole affair was a hoax, they demanded the return of their parcels. This created arguments and even, on one occasion, a fight with the police. A particularly subtle hoax was an expertly forged official notification sent to 208 industrial works, calling for the celebration of 2 May as a holiday – the day before the Polish national holiday – by order of Hitler. In Warsaw, some thirty-seven works interrupted work and in Pruszków, in the railway repair workshops, 9,000 workers downed tools to celebrate the day!

In an attempt to stop the distribution of pamphlets and leaflets, the Governor of Warsaw, in a circular dated 8 May 1942, stressed that it was the duty of every German to report each individual instance and to hand over these 'heavily camouflaged *Hetzschriften* [hate publications] to the authorities' without reading them first! The propaganda section of the AK pounced on this admission to observe that 'the chief objective of the scheme had been achieved – i.e. the steady undermining of confidence to [*sic*] genuine publications and circulars'.

The Spectre of Communism: Communist Partisan Bands, 1941–1942

In July 1941 Stalin, facing the implosion of the USSR, appealed to the large numbers of Red Army soldiers stranded or escaped from POW cages behind the German lines to form

> guerrilla units [. . .] to blow up bridges and roads, damage telephone and telegraph lines, set fire to forests, stores and transport [. . .] In the occupied areas conditions must be made unbearable for the enemy and all his accomplices. They must be hounded and annihilated at every step and all their measures frustrated.

The Polish Underground 1939–1947

While both Stalin and the Underground State had the same priority – the destruction of the Germans – there were serious tactical disagreements. The Russians were pressing for large-scale partisan warfare in Poland, or even open revolt, as early as September 1941, but as we have seen, the AK wished to postpone any uprising until Germany was on the brink of collapse. As General Kukiel, the Minister of National Defence in London, was to observe a year later: 'a premature uprising would leave Poland dead as a spent bullet'. In the Polish borderlands, the Russians also became increasingly reluctant to cooperate with the Home Army unless it subordinated itself to ultimate Soviet control.

By late summer, partisan bands were beginning to collect in the eastern borderlands of Poland, and in September the Red Army started to parachute in trained officers to discipline and lead them. During the winter of 1941–2, after the repulse of the Germans before Moscow, it became possible to establish the Vitebsk Corridor, which allowed a trickle of supplies and men to reach the partisans in eastern Poland and the Ukraine. In May 1942, the Central Staff for Partisan Warfare was set up in Moscow, composed of Red Army and Byelorussian Communist Party personnel. This enabled the USSR increasingly to coordinate and control the Communist-dominated partisan bands in Lithuania and Ukraine, and in the eastern parts of the General Government. The partisans were organized into detachments or *Otrady*, four or five of which formed a brigade with its own commander and usually political commissar. A detachment could number anything from 50 to 200 partisans. In Eastern Poland, the *Otrady* were composed of escaped Soviet POWs, many of whom were in fact from the Far Eastern territories of the USSR, Communist-inclined Poles, Ukrainians, and Jews who had fled the ghettos. In May 1942 Dr Klukowski confided in his diary that it was 'nearly impossible to find out who the partisans were: Polish, Russian, even German deserters or plain bandits'. The Soviet Air Force was able to make regular airdrops of supplies, weapons, radios and specially trained commandos as far west as Chełm, Zamość and Lublin, as well as the Holy Cross Mountains in Kielce province.

In an attempt to improve the efficiency of the partisans, a training school was set up in Russia, and in August 1942 their brigade commanders were ordered to fly back to Moscow to report to Stalin himself. They were given a lecture on the importance of recruiting more partisan fighters, and told that the movement needed to be both more aggressive and better disciplined, and should concentrate particularly on the destruction of the German lines of communication. Stalin's guidelines to the partisans operating west of the German lines were summed up in five terse slogans:

Fulfil your partisan oath
Carry iron discipline
Guard your partisan secrecy
Have your weapons at the ready
Recruit for the partisan cause

[A. Levine, *Fugitives of the Forest*, Stoddart, Toronto, 1998, p. 164]

The reports flooding in to the Commander of the German Security Service, the SD, in Lublin province from 1942 onwards give a picture of increasing turmoil. Daily, marauding groups of partisans or 'bandits' as the Germans invariably called them, demanded food from the local farms, seized weapons and money and assassinated informers or resisters. Sometimes the groups numbered well over fifty men. According to the Forest Security Office at Biłgoraj (in Janów County) there was, for example, near Ulanów, 'a very well armed Russian group of seventy bandits', who were terrorizing the local woods and foresters. Another German report dated 29 September observed: 'the number of incidents and robberies can no longer be calculated since the minor incidents are usually no longer reported. The victims are afraid that if they report the incidents they will be punished by the bandits.'

For the handful of Jews who managed to escape the ghettos or the death squads, the forests and swamps of Eastern Poland and the Ukraine were a blessed refuge, where there was a chance of safety if they joined a partisan band. A fascinating account of partisan life can be read in the memoirs of Yosel Epelbaum (Joseph Pell), a Polish Jew who managed to flee the Manievich ghetto in Volhynia. He was fortunate to make contact with a Partisan group under the leadership of a former Polish Communist spy, Józef Sobiesiak (whose *nom de guerre* was 'Mak'), which was composed of Russians, Poles and 'anti-Fascist' Ukrainians. 'Mak' set up a 'forest republic' in the swamps north of the Manievich forest, which provided ideal protection against a modern mechanized army. Within a few months, his group increased to over 500. Unlike many guerrilla leaders, he was ready to accept both Jews and civilians.

In a report dated 17 July and sent to London by the AK, the achievements of these partisan groups was played down. It observed that so far no attempt had been made by these bands seriously to disturb communications, and that their usual objects of attack were only small police stations or isolated Germans. It is true that, initially, efforts to disrupt railway traffic were primitive and often involved levering off lengths of track with a crowbar – a temporary expedient as the tracks could be speedily repaired – but in the course of the winter of 1942/3, better equipment arrived from the USSR, and by the spring of 1943 partisan groups had crippled the whole railway network of Northern Volhynia. The effectiveness of those partisan groups that accepted Soviet control also improved when Soviet officers were parachuted in to command them. In late 1942, for example, Anton Brimsky, a colonel in the Red Army, together with a political commissar, was parachuted into north-central Volhynia to coordinate the disparate partisan groups there. Brimsky imposed a rigorous personal discipline on the partisans, insisting that they should wash outside every morning, regardless of the temperature, and shave their beards. Partisan schools were also set up in the woods, where new recruits were trained. In July 1942, Klukowski received 'information about well-equipped forest units, some even mounted, about military exercises and even shooting ranges'.

The marshlands and the densely wooded terrain in Eastern Poland, which had helped protect Polish troops in the autumn of 1939, were more favourable to partisan warfare than the flat agricultural land and cities of Central and Western Poland. The partisans were able to construct log cabins, known as *Ziemlanka* inside excavated pits, which just about gave them the necessary protection during winter. The walls were lined with cowhides to keep out the rain and the snow, and the pitched roof, made of logs camouflaged with hay, straw and branches, only rose three or four feet above ground. Yosel Epelbaum's group constructed some dozen of these, in which, at night, in each cabin, two rows of fifteen people slept. In the centre aisle, most *Ziemlanka* had a wood-burning heater, ventilated with a pipe constructed from tin cans. Food was foraged from the farms and, apart from potatoes, mostly consisted of meat, which was cooked in 50-gallon barrels cut in half. Pigs were the favourite target because salted pork provided an excellent food reserve, essential for winter survival.

The Home Army and the Government-in-Exile viewed these developments with considerable misgivings. First of all, they were conscious of how they provoked a bloody German backlash for, as they saw it, relatively little gain. Józef Retinger, Sikorski's adviser, claimed in October 1942 that there was hardly a village in the whole of Lublin province where people had not been killed by the Germans, while in the Pripet

Campaign Chronicle

Marshes an appalling bloodbath took place that caused one former SS member of the Estonian Legion, who had participated, to observe in 1945 that: 'It seems as if history had done a retrograde movement of a thousand years into the period of the plundering expeditions of the demented, bloodthirsty, Asiatics.' The Home Army and the Government-in-Exile were convinced that such atrocities were the German reaction to Soviet appeals for an uprising, which they viewed as premature. In May, Edward Raczyński, wrote without effect to the Soviet Ambassador in London, begging the USSR to limit the build-up of its anti-partisan activities.

In January 1943, SOE received from 'a most secret' source a list of what the Home Army considered were Soviet aims in Poland:

- Military Intelligence and sabotage–guerrilla activities
- Preparations for an armed rising to relieve the Soviet rear
- Creation of a state of feeling favourable to the USSR
- Combating of elements opposed to Communist action
- Creation of anarchy in Poland so as to enable 'K' (i.e. the Communists) to seize power and also to justify foreign intervention

[NA, HS4/138]

Soviet action was two-pronged: as well as organizing guerrilla activities, it also aimed, through the KPP (Polish Communist Party) and the PPR (Polish Workmen's Party), to penetrate independent Polish organizations, such as the AK and the political parties. As early as July 1941, the VI Bureau in London received, much to its alarm, news that a Russian NKVD colonel had established himself in the Warsaw Ghetto. In the summer of 1942, the PPR was engaged in recruiting workers in the industrial centres. It also formed a para-military section, the People's Guard (GL), which trained groups to cooperate closely with the Soviet-led guerrilla bands. In its three Underground papers it agitated for an immediate armed uprising, and emphasized that only the USSR could save the Polish nation. These papers also gave prominence to news broadcasts by the *Kościuszko* broadcasting station in Moscow, which never ceased to urge immediate insurrection and accused the AK and Government-in-Exile of betraying Poland.

By the summer of 1942 the potential Communist threat to future Polish independence was clearly visible, but at this stage Communist influence was, for the most part, confined to the eastern districts of

Lublin Province. However, should the USSR be in a position to drive the Germans out of Poland, the situation would be very different.

The Zamość Crisis

The German resettlement policy in Zamość County finally compelled the AK to risk limited guerrilla warfare. In the spring of 1942 Globocnik, the head of the SS and police in Lublin, announced that Lublin would soon become a purely German settlement area, which would form a bridge between German settlements in the Baltic and those in Galicia and Romania. On 12 November, Himmler ordered that Zamość County should become the first German colony in the General Government. The inhabitants of eight villages were then forcibly evicted. There was, initially, little opposition, as the villagers had been completely surprised. Further evictions followed: over 100,000 Poles were forcibly moved to transit camps in two waves – November 1942 to March 1943 and June to August 1943 – and replaced by some 13,000 ethnic Germans. Altogether this amounted to the expulsion of over 30 per cent of the local Polish population and Zamość was renamed '*Himmlerstadt*'. General Rowecki reported to London on 23 December that

> the peasants were being sent to prison camps and thence to labour camps or deported into other districts. Some are simply being sent away. Families are being parted in such a way that small children under the age of six are being taken to Germany, mothers who do not give up their children are being killed. The old and sick are sent to an unknown destination. A transport of the latter was reported heading for Oświęcim [Auschwitz].

[NA, HS4/316]

Rowecki, like many of his countrymen, feared that the Zamość evictions were but the prelude to deportations and massacres similar to those the Jews had already suffered. He told his Government in London that 'the Poles would not allow themselves to be led away and destroyed, but would at all costs fight', and ordered immediate active resistance and large-scale subversive activities throughout the whole Lublin district. Rowecki also asked for air support for the operations in Zamość and offered to send London a list of targets for the RAF.

Once they overcame their surprise, the inhabitants, however, reacted spontaneously. Dr Klukowski noted on 7 December that 'many villagers are forming their own units with only one goal, revenge'. In early December, sections of the Peasant Battalions (BCh), Soviet partisan groups and the AK began to attack the new settlers, railroads and bridges, as well German road traffic. The scale of opposition to German plans in Zamość escalated into partisan warfare throughout Lublin province and forced the Germans to interrupt their resettlement programme.

The reaction of the Polish Government in London, however, was decidedly muted. The message from Mikołajczyk, the Interior Minister in the London Government-in-Exile, which was transmitted to Poland on the wireless, was so cautious that many Poles interpreted it as giving instructions to remain passive. On Christmas Day, the Polish Cabinet informed the Commander of the Secret Army that 'at all costs he was to localize the action and prevent it spreading to other districts'. It also decided not to approach the Russians, as they might find this an excuse for large-scale parachute operations that would escalate the revolt. Instructions were sent emphasizing 'that all counter measures were to be made to seem like self-defence, so as to avoid unnecessary reprisals being taken against the civilian population in Warsaw and elsewhere'. To deter the Germans, the Poles urged that a specific campaign of reprisal bombings of targets within Germany should be carried out by the RAF. While this was turned down, the Air Ministry agreed in principle to accelerate dropping operations over Poland, even if they had to be carried out in the 'non moon period'. Also, direct wireless communication with Zamość was to be opened up.

Polish Resistance in France

While the main preoccupation of the Government-in-Exile was inevitably Poland, the 'Adjudicate' and 'Angelica' (*see page 52*) organizations in France continued to be developed. By August 1942 'Angelica' controlled about 5,000 agents and was carrying out an effective propaganda campaign, as well as feeding London with useful information. Sikorski told Lord Selborne on 26 August 1942 that it was keeping alive 'the morale not only of the Poles but also of numerous Frenchmen with whom it is in contact'. It also managed to publish three secret papers in Polish, which had a circulation of over 25,000, as well as numerous leaflets in French.

'Adjudicate', on the other hand, had suffered a disaster and all its 180 members had been arrested, while its head had been compelled to escape across the border to Spain. Inevitably, this was a serious threat to the future of the Polish Underground activity in France, and prompted Sikorski radically to restructure the whole organization. The military side of the organization was now to be directed by a senior officer resident in France. The civilian side, which was to cover matters relating to propaganda and information, the psychological preparation of the Polish population in France for the coming second front, and the planning of strikes and industrial sabotage, as well as counter espionage, was renamed 'Monica' and was to be the responsibility of Mikołajczyk at the Ministry of the Interior. Sikorski informed Selborne on 26 August that the overall guiding policy of action in France was not to initiate premature action, which would almost certainly provoke reprisals from the Germans 'on the part of their hosts'. As in Poland, 'action must be reserved for the moment of decisive armed intervention' by the Western Allies. Ultimately, Sikorski calculated that three divisions of Polish troops could be created 'from among 80,000 recruits already called to the colours in 1940'. SOE's assessment in December 1942 was rather more cautious. It calculated that there were about 5,000 officers in the internment camps in Vichy France, and about 50,000 able-bodied men capable of military service scattered throughout the whole country, of whom probably only about one-third would actually be available. They would also have to be armed.

Ambitious Diplomatic Schemes

On 19 February 1942 Jan Librach, who was responsible for mobilizing Polish minorities abroad, made an interesting proposal to Gubbins. He argued that the Government-in-Exile, on the basis of its contacts throughout the Continent and its 'special position' among the émigré Allied Governments in London, was well suited to act as an 'honest broker' if any of the lesser Axis powers (such as Hungary or Romania) wanted to make a separate peace with the Western Allies in an attempt to 're-insure themselves against: (a) a German defeat, and (b) the full implications of a Russian victory'. He consequently suggested that 'Peter' (his *homme de confiance*) should approach the representatives of these countries in Lisbon and request courier facilities, the occasional use of the diplomatic bag to and from Poland, and permission for Polish agents to organize internal dissident elements. In the event of a German collapse, Librach was convinced that these dissidents would be able to negotiate reasonable terms with the Western Allies, while the Poles, who had now 'made their peace' with the Russians, would also be able to act as mediators between these states and Moscow. Optimistically, he believed that, with the help of the British Government, Poland would be able to act as a brake on Russian ambitions. He argued that these allies and satellites of Nazi Germany all had a common interest in preventing, as far as possible, the Russians' 'Drang nach Berlin' ('push to Berlin'), which would be the immediate outcome of an Allied victory. Gubbins was struck by how Librach felt confident enough to approach representatives of foreign governments already at war with Great Britain and 'initiate secret and far-reaching conversations!'

Deteriorating Relations Between the Polish Government-in-Exile and the USSR

After the great Soviet victory at Stalingrad in January 1943, confirmed in the summer by the equally decisive German defeat at Kursk in August, it became clear that the future of Poland would increasingly be decided in Moscow rather than London or Washington. Each stunning victory of the Red Army both reduced the will of the Western powers to intervene in Poland and, indeed, made it more difficult to do so. On 1 March Stalin reasserted Soviet claims to the Polish territory that had been annexed by the USSR in September 1939, and the Soviet Ambassador in London, Ivan Maisky, informed Anthony Eden, the British Foreign Secretary, that the Soviet Union would only tolerate a government in Warsaw that was friendly to itself, thereby, as he said, ruling out the London Poles.

Katyń

This divide between Moscow and the London Poles was intensified by the announcement on 13 April 1943 of the discovery by the Germans of the bodies of several thousand Polish officers, who had been captured by the Red Army in September/October 1939, buried in mass graves near Katyń. At the beginning of April, the Germans took a delegation of nine Poles to see for themselves the several thousand decomposing bodies still bearing Polish military insignia. The AK sent its own observer to assess the findings. Working amongst the exhumers for a few days, he came to the conclusion that, in the particular mass graves opened up, 'only' about 4,000 bodies were interred. However, there was not a shade of doubt that they were former Polish officers. The observer reported that 'all the shots had been fired in the same way: at the base of the skull where it joins the neck'. He also noted in about 'fifteen or sixteen cases evidence of what they must have gone through before death'. Some of their overcoats had been pierced by what were probably bayonets, other bodies had broken jaw bones and 'in some cases the greatcoats wound round their heads were filled with sawdust'. This was, as the AK's observer pointed out, probably a method of killing those who were struggling for their lives:

'when they breathed in the sawdust, it would stifle them'. He also brought back to General Rowecki a selection of personal papers, including the diary of a close friend of a colonel on the AK's staff. A handwriting expert compared the handwriting in it with some of his notes made before the war at staff college, which the colonel still had in his possession, and they were found to have been written by the same hand.

General Sikorski, who was seen by many of his officers as a dangerous appeaser and pragmatist towards the USSR, was in the Middle East when the news of the Katyń discoveries broke. It was therefore left to General Kukiel, the Minister for National Defence in London, to issue a detailed account of the Soviet–Polish correspondence on the fate of the missing officers. The Poles showed considerable restraint. Their approach was well summarized by the émigré paper *Dzień Polski* on 15 April. It conceded that German accusations of Soviet atrocities might only be 'one more lie [...] aiming at driving a wedge into Russo-Polish relations'. On the other hand, there was no denying that, as the fate of the Polish officers in Kozielsk and Starobielsk was still unknown, German propaganda could only be neutralized by the Soviets proving 'that the German reports are false and by answering the question: "WHAT HAS HAPPENED TO THE POLISH OFFICERS FROM THE PRISON CAMPS AT KOZIELSK AND STAROBIELSK?"'

Stalin reacted to these requests by seeing them as evidence of an anti-Soviet campaign and as collusion between Hitler and the Sikorski Government, and consequently broke off diplomatic relations with it. Inevitably, at a time when Soviet forces were asserting their superiority over the Germans, this made the prospect of future cooperation between the USSR and the London Poles even more remote. Stalin followed this up by two decisions that challenged the legitimacy of the Polish Government-in-Exile. He announced the formation of a new Polish organization in the USSR, the Union of Polish Patriots (ZPP), the leader of which, Wanda Wasilewska, claimed in a radio broadcast on 28 April that the Sikorski Government had no right to represent the Polish people. Stalin also gave permission for the creation of a fledgling Polish Army to be formed under General Zygmunt Berling (*see page 126*).

Potentially, both these actions had profound importance for the future of an independent Poland. Sikorski realized that his Government would have – by hook or by crook – to re-establish diplomatic relations with the USSR, if there was to be any chance of ever recreating an independent Poland after the war. His death on 4 July, when his plane (which was carrying him back from Gibraltar after a visit to Polish troops in the

Campaign Chronicle

Middle East) crashed, could not have come at a worse time. It removed the one man of stature in the Polish Government who symbolized the spirit of Poland and whom Churchill respected. He was, to quote the historians Coutouvidis and Reynolds, 'an irreplaceable Polish asset' in the international community. As prime minister, he was replaced by Stanisław Mikołajczyk, who had little experience of international affairs. General Sosnkowski, who had resigned over the Polish–Soviet Treaty in July 1941, was made commander-in-chief of Polish forces.

Anglo-American Appeasement of the USSR

Inevitably, Stalingrad and Kursk altered the relationship between the Western Allies and the USSR. By the autumn of 1943 it seemed likely that Stalin would drive the Germans out of Russia and liberate Poland without any help from the West. The danger for Britain and America was that Stalin might then decide to stop short of assisting them in the final destruction of Germany. It therefore became increasingly important to appease the Soviet Union and bind Stalin firmly into the Grand Alliance. At the Moscow conference of foreign ministers in October, and the subsequent meeting between Churchill, Roosevelt and Stalin at Teheran in November, both Western leaders agreed to the Soviet annexation of territory up to the Curzon Line and Polish compensation in the west at the cost of Germany. In January 1944 an anonymous circular was posted at Paddington Station, which accurately summed up the dilemma in which Poland now found herself:

> None of the Anglo-Saxon states has either the will or the strength to resist Russia;
>
> Russia is an element without which the speedy defeat of the German Reich would be difficult;
>
> Every Russian demand which is not in disaccord with the principle of legality in international relations must be acceded to;
>
> The Curzon Line – as a basis for discussion – has already once been recognized as equitable by the Anglo-Saxon world.
>
> [NA, HS4/138]

The final blow to the Poles' chances of emerging at the end of the war with their frontiers intact was the decision by the Western powers to invade France rather than attack Germany through the Balkans. This effectively ended any Polish hope that Western troops would ever reach Polish soil. The only hope the non-Communist Resistance in Poland and the London Government-in-Exile now had of creating an independent Poland was to cooperate with the Red Army and set up de facto control of the liberated areas. This, of course, assumed, optimistically, that the Red Army would tolerate such action!

The State of Poland, January 1943–August 1944
In the eighteen months up to the outbreak of the Warsaw Uprising in August 1944, the German administration of the General Government came under increasing pressure. Klukowski noticed that in Zamość, the Germans were drinking heavily, and that the German mayor was attempting to make his apartment more secure, from which he deduced, rather prematurely in May 1943, that 'we are coming to the last days of the occupation'. There is no doubt that Poland was slowly slipping into anarchy. In August, the VI Bureau in London, on the basis of several reports from Poland, observed that 'conditions of safety in villages are deteriorating steadily, while in towns, in spite of greater opportunities for the employment of the police, no improvement is noted'. After his escape from Poland, Corporal Jeffery (*see page 81–3*), during his debriefing in London in March 1944, painted a bleak picture of an increasingly corrupt and insecure occupation regime. According to Jeffery, many Germans were already organizing a way of escape from Poland when the inevitable collapse came 'by providing themselves with Polish *Kennkarten* [identity cards] and emergency addresses, so as to lose their German identity immediately in case of need'. A certain number were also busily trying to cultivate Polish contacts, 'who would vouch for them as "good Germans" when the time came'.

Governor Hans Frank drew the conclusion from this mounting chaos that the Reich should use the Katyń affair to end its policy of terror towards the Poles. With Goebbels' support, he urged Hitler to order an increase in food rations, the ending of public executions of the elderly, women and children, and an improvement in the treatment of the Poles forced to work in the Reich. Even the Security Police and the *Gestapo* tentatively conceded the need to come to terms with the AK, but little came of this policy apart from a few gestures, such as the opening of the Chopin museum and the printing of millions of anti-Soviet propaganda pamphlets. The Poles easily saw through the clumsy German efforts and – despite British fears – once again no Polish Quisling appeared.

Campaign Chronicle

Mass arrests continued to be a common feature of Polish life, whether in Kraków, Lublin, Warsaw or Zamość. As a Polish teacher in Kraków all too accurately recorded in her diary just before Christmas in 1943, 'when you leave the house, you never know if you will get back. There are perpetual round-ups.' A month earlier she wrote:

> For each German killed, ten Poles are shot in the street. They make an announcement on the radio where and at what time the executions will take place, so that people can go and watch; they give the surnames of the poor wretches and their ages. After a few hours they clear the bodies away and sprinkle sand on the blood and brains left on the ground. People take flowers and candles to the spot.
>
> [K. Stankiewicz, IWM, 83/10/1]

By early 1943 the Germans were operating massive drives to conscript labour. In March 1943, for instance, nearly 20,000 workers were sent to the Reich from the Warsaw district alone. Within the annexed areas all eligible Poles on the *Volksliste* were enlisted into the German Army and reprisals were taken against the families of those who deserted. The economic situation also steadily worsened. Farms in the eastern provinces, particularly, were regularly attacked by partisans and 'bandits'; and throughout the General Government, food production was hampered by lack of manpower. Increasingly, the food quotas demanded for the *Wehrmacht* grew more onerous and drove the peasantry into the arms of the partisans This inevitably resulted in a steep increase in food prices. The German Governor of the Warsaw district observed in a report in April 1943 that 'without exaggeration [...] a worker is not interested in his pay'. The average worker's wage was 30 *złoty* a week, while 1 kg of butter cost 250 *złoty* and a kg of bread, 12.50.

On the one hand, the Germans were still strong enough to exact ruthless reprisals on the population, but on the other they were powerless to stop the General Government from sliding into anarchy. The Poles, particularly in the eastern provinces, faced the worst of both worlds. In the Lublin area mass evictions from the villages only encouraged growing attacks from Soviet-controlled partisan groups, who would often attack the remaining Polish farms and settlements; while in Volhynia and Eastern Galicia the Poles were subjected to a policy of 'ethnic cleansing' by the Nationalist Ukrainians. All this, of course, was conducted against the background of the horrific elimination of the ghettos and the Holocaust.

The Polish Underground 1939–1947

In May 1943, for example, Klukowski observed a 'long train loaded with Jews' pass through Szczebrzeszyn in the direction of Chełm: 'During the journey some of the Jews try to escape by jumping from the train, but guards shoot them to death.'

The Streamlining of the Underground State

The increase in sabotage and Underground activity since the commencement of *Barbarossa* led first to the subordination of the two sabotage units, the Union for Revenge and *Wachlarz*, to the Directorate of Diversion (*Kedyw*), which, together with the Propaganda and Psychological Warfare Sections, was placed, in the autumn of 1943, under the newly formed Directorate of Underground Resistance, headed by the Commander of the Home Army. As this led to overlapping and a degree of duality with the Directorate of Civil Resistance, both organizations were later merged under one common name, the Directorate of Underground Struggle, which took over responsibility for the struggle against the Germans. The Directorate consisted of the Commander of the Home Army, the Chief of Staff, the Chief of *Kedyw*, the Chief of the Bureau of Information and Propaganda, and the Director of General Resistance.

Assassinations

The AK carried out an increasingly daring programme of assassinations. Between January 1943 and June 1944, 2,015 *Gestapo* agents were eliminated, while an attempt on the life of Hans Frank only narrowly failed, when the first three coaches of the train he was travelling in were destroyed. All German officials were targets if they had a record of brutality. In Warsaw, for example, Kurt Hoffmann, the chief of the Labour Recruiting Bureau, was assassinated, as was the billeting officer, Braun. In Kraków, on 20 April, two bombs were thrown at the car of the General Government's Head of the Security Police, SS General Krüger, severely wounding him.

The most successful of the assassinations carried out by the Resistance was that of SS Major-General Kutschera, who had been appointed Head of the Warsaw police in the autumn of 1943, in an attempt to defeat the Underground. Initially, he appeared to achieve success through a brutal policy of mass reprisals. It therefore became vital to eliminate him. Bór calculated that at least 200 hostages would have to pay the price for his death, but he was convinced that his assassination would deter his successor from pursuing the same brutal policies. It took three months to

Campaign Chronicle

plan this operation. A special *Kedyw* (partisan) unit had to be formed under a young lieutenant, code-named 'Lot', just twenty years old, who had already carried out several successful missions. Kutschera's lifestyle and routine also had to be studied minutely so that the right place for the assassination could be found, which in the end was just outside the SS headquarters. An account of the events of 1 February 1944, albeit second hand, was later given by Corporal Jeffery to the SOE in London:

> At 08.30 hours on the morning of the execution, members of the Polish Underground forces, armed with machine pistols and grenades concealed in cases and in their clothing, took up positions covering Ujazdowska Street. A concierge came out of the gate of a house and saw one of the men fumbling with his weapon. He was told to stay where he was and not to re-enter the house or he would be shot.
>
> Kutschera's car arrived as usual at the gates of his office and stopped while the German sentry removed the bar. At this moment a car containing members of the Polish Underground forces arrived and immediately shot the sentry as he was opening the gates of the building. Grenades were thrown at Kutschera's car, resulting in the immediate death of Kutschera and the other occupants of the car.
>
> The Germans inside the building, hearing the shooting, rushed out and a battle commenced between the Germans and the covering parties. Two of the covering party were killed immediately but the attackers were able to withdraw, taking their casualties with them.
>
> [NA, HS4/255]

They managed to take Lot and one other wounded colleague to hospital, where they were later whisked away to safety to avoid the *Gestapo*, but their wounds were to prove fatal. The two other men in the car, Sokół and Juno, drove back into the city but ran into a police cordon at the Kierbedź bridge:

> In a flash, Sokół and Juno leapt from the car, climbed the iron balustrade and jumped into the river 100 feet below [...] They disappeared, came to the surface, and started swimming rapidly downstream. Bullets splashed all around them. Sokół was the first to be killed. Juno continued to struggle on. Silent crowds watched with bated breath from the banks. Then the sound of a motor boat was heard [...] The police boat gained on him swiftly. Shots fired at close

range could now be heard. Once more the body of the mortally wounded young man appeared on the surface and then sank.

[Bór-Komorowski, p. 159]

The first day of February was an impressive day for the Liquidation Section of the Underground Army. At the time that Kutschera was killed, Lubert, chief of the Investigation Section of the *Arbeitsdienst* (Labour Conscription) in Warsaw, was approaching his office accompanied by a colleague, when they were suddenly stopped by two men armed with pistols, who ordered them to put their hands up. Lubert was killed instantly by a bullet in the head, while his colleague was allowed to flee. The two assassins then disappeared and Lubert's body was taken into the office. In June there was a further success when Franz Witek, the chief of the Kielce *Gestapo*, was shot outside his offices. Previously there had been an attempt to poison him, but this had only induced a slight illness!

The *Gestapo* Fights Back

The *Gestapo* also had its successes. Sometimes its agents were able to penetrate sections of the Underground and, under the cover of being loyal Poles, were able to betray its members. Between 1 September 1943 and 19 February 1944, some 14,221 members of the AK were arrested or killed. In April 1944 a *Gestapo* agent posing as a member of the Resistance managed to discover a whole network of contacts involved in the dispatch of information to London, and in Warsaw alone this resulted in the arrest of twenty-two people. That same month, however, the Underground managed to trap one of its own agents, Kasprzycki, who had betrayed members of a network extending into Germany. Headquarters instructed his interrogators on 14 April 1944 that, since Kasprzycki had not hesitated to reveal to the *Gestapo* all he knew of the work of the Polish Underground and of persons working for it, including even his skiing friends,

> have no scruples in applying German methods of interrogation to him, since it is, for obvious reasons, of the utmost urgency that we should be informed of the degree of penetration by the Germans as well as methods used by the Germans for this purpose.
>
> [NA, HS4/274]

The Germans' greatest success was the capture of General Rowecki on 30 June 1943, just after he had entered what was assumed to be a safe flat on Spiska Street in Warsaw. Rowecki had been betrayed by Ludwik Kalkstein (alias 'Hanka' – an Intelligence officer in the AK), Kalkstein's brother-in-law, Świerczewski (alias 'Genes'), and Świerczewski's fiancée, Blanka Kaczorowska (alias 'Sroka') – all of whom were *Gestapo* agents. Before plans for Rowecki's rescue could be attempted, he was removed to Berlin for interrogation. He rejected outright any proposals that he should collaborate with Nazi Germany against the USSR, and was in due course moved to Sachsenhausen concentration camp, where he was murdered on 2 August 1944. Świerczewski, Kalkstein and Kaczorowska were sentenced to death for high treason by the Underground state, but only Świerczewski was hanged. Kalkstein joined the SS and Kaczorowska escaped execution because she was pregnant.

On 1 July, Bór was informed from London that he was now commander-in-chief of the Home Army.

Intelligence, 1943–1944

The Poles continued to supply the Allies with detailed and accurate Intelligence. It was sent to London, as we have seen, by wireless and couriers travelling through Hungary, the Balkans, Switzerland and Sweden, to whom elaborate codes and instructions were given. The couriers were passed from hideout to hideout. Before they were deemed *bona fide*, they had to participate in a coded dialogue. For instance, in Berne, in May 1944, couriers were given detailed instructions for finding their way to various safe houses. To gain access to one of these, which was '100 metres from the [tram] stop opposite Brasserie de la Chapelle', and situated in the garret of a large basement house, where a certain 'Mr B.' and his wife lived, the courier was instructed to say (according to an English translation later made for the SOE by the VI Bureau): 'Is John from the Forest at home?' Mr B. would then reply: 'This lame one.' As a security or 'second check', the courier would then say: 'Lame and blind.'

With the opening up of supply bases in Southern Italy in late 1943, it became easier to dispatch stores and personnel to Poland. As the need for detailed information grew, good radio operators became ever more vital and were regularly parachuted in. Jan Cias, for instance, volunteered for special duties in Poland after serving in a Polish signals company in England. After attending a series of British courses and then a five-week course organized by the Polish VI Bureau, he was given a new set of identity papers, which included a *Kennkarte*, birth certificate, and a leave pass from a firm in Radom, as well as two addresses – one in the Lublin area and the other in Warsaw. In December 1943 he sailed with a group of forty others from Liverpool to Algiers, and thence to Taranto. On the night of 12/13 April 1944 he and three other men flew to Poland and were dropped about 7 km from Lublin. He was, as he later recalled when he returned to London almost a year later, received by a cadet officer and a unit of twenty-five men, who immediately took charge of the material dropped by the plane. The four men were then marched through the night to a village, where they were hidden during the day. The following night they were taken to the Underground Area Commander, and Cias and a fellow parachutist, one Zielichowski, were whisked off to Lublin 'by taxi' and hidden in the house of a prominent member of the Underground, who was also the Director of the Local Mechanical College. The other two men arrived later in a lorry. The next morning, Cias and Zielichowski were collected by the Area Commander's sister and taken by train to Warsaw. There he was guided from safe house to safe house, given a new set of papers – as those he had brought with him from London were not considered to be perfect – a *Kennkarte* and an *Ausweiss* (pass) from a German garage in Warsaw, issued in the name of Jan Kawka. He was also thoroughly briefed on the current situation in Poland.

On 23 June he was taken by a courier – a certain Miss 'Wiesia' – to Kielce to operate a special wireless transmitter, which was at the sole disposal of the Government Delegate in Warsaw. It was guarded by a squad of seventeen men and hidden in a room in a saw mill where only Poles worked. On 28 June Cias managed to establish contact with London and began the regular transmission of messages from the Government Delegate, which were brought at least once a week by Wiesia. He was supposed to be replaced by a wireless operator from Warsaw and to return to work in the capital, but this did not happen because the Germans discovered one of the Warsaw transmitters and arrested three of their operators. Cias therefore remained in Kielce for the duration of the Warsaw Uprising. He was seized by the Germans in October but managed to escape from prison before being interrogated by the *Gestapo*. He also evaded capture by the NKVD in March 1945 by assuming the name and identity of a dead British POW (*see page 188*).

Aircraft and Ballistic Rocket Projects
As German factories were moved into Poland to escape the Allied bombing offensive, the demand for detailed information about what they were

Campaign Chronicle

producing grew in London. For instance, to take just one set of messages coming from the Polish VI Bureau to the Home Army on 16 May 1944, the Poles were expected to find out about:

what kind of changes are to be made in the He-177, the position of the aircraft factory in Rendsburg. The Focke-Wulf factory in Bremen has been brought in parts to Poland. You will find out where.

[NA, HS4/303]

These detailed shopping lists for information show how dependent the Allies had become on Poles to supply vital information for the bombing campaign. Of decisive importance, however, was Polish information about the German ballistic rocket projects, the V-1s and V-2s. By early 1943 the Germans had at least 15,000 conscripted workers toiling on these projects at Peenemünde: by the spring, the AK had already received reports from a couple of Polish labourers working there. The information was then sent to London. A few months later, in August, an Air Ministry Intelligence report referred to information received on 30 March as emanating from 'a most reliable and expert source, which had proved most valuable over a long period'. Information from agents in France, Luxembourg and Belgium all confirmed these Polish reports.

In the night of 17/18 August, the RAF launched a bombing raid against Peenemünde, which failed to halt production but nevertheless persuaded the Germans to shift production to the massive underground Mittelwerk plant near Nordhausen in Central Germany. The actual testing ground was moved to near the site of the razed village of Blizna, in the SS training base of Heidelager, in south-west Poland, where the first rocket was launched on 5 November 1943. By early 1944 rockets were being constantly sent to Blizna for experimental launching. The AK monitored the trials but were unable to give any information on how they were launched. They were usually fired off in a northerly direction and landed near Warsaw, Lublin and Radom. German motorized units were quickly informed and managed to retrieve the rockets before the AK reached them.

However, on 20 May 1944, when a V-2 rocket fell on the marshy ground bordering the River Bug near Sarnacki, about 75 miles east of Warsaw, the AK at last managed to retrieve a rocket before the German recovery unit arrived. A local AK unit successfully concealed the rocket from the German search parties, and then managed to load the missile onto a horse cart and take it to be stored in a barn in the nearby village of Hołowczyce-Kolonia. Here, Antoni Kocjan of the AK Research Committee organized a group of experts to photograph and make drawings of the rocket. There was a moment of acute danger when Kocjan was arrested by the *Gestapo*, but despite torture he betrayed nothing. From the British Government, via the VI Bureau, a series of detailed questions were sent to the Government Delegacy for forwarding to the Research Committee.

On 13 June, a V-2 test rocket fired from Peenemünde crashed near Malmö, Sweden. The Swedes allowed British agents to inspect the rockets and fly parts back to Farnborough on 16 July. This coup did not make the Polish discoveries any less valuable, as they were needed for comparison purposes to see whether the remote-control system of the Malmö rocket was just an experimental one-off or the standard control system for all V-2 rockets. It consequently became vital to arrange, through Operation *Wildhorn* III, the transport of key sections of the rocket from Poland to England. On 25 July a Dakota took off from Brindisi carrying a number of Poles, nineteen suitcases of equipment, mail and a considerable sum of money. The plane landed on a site known as 'Motyl' or 'butterfly', 12 miles north-west of Tarnów in Southern Poland. The site was far from safe, as the approach roads to the landing were jam-packed with German troops and vehicles retreating from the Soviet advance and, furthermore, two Fieseler Storch reconnaissance planes had already touched down on the site a few hours earlier!

The passengers and the packets were quickly unloaded and then on came the cylinders containing the rocket parts and the returning passengers, amongst whom were numbered the Socialist politician Tomasz Arciszewski and Józef Retinger, who had been Sikorski's adviser. Nearby, in the village of Wał Ruda, German troops were billeted but mercifully took no interest in the proceedings, assuming, one imagines, that the plane was German. It took four attempts for the Dakota to take off. The first time the brakes jammed. Then, when that was fixed, its wheels sank into the soft ground. Planks were brought out from a barn and pushed under its wheels. Finally, after two attempts, this at last worked and the Dakota was able to take off. As the historian Jonathan Walker observed, 'even the take-off din from the twin Pratt and Whitney engines failed to alert the slumbering *Wehrmacht*'.

The parts were handed over to the VI Bureau in London, which translated the reports and gave the rocket parts to the scientists. On 6 August the Russians occupied Blizna, but Information continued to flood in from Polish agents in France. The Polish Ministry of the Interior informed

Lord Selborne on 3 August that between 23 June and 1 August, eighty-five messages had been

> received from our organization in France and dealing with a/ The location of the flying bomb sites, b/ The location of the flying bombs' dumps, c/ Observed results of air bombing of the sites and d/ Transportation of the flying bombs.

[NA, HS4/317]

The Communist Challenge, 1943–1944

In the post-Stalingrad world, where Russia had the Germans on the run, but the Western Allies had not even yet established a military presence on the continent, the AK's links to London were its Achilles' heel. The AK certainly dominated the Resistance in German-occupied Poland, but once Soviet troops moved in, only international agreement could, in the final analysis, guarantee an independent Poland.

The PPR (the Polish Workers' Party) had the great advantage of having close links with the Kremlin. It claimed to be independent and patriotic but in practice took orders from the small Polish Communist Party, the KPP. In the eyes of the AK, the PPR was a Soviet agency. In the towns it sought to attract the workers and radical intellectuals, and in the countryside it targeted the poorer peasants, the landless farm labourers, and the deportees. In early 1943 it was estimated that the PPR was strongest in Warsaw, Łódz, Kraków, Tarnów and in the eastern districts of the General Government, where it received support from Soviet partisans. Talks did take place between the AK and PPR in April 1943, although on whose initiative it is hard to determine. Both organizations agreed, in principle, on a unified military effort, but the talks collapsed, not surprisingly, when the AK insisted that the PPR must be completely independent of any outside power and recognize Poland's 1921 frontiers.

A stream of AK reports to the VI Bureau showed how 'the Soviet agencies operating in Poland through Soviet partisans, the Polish Workers Party, loose groups and Communist centres [had] ... attempted to penetrate into the Polish Underground Movement in order to gain knowledge of the names of key leaders so that they could betray them later to the *Gestapo* or else liquidate them themselves.'

The Polish Underground 1939–1947

In July 1943 the delegates of the PPR and the commanders of the People's Guard (GL) had met in the district of Siedlice to discuss plans for the liquidation of the leaders of the Polish Underground Movement. These were then sent for approval to the PPR's Central Committee with the instructions that 'additional exact lists' should be drawn up. Throughout the winter of 1943/44 there was a stream of reports being transmitted to London of kidnapping and assassinations of AK officers and prominent anti-Communists in the Underground by the GL.

The political actions of Soviet agencies took different forms in different parts of the country. In the eastern provinces, relying on Soviet partisan bands and agents, they acted 'on the ground of accomplished facts', that is the plebiscite of 1939, which was alleged to have declared overwhelming public support for the annexation of the Soviet-occupied zone (*see page 21*). According to one AK report of 11 October 1943, a Soviet band under one Pylyplenko – who had been in 1939 a member of the Town Council of Zhitomir, on the Polish–Ukrainian border – arrived in the district of Łuck and, far from spending his time fighting the Germans, he and his followers merely organized meetings demanding union with the USSR.

In Central and Western Poland – where there were few Soviet partisan bands – little was said about the eastern territories. Rather, the message was that only the USSR could liberate Poland from the German yoke, while Britain and the USA were merely pursuing their own selfish goals. The paper of the PPR, the *Robotnik*, declared, for instance, on 23 September 1943, that 'The war against the Nazis has become for England and America a screen behind which the two powers are preparing for a counter-revolutionary dictatorship of AMGOT (Allied Military Government for Occupied Territories) in Europe.' Apart from sowing mistrust against the Western powers, the 'Government of the Colonels' in London and the AK were the targets of constant vituperation and hostile propaganda both in the press and the Moscow-controlled Radio Kosciuszko.

In November 1943 the PPR published, with the consent of Moscow, its political programme, which promised the reconstruction of an independent and democratic Poland, where the landed estates would be broken up and the big factories, banks and mines would be managed by workers' committees. In January 1944 – days after Red Army troops crossed the pre-war Polish–Soviet border – the PPR declared that it would set up the KRN (Homeland National Council), which would be a network of local councils aimed at bringing together sympathizers of the PPR's policies in anticipation of forming a government in Poland once it was liberated. This was accompanied by the announcement of the formation of the People's Army (AL), the military arm of the PPR, which was immediately denounced by the Underground Directorate as treason to the existing Polish state. Nevertheless, PPR and Soviet propaganda certainly achieved some success. According to a report in January 1944, from a 'North European' businessman who paid periodic visits to Warsaw and made a point of talking to factory workers, the opinion was often expressed by them that 'it is only the Russians who have succeeded in beating back the common oppressor'. The successes of the Western powers in Africa and Italy and the bombing of Germany had apparently made little impact.

In view of opinions such as these, it was not surprising that the AK decided in January 1944 to set up a special organization, 'Antyk', to place Communist and fellow travelling organizations under surveillance. In November 1943 Bór had come to the conclusion that the AK had been penetrated by Soviet agents and informed Sosnkowski in London that he had begun to prepare 'in the greatest secrecy' a new Underground organization called NIE (an acronym for the Polish word for Independence, 'niepodległość') that would function in the event of a Soviet occupation.

Jewish Resistance and the Poles

How should the Jewish resistance in Poland be assessed? Should it be viewed as part of the Polish resistance or was it a distinct and independent movement? For both the Poles and the Jews, the Germans were their main enemy, but as Shmuel Krakówski, the historian of the Jewish resistance movement in Poland, writes, there were 'different roads that brought Jews and non Jews into the Underground movement, their basically different purposes, their sometimes unidentical enemy and their totally different relations with the local population all make for the distinction'. Although the Poles faced draconian laws and, if the Germans remained victorious, permanent eclipse of their culture and the destruction of their elites, the Jews after 1942, at the latest, faced total and immediate extermination whether they cooperated with the Germans or not. For the Germans they were cunning and dangerous sub humans to be totally eliminated. The Slavs arguably also faced extinction but over the long term. In their desperation those Jews who survived and joined the partisans also tended to see the Russians and the GL as their protectors against both the Germans and the 'Nationalist' Poles.

In September 1939 there were some 3.5 million Jews in Poland. They were forced by the Germans to wear armbands marked with the Star of David, had much of their property confiscated and, in 1940–41, were herded together into ghettos. They were, too, made liable for compulsory labour. Initially, like the vast majority of Poles, the Jews tried to survive through a mixture of economic and cultural resistance and accommodation with the Germans. To survive they had to buy food on the black market. Within the ghettos the overwhelming majority of Jews came to the conclusion that the only practical policy was total submission to the Germans. To quote Stefan Korboński, in his book *The Jews and the Poles in World War II*, their 'watchword was: This is not our war, it's the war of the Poles against the Germans.'

There were, of course, exceptions to this attitude, especially amongst young Jews. In late 1940 the ZWZ appointed Major Alojzy-Dziura-Dziurski liaison officer with all Jewish military units. Under the camouflage of being a German inspector of epidemics, he was able to establish contact with the small Underground movements in the ghettos. In Warsaw he met Lieutenant Zych, the ghetto military leader, and advised him to build up a cadre squad, based on the twenty-one men he had so far recruited, as a future source of platoon leaders. In Częstochowa Ghetto, representatives of several Underground organizations met in August 1941, but a common plan for action did not emerge because the activists were arrested in April 1942. In Kraków, contrary to the other ghettos, the activists – a group of young Zionists and intellectuals – came to the conclusion that resistance was impossible within the ghetto, as the area was too small, and decided to shift resistance to the city itself and become 'urban guerrillas'. In December 1941 they set up a training camp in a farm outside the city.

In 1942 the ghettos began to be emptied when transports to the extermination camps of Auschwitz, Treblinka, Sobibor, Belzec and Chełmno were organized. The evacuation of Jews in the Warsaw Ghetto to Treblinka started on 22 July, and within two months 300,000 out of the total population of 400,000 had been moved. Rumours soon emerged about their destruction in the gas chambers, and it became belatedly very clear that accommodation with the Germans had failed. To avoid this fate, there were only two options for Jews in Poland or indeed elsewhere in occupied Europe: either to die fighting or to flee.

The Warsaw Ghetto Uprising, April–May 1943

As soon as the Germans temporarily discontinued the deportations on 13 September 1942, the 'Jewish Fighting Organization' (ZOB) in the Warsaw Ghetto decided to prepare for the next round-up. Unlike the

Campaign Chronicle

Polish Underground, the Jews could not look forward to eventual victory. Faced with overwhelming German might and the German extermination policy, all they could do was to kill as many Germans as possible and, in the end, in the words of Mordechai Anielewicz, leader of ZOB, 'die like homeless dogs'. ZOB had first to win round the various political factions within the ghetto to the idea of armed defiance by setting up the Jewish National Committee to act as a coordinating group, and to persuade them to join ZOB. Although the Socialist Bund and the Zionist Revisionist Movement refused to join the Committee, both groups accepted the need for armed struggle. ZOB then began to recruit, organize and arm its members. By April it managed to form twenty-two combat groups. The Zionist Revisionist Movement formed a separate military organization, the Jewish Military Union, which consisted of at least another ten groups. Altogether, these forces numbered a little over 1,000 combatants.

Training and arming them was a difficult task in the ghetto and both groups approached the AK and the GL for help. Initially, Rowecki was wary of too close a cooperation, as he suspected Communist influence within the ghetto and feared that Soviet agents would attempt to trigger a premature uprising in Warsaw itself. By December, however, Mordechai Anielewicz was able to reassure the AK that ZOB forces were under a tight rein, and its leaders visited a secret AK training school on Marszałkowska Street, where they were given training in arms and explosives and the manufacture of incendiary materials, mines and grenades. Through its contacts with the Polish Underground movements and the black market, ZOB managed to accumulate a modest cache of arms, which included at least one light machine gun and one sub-machine gun.

On 18 January 1943 the combat units were unexpectedly given a chance to practise what they had learnt when German forces re-entered the ghetto to resume deportations. The Germans speedily gained the upper hand, but after three days withdrew from the ghetto, presumably hoping to achieve their aims later in a more 'peaceful' manner. The AK, however, was so impressed by ZOB's resistance that it significantly increased the amount of weapons it supplied to the ghetto, although this was still a drop in the ocean. ZOB had absorbed some important lessons for the future. Zivia Lubetkin, its only female member, later observed:

We learned that it was most important to put the people into a kind of military barracks, to plan the uprising so that all the groups would be ready in their positions, and to make sure that each company commander, each area commander, and each fighter would know what to do, so we would not be surprised when the Germans renewed action.

[Krakówski, *The War of the Doomed*, p. 182]

This happened at 6 a.m. on 19 April, when some 2,000 SS troops, police, and a Ukrainian battalion, which had been trained at the special SS camp at Trawniki, accompanied by armoured vehicles, entered the ghetto along its two main streets, Zamenhof and Nalewki, in closely bunched columns, indicating that the German commander, Colonel von Sammern-Frankeneg, assumed that the ghetto forces would favour a frontal confrontation. In fact, quite contrary to these assumptions, the rebels opened fire from prepared positions. The column, marching along the Zamenhof, was ambushed and actually forced to retreat. It now dawned on von Sammern that he was faced with a carefully planned defence. He was replaced by SS Major-General Stroop, who rapidly re-organized the German forces and, after a six-hour battle, forced the insurgents to retreat from their prepared positions. That afternoon, over the roof of the head-quarters of the Jewish Military Union, two flags were raised: the Polish flag and the blue and white banner of the JMU, which is the flag of the present state of Zionist Israel. For four days these flags were seen from the surrounding Warsaw streets, the propaganda value of which was immense and made a deep impression on the Warsaw Poles.

On the second day, the focus of the fighting was in the central ghetto and, in what was known as the Brushmakers' Quarter, the area of the Toebbens and Schultz factories. The Germans again had only limited success. By the evening the rebels were still left in control of the Brush-makers' Quarter and most of the area around Toebbens' factories. Stroop broke off battle, fearing heavy losses in night fighting, and withdrew his troops while reinforcing the outer encirclement. It was on the third day that the turning point came. Stroop decided to burn the rebels out, first of all in the Brushmakers' Quarter and then systematically throughout the ghetto. By 22 April, the fourth day, almost the entire area of the central ghetto was a sea of flame. Zivia Lubetkin later commented, 'We had to fight not against the Germans, but against the fire'. Yet even so, the combat groups in the central ghetto managed to retreat through the Underground passages and tunnels and organize new defensive positions in buildings to the rear, which were not yet burnt down.

On the fifth day, Stroop once again changed his tactics and divided the ghetto into twenty-four sectors. His troops were ordered to comb through them, destroying the defence positions, seizing the people found in hiding, and blowing up any shelters that were discovered. Stroop was optimistic that these tactics would rapidly end the fighting, but on the sixth day fighting still raged for another twenty-four hours around the various defensive points in the ghetto. The following day, 25 April, Stroop called in the *Luftwaffe* to drop incendiary bombs and, in his own words, a 'sea of flames was seen over the ghetto'.

By the end of the first week, the Germans had managed to destroy the insurgents' positions within the ghetto. During the second and third weeks, battles were fought for the control of the bunkers, which methodically the Germans discovered and destroyed. On 8 May the Germans found the bunker where Anielewicz and about 100 members of the ZOB were sheltering. They used smoke candles to force them out, and shot the great majority, who were unable to escape. Mopping-up operations continued for at least another two weeks, and only a very small number of fighters were able to flee to the woods to join partisan groups outside Warsaw.

In this desperate and dramatic insurgency, both the AK and GL played, of necessity, a marginal role. For the AK, the crucial policy was to conserve energy and not let the insurgency spread to the 'Aryan' side of the ghetto before the time was ripe. By and large, the Jews understood this position. Nevertheless, limited amounts of arms were delivered. Some assistance was also given during the uprising. Captain Iwanski, for instance, brought into the ghetto (via a tunnel) arms, ammunition and food for the Jewish unit on Muranowski Square on 25 April. Three days later this same tunnel was used by some of the combat groups in an attempted escape organized by Iwanski, but most were gunned down outside the ghetto by German troops.

Resistance in the Other Ghettos
In Białystok Ghetto there was a short period of armed opposition when its liquidation began during the night of 15/16 August 1943. The Jewish Fighting Organization within Częstochowa Ghetto planned to establish partisan units, which would sabotage German efforts from outside the ghetto, but on 25 April it was taken by surprise by the speed of the German round-up and unable to put up an effective opposition. Elsewhere, in the smaller ghettos, any large-scale armed opposition was impractical and the only alternatives to the gas chambers for the Jews were either to escape into the forests to join the partisan units, or to hope that somebody would show mercy and grant them safe shelter.

The Polish Underground 1939–1947

Żegota and Polish Assistance to the Jews

Some Jews received help from 'Żegota', an organization operated under the patronage of the Polish Government-in-Exile by the Government Delegacy in Warsaw. Its purpose was to give Jews who had escaped from the ghettos – or indeed who had managed to survive outside them – forged documents and secure hiding places, which, of course, had to be paid for. The historian Jan Grabowski calculated that 'a paid Jew needed at least 2,000–3,000 *złotys* per month to pay for shelter and rent'.

Most of the Jews who survived were saved by Poles who had no link with Żegota. Usually they had to pay for forged documents to show that they were gentiles. To take one example: to obtain forged birth certificates in 1942, the father of Kitty Felix had to pay a priest with jewellery with which a dentist in the Lublin Ghetto had filled her back teeth. In the end, after Kitty and her mother had received the necessary papers, the priest came to the paradoxical conclusion that they would be safer if they were rounded up with a transport of Poles and sent to work in Germany. For a time this was successful, so Kitty was given an office job in an I.G. Farben factory but in the end she was betrayed by a spy and sent to Auschwitz.

The motives of at least some Poles hiding the Jews are a matter of controversy. One survivor, Mietek Pokorny, was convinced that

> the fate of the Jews who succeeded to escape to the Aryan quarter did not deserve to be envied [. . .] They found themselves amidst a hostile population in constant fear of extortions or being discovered [. . .] The Poles considered the Jews concealed by themselves as their legitimate slaves.
>
> [Mietek Pokorny (Parker), IWM, PP/MCR/378]

Of course, this is, to say the least, a sweeping generalization. There were numerous Poles who hid Jews for altruistic reasons and paid for this with their lives. As Jan Grabowski observed, 'Some helped because of greed, others because they had a heart of gold.'

Partisan Operations: the AK

The year 1943 was a turning point in the AK's development. In response to German efforts to create a colony in Zamość, the AK decided to form partisan units to defend the Polish population. Both the ZO (the Union for Revenge) and *Wachlarz* were absorbed into a new organization

ef Piłsudski (1867–1935).

zimiersz Sosnkowski (1885–1969).

Wadysław Sikorski (1881–1943).

Michał Tadeusz Karaszewicz-Tokarzewski
(1893–1964).

Stefan Starzyński (1893–1943?).

Witold Pilecki – veteran of Auschwitz and th Warsaw Uprising. Executed by the Soviet NKVD in 1948.

Henryk Dobrzański, alias 'Hubal' (1897–1940).

Franciszek Kleeberg (1888–1941).

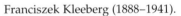

adeusz Bór-Komorowski (1895–1966).

Stanisław Kopanski (1895–1976).

Władysław Rackiewicz (1885–1947).

Stefan Rowecki, alias 'Grot' (1895–1944).

Jan Karski (1914–2000).

Colin Gubbins (1896–1976).

Hans Michael Frank (1900–1946).

Arthur Seyss-Inquart (1892–1946).

Erich Julius Eberhard von dem Bach
(1899–1972).

partisans.

Katyn massacre – exhumation of bodies 1943.

Two views of AK partisans.

Jewish partisan group active in the Nowogródek region.

Partisan Group 'Zbeda'.

'...delman' Partisans – Jewish fighters active in the Lublin region.

...arsaw Ghetto – civilians being marched off.

AK insurgents during the Warsaw Uprising.

Two views of AK insurgents during the Warsaw Uprising.

Two views of AK insurgents during Warsaw Uprising.

insurgents during the Warsaw Uprising.

AK child-fighters, Warsaw 1944.

AK nurse, Warsaw 1944.

rman troops deploy during
Warsaw Uprising.

Oskar Paul Dirlewanger
(1895–1945).

German Stuka bombs Warsaw's Old Town.

Warsaw in ruins after the uprising.

Campaign Chronicle

known as the Directorate of Diversion or *Kedyw*, which now took on the responsibility for setting up, training and controlling Home Army partisan units (*see page 100*). By June 1943 there were at least forty such units of 30–100 men in Poland. They were based primarily in the great forests around Lublin, Kielce and Sandomierz, and in the Tuchola Woods in Northern Poland, all of which gave them security and enabled them to set up training camps.

Major Alojzy Dziura-Dziurski's memoirs include an informative account on the formation and training of a *Kedyw* partisan group. In September 1943 he was given responsibility for training an elite group of men who would become future partisan commanders. The training camp was set up in the Przysieka Woods, some 50 miles north of Kraków. His group, which took the name of a legendary hussars captain, 'Skrzetulski', consisted of four units, each of twelve men led by an officer: the Assault, Liquidation, Reconnaissance and Support Units. There were also five sections: Command, Communication, Supply, Medical and Transport. This last section was the largest, as it consisted of sixteen horse-drawn wagons, which were specifically adapted to move along country lanes inaccessible to motor traffic. The group's arsenal consisted of 'one heavy machine gun, three light machine guns, twelve sub-machine guns, thirty-two pistols and sixteen shotguns for the wagon drivers'.

The High Command never forgot that the real aim of the AK was an uprising to seize control of Poland at the moment of German collapse. It was wary of attacks that would only attract German reprisals against the civilian population. Consequently it impressed on *Kedyw* leaders the need to launch an attack only after careful preparation, and in areas that were thinly populated, mountainous, thickly wooded or marshy. Above all, surprise was vital. As a 1942 AK training manual entitled, *Notes on Guerrilla War* stressed, where possible night attacks were the best option, but where this was not possible it was 'very desirable to make use of enemy uniforms'. On withdrawing, partisan leaders were advised that 'it is essential to cover up well all traces along the real routes of withdrawal and to make decoy traces on false routes'.

Given the AK's desire to protect the population from robbers and bandits, as well as from the German terror, the *Kedyw* pursued – in contrast to the GL and the Soviet-led guerrilla bands – a relatively cautious and, above all, targeted policy. Thus, in Janów County, specific instructions were issued by the local AK Command to the effect that 'during operations to capture weapons, carried out primarily against the German police, unconditionally disarm and do not kill'. An example of this policy being implemented can perhaps be seen in February 1943 when, in a village near Szczebrzeszyn, the director of forestry and a German forest inspector were (according to Dr Klukowski) stopped 'by some armed men', who took all their money, papers, and clothing, leaving them in their underwear. This policy was pushed to its logical extreme in 1943 by Major Dziura-Dziurski, who was determined to remove from his district three German execution units (*Einsatzkommandos*), probably amounting to some 3,000 men. He came to the conclusion that he should first attempt diplomacy and actually sent a letter to the *Kreishauptmann* (district head) demanding their withdrawal, 'otherwise no German would be safe', as the Polish partisans would mobilize and fight them. The Germans did in fact withdraw, but Dziura-Dziurski was fiercely criticized by his commanding officer, Inspector Bolko, and even by the Government-in-Exile for negotiating with them. In the Lublin area, *Kedyw* units were faced with defending the population from a two- or even three-pronged attack: first of all, around Zamość, there was the forceful deportation of Poles to make way for German settlers; then there were the repeated bandit thefts, as well as escalating raids by the partisan groups composed of Polish Communists, fugitive Jews and Soviet partisans (often under the leadership of an NKVD officer).

Throughout 1943 the Germans persisted with their resettlement policy. Klukowski's diary for this year contains constant references to the forced evacuation of the villages. He observed on 17 May Germans moving into the villages of Wieloncza and Zawada and noted that 'everywhere you can see young German boys in *Hitlerjugend* [Hitler Youth] uniforms'. The name of his own home town of Szczebrzeszyn was renamed *Hauptdorf* [main village] Szcz and was the administrative centre of thirty-one villages and colonies, of which thirteen were now German. Yet, as fast as the Germans colonized, the partisans attacked the settlements, stole the livestock and, in some cases, burnt whole villages down.

The *Kedyw* were most active in Eastern Poland and in the Ukraine–Polish borderlands. Information received in London in March 1944 gave a detailed list of recent actions, which included attacks on German out-posts, police stations, the taking of Rudomino, near Wilno (where the garrison actually surrendered), and the derailing of the Lublin–Stuttgart train with the loss of about 200 soldiers. Yet, to put this into perspective, between February and July 1944, NKVD commandos and Soviet partisan units were responsible for more damage than all the Polish Underground groups combined since October 1939.

Campaign Chronicle

Until the early summer of 1944, sabotage of the German lines of communication still remained the most effective weapon the AK could deploy. To counter Communist accusations that the AK was sitting on its hands, the Polish Ambassador to the USSR, Tadeusz Romer, during a lengthy discussion with Stalin lasting from 10.25 p.m. to 1.40 a.m. on 26/27 February 1943, proposed a plan drawn up by the Home Army and approved by Sikorski for 'a simultaneous disruption for at least a few days of all railway lines accessible to us and leading from Germany to the Eastern front'. This covered some 85 per cent of the railway lines supplying the front. Stalin, now in a strong position after Stalingrad, had no need for Polish assistance and advised against its execution, for the time being, anyway, on the patently insincere grounds that it would cause heavy Polish losses.

Operation *Tempest*

By the autumn of 1943 it was becoming obvious that it would be the Russians who would liberate Poland. How should the AK plan for this increasingly likely contingency? On 27 October the Government-in-Exile issued two sets of instructions to General Bór:

   I. If by any chance Soviet–Polish diplomatic relations were restored, then the Poles would carry out 'intensified sabotage-diversion operations' (given the name of 'Operation *Burza*' or 'Tempest') behind the German front in collaboration and liaison with the Red Army.

  II. However, 'Should diplomatic relations remain severed', the Home Army was still to carry out the *Burza* Plan but 'with the one difference that the administrative authorities and the armed forces should remain underground and await further decisions from the Polish Government'.

[Bór-Komorowski, pp. 175–6]

Bór rapidly pointed out that the second alternative was hardly practical. How could his troops 'emerge for battle with the retreating Germans and then crawl back into hiding'? Unilaterally, he amended his instructions with the approval of the Government Delegate in Poland and ordered his local commanders, in the event of a Soviet invasion, to reveal themselves and cooperate with the Red Army against the Germans, but to make clear that they were representing the Polish Government and that the AK was a component part of the Polish Army, which owed its loyalty to the commander-in-chief in London. It was not until February 1944 that this was confirmed by the London Government.

At the end of November 1943, Bór issued the order for Operation *Tempest*. In essence, it envisaged extensive sabotage of rail and road communications and large-scale guerrilla operations at the rear of the retreating Germans. Starting in the east, in January 1944, this rippled across Eastern Poland, coming to a bloody climax in Warsaw in August. Politically, the Poles also hoped that these actions would impress the USSR and give Poland sufficient military stature to gain a place at the negotiating table when the time came at the end of the war to consider the future of Poland.

Supplying the AK from Italy

Implementing *Tempest*, however, would require supplies and money. The Poles received equipment from three sources: secret arms dumps made in 1939, weapons and material flown in from Britain, and weapons and munitions either seized or paid for illicitly from German soldiers, of which the last source was by far the most productive. In March 1944, the Poles pushed hard to be allowed to search for captured German material in dumps in Italy but ran into red tape, as no ruling had yet been made on that point.

Although the British Chiefs of Staff pursued a policy of considerable parsimony towards Poland as far as supplies went, the real problem was still lack of planes to fly missions to Poland, and even when on moon nights such flights were possible, interruptions due to bad weather and enemy action were frequent. An added hazard, so SOE was warned by the VI Bureau in February 1943, was that even if the flights reached the correct dropping points, agents who had just been parachuted in 'must be prepared on landing to fight with the reception committee against groups of Soviet saboteurs, who are constantly trying to raid their secret stores of materials'.

In September 1943, when flying operations to Poland again began, the northern route had become extremely hazardous, as planes had to traverse the German night fighter and AA belt stretching from the north of Denmark to Central Germany. Out of a total of twenty-two planes sent to Poland in September, six were shot down. In October, on the first day of the moon period, an attempt was made to vary the route and, at the request of the Poles, to increase the number of flights. The Poles optimistically organized sixty reception committees composed of 2,000 men, but all except six of these were out of range. It was consequently decided to switch the flights to Poland to fly first of all to North Africa and then to Brindisi in Southern Italy. By the beginning of January 1944, 1586 Polish Flight was established in Brindisi. Together with 138 Squadron RAF, it formed 334 Wing.

Operationally, the new venture was not initially a success. In the first three months of 1944 weather conditions only allowed three nights on which operations could proceed. As an SOE memorandum pointed out, this pitiful scale of support barely enabled the Poles 'to maintain the activity of the Secret Army at its present level, which may be described as continual but sporadic sabotage and isolated guerrilla activity mainly for counter-reprisals'. However, in April and May 1944, any doubts about the feasibility of this decision were dispelled when better weather enabled the dropping of 104 'operators' and 17½ tons of stores, which was more than twice the weight sent over in the previous three years.

The Wildhorn *Operations*

The RAF's 334 Wing was also able to organize three pick-up operations on 15 April, 29 May and 25 July 1944, code-named 'Wildhorn I, II and III'. They were hazardous in the extreme, as they involved flying an unarmed Dakota hundreds of miles from the Brindisi base in Italy to land on a strip prepared by the AK. The first operation was lucky to succeed, as the airstrip was too short. The plane also landed in the middle of a German counter-insurgency operation: the AK lost forty men defending the strip but the plane was able to get away safely with five passengers, one of whom was General Tatar, alias 'Tabor', who was to take over the post of deputy chief of the Polish General Staff in London. For Wildhorn II an airstrip at the site known as 'Motyl' or 'Butterfly', just north of Tarnów, was chosen. The operation was a success, although Retinger, who had been parachuted into Poland in April 1944, failed to turn up. He did manage to reach 'Motyl' for Wildhorn III, which was a cliff-hanger, as the plane with its invaluable load of V-2 parts was only able to take off after the third attempt (*see pages 105–6*).

The Polish Underground 1939–1947

To illustrate this point, between 1941 and 1943 only 13,735 lbs of explosive were dropped, while in April 1944 alone 17,470 lbs were dropped and in May, 13,420. For the first time a limited number of light machine guns, sten guns and anti-tank rockets (PIAT) were also dropped. This was certainly a welcome addition to the AK's stores of weapons and explosives, even though it was, of course, still not nearly enough.

Operations *Jula* and *Ewa*, April 1944

Once the Red Army crossed the pre-1939 Polish frontiers in January 1944 (*see page 125*), the AK had to counter constant efforts by Soviet propaganda to minimize its contribution to the liberation of Eastern Poland. Consequently, in order to refute this propaganda and show that the AK Command still controlled the Resistance as a whole in Poland, General Sosnkowski informed Bór that the military situation on the south-east front made it 'advisable', in what was called Operation *Jula*, to cut German rail communications on the lines running east–west from Kraków through Przemyśl, from Bielsko to Lwów, and also the line from Łódź to Lwów. About 28 March the plan was signalled to London with permission requested to implement it. This arrived on 2/3 April and the action was carried out between 6 and 9 April. The operation was a classic of its kind: at the cost of just three wounded:

> A span of 150 feet of the railway bridge over the Wisłoka on the Przeworsk–Rozwadów was blown up, which stopped traffic for forty-eight hours.
>
> Explosives were detonated under a passing munitions train at Rogoźno and rescue transports were delayed by automatic mines. The traffic was only resumed on the line after thirty-four hours.
>
> Another munitions train was blown up on the Jasło–Sanok line near Nowosielce, which resulted in thirty-three hours' stoppage.
>
> [Bór-Komorowski, p. 190]

Jula was a relatively minor operation, but in preparation for *Overlord* – the invasion of Normandy – the Home Army was ordered to prepare 'Operation *Ewa*', aimed at cutting off simultaneously all main lines running east–west from the Kraków area to Lwów, as well as the lines running north-west to south-east from Łódź, and Warsaw to Lwów. Sosnkowski also ordered the AK to prepare plans for interrupting communications around Warsaw, Silesia, Pomerania, and on the Białystok junctions. These plans were never executed because they depended for their effectiveness on close coordination with a Russian attack in south-east Poland. Both *Jula* and *Ewa*, as the SOE recognized, were 'primarily political rather than military operations', as they were arranged to impress the Russians. By the time Allied troops landed in Normandy on 6 June, the Underground's role in disrupting German communications and troop movements in Poland was rapidly becoming less important in light of the Red Army advance towards the Bug.

Partisan Operations: GL/AL and the 'Forest People'

The People's Guard (GL) was a latecomer to the Resistance. Up to June 1941 all pro-Soviet groups in Poland had supported the Nazi-Soviet Pact, and therefore played no role in the Resistance. The GL was created in January 1942 by the Polish Workers' Party (PPR) and therefore came on the scene only after the structure of the ZWZ/AK was in place and the Underground State constructed. The AK had created an extensive network of Underground units that it was able to train in preparation for the national uprising, and it had its own supplies of ammunition. It was also determined to enrol all the disparate Underground units under its own banner. The GL, on the other hand, lacked weapons, numbers and training. It initially tried to recruit disaffected members from the AK, BCh, and even the Nationalists, but with very little success. Its natural allies were fugitive Soviet POWs and Jews who had fled to the forests to escape the Holocaust. By December 1942 it had managed to create an organization that divided Poland into seven administrative areas based on Warsaw, Lublin, Radom-Kielce, Kraków, Łódź, Silesia and Lwów; but early in 1944 its command structures were seriously weakened when the *Gestapo* arrested many of its activists. In January 1944, in an attempt to unify left-wing and progressive forces, the Armia Ludowa (AL) was formed, which the members of the GL joined.

SOE sources in London in February 1943 put the number of Communist partisans at about 10,000 in Eastern Poland, but approximately 5,000 of these were Soviet POWS or deserters. The PPR – the members of which, at least nominally, belonged to the GL – hoped to attract support for the GL by pursuing (in apparent contrast to the AK) an active policy of resistance. For instance, on 1 July 1942 an article published in the PPR paper *Trybuna Wolnosci* thundered that the war could not be won 'by patience alone'. In October 1942 a bomb was lobbed into one of the

The Polish Underground 1939–1947

German coffee houses in Warsaw, which caused a number of casualties and made considerable impact on Polish public opinion. The PPR, however, put most of its energies into setting up partisan bands in Eastern Poland. Until the Soviet commandos arrived in force in early 1944, the GL/AL's guerrilla and sabotage attempts were often distinctly amateur and merely resulted in the Nazis wreaking fearful revenge on the countryside. GL/AL partisan groups continued to live off the land, which necessitated seizing food by force from a largely unsympathetic peasantry already burdened by massive German demands. Refusals were often rewarded by arson and murder. On this bandwagon climbed an insalubrious assortment of crooks and bandits, who often posed as members of one Underground group or other. Frequently, the villagers took to the woods to escape the almost nightly attacks.

The GL/AL also conducted a vicious class war to rid Poland of elements hostile to Communism. They targeted prominent members of the AK and local landowners. Some ten years later, in 1954, a former senior GL/AL officer in Janów openly admitted that

> I was in an organization that was to fight against the Germans, but instead we were murdering Poles and Jews. We were told that the struggle against the reactionaries and the NSZ was more important than the struggle against the Germans.
>
> [M.J. Chodakiewicz, p. 197]

This policy was reinforced by Soviet partisans operating within Polish territory and the Central Bureau of Polish Communists in the USSR, which remained suspicious of the political 'reliability' of the PPR. In the summer of 1943 the Bureau requested Stalin to send units of party activists into Poland, who had received their political training in the USSR. In August 1943 one of the first of these bands was commanded by Leon Kasman. When it entered the Lublin district, it was challenged by the local GL commander, Milolaj Demko, alias 'Mieczysław Moczar', to subordinate itself to his own group but refused outright. It also refused to acknowledge the authority of the head of the PPR.

The Soviet partisan bands, in cooperation with the GL/AL, were determined to take over the control of Polish Volhynia in the winter of 1943/44. Reports coming to London painted an alarming picture. In February 1944, for instance, the Government-in-Exile was informed how, near Łuków, a detachment of the People's Guard, under the command of a Soviet Sergeant named Fiodow [was] attempting to take over the control of the district and to liquidate the Secret [Home] Army. The commander of a unit of the Secret Army, 'Mir', was summoned by the partisans to attend a meeting under threat of death.

[NA, HS4/138]

The same report also contained information that, on 20 December 1943, three officers (including 'Bomba', the commander, and ten other men of his AK unit) were invited to a Soviet partisan headquarters in Bronisławka and told bluntly that they, too, were to disband and leave the district. They were not shot on the spot, 'owing to the preparedness of this unit'. However, 'Bomba' was again summoned to the headquarters of General Schytov and this time killed. A few weeks later, on 8 January, the Commander of the Home Army in the region of Przebraże, together with a Doctor Pieta and one orderly, was invited to the Soviet camp to discuss cooperation. A week later, an AK patrol found all three dead with bullet holes in the back of their necks. The most chilling evidence of Soviet intentions was found by the AK in 'Copy No. 7' of a secret order issued by the Commissar of the 'Stalin Brigade', in the possession of the political commissar of the Chapaev Soviet Partisan Unit. This was an operational order dated 30 November 1943, informing the unit that 'all Polish Legionary partisans' in their area were to be seized and sent to an internment camp. Those who resisted were to be shot on the spot.

Although the Russians did not completely trust the GL/AL, it was a pawn in their hands. For instance, in the autumn of 1943 the district leader of the People's Army sent a number of Jewish partisans to the town halls of Lubartów and several other towns to seize all the records of the inhabitants, as the Germans were planning a fresh conscription drive for labour in the Reich. They were to set fire to the offices so that it would look as if the books had been burnt. The operation succeeded but, as one of the Jewish partisans, Ephraim Blaichmann, realized later, the 'ultimate goal was to send the books to the Soviet side to help them, after the liberation of Poland, to uncover Polish collaborators'.

The anarchy in the great forest regions of Eastern Poland was one of General Bór's greatest problems. It threatened both the effective execution of diversionary activity and the organization of larger operations when the time was ripe. By the autumn of 1943, as Ralph Smorczewski later remembered, 'the scale, variety and number of raids was becoming frightening and unbearable'. His father's estate was protected by the Germans billeted in his house (*see page 80*), but his neighbours were attacked four times by the same bandit gang and threatened initially with being soaked in petrol and set on fire. Each time the group left with a pig and a considerable sum of money. This was one of the milder incidents. In the Miechów area, north of Kraków, for instance, a Communist partisan group led by one 'August II' made a habit of raping all aristocratic women when it raided the manor houses. It also robbed and then clubbed to death a well-known local miller. With incidents like this occurring so frequently, it was no surprise that Dr Klukowski chronicled on 3 October 1943 that 'Every day what we see around us are assaults, robberies and killing'. In attempt to control the situation, Bór issued, on 15 September 1943, an order for area AK commanders to intervene with force, when necessary, against 'these plunderers or revolutionary robbers'. The problem was that it was not always easy to distinguish between the various bands because, as Smorczewski later explained, 'members of one band intermingled with the members of another, which ever seemed more profitable, so even the true patriotic units had shady elements amongst them'.

Even before this order, the AK had begun to harass the GL, Jewish and Russian partisan groups. As early as June 1943, Moczar, the GL partisan commander in the Lublin area, wrote: 'our units are now forced to fight on two fronts. The Underground [AK] leadership is organizing units whose role it is to wipe out "the Communist gangs, prisoners of war and Jews".' While Bór's order did give some legitimacy to the shooting of GL/AL, Jewish and Soviet partisans by AK personnel, much of the violence was carried out by NSZ groups. In August 1943, it seems likely that an NSZ group hacked a GL unit to death with axes in the district of Janowiec near Lublin, and a month later, according to Frank Blaichmann's memoirs, another band slaughtered twenty-six Jewish partisans in the Borowa Forest. This inevitably provoked retaliation and a spiralling of violence and tit-for-tat assassinations. One Jewish group, under Shmuel Jegier, which operated under the auspices of the GL/AL, executed with the latter's agreement Poles who were guilty of the murder of Jews. At times the AK tolerated this policy. Blaichmann recounts one case where, after his group burnt down a farm in retaliation for its owner's betrayal of Jews to the *Gestapo*, its leaders were called to a conference of the Home Army and the Peasant Battalions. The Jews took members of the GL/AL to act as witnesses to the proceedings. After Blaichmann had explained what had happened, the AK accepted the situation.

Campaign Chronicle

In Janów County, as Mark Chodakiewicz has shown, the AK 'oscillated between populist leniency and Nationalist ruthlessness'. In March 1944 the local leadership ordered the liquidation of eleven people: 'members of the PPR and [. . .] of a robber band, whose activities have threatened Polish conspiratorial life and have terrorized society'. In the Miechów region 'Kmita' (Major Dziura-Dziurski) was initially prevented ('for political reasons') by his superiors from liquidating the leaders of the Communist Partisan Group 'August II', although, in the end, he disobeyed orders 'irrespective of political consequences'. Even so, he had considerable respect for the local secretary of the PPR 'as a true Polish patriot'. Arguably, relations between the GL/AL and the AK can at best be described as 'armed neutrality', even though at times there is some evidence of cooperation in face of German aggression.

The Red Army Enters Polish Territory

In January 1944 the Red Army resumed its great winter offensive. One thrust was made from Leningrad towards Latvia, while a more rapid advance was made in the south across the Byelorussian–Ukrainian frontier. During the night of 3/4 January, Soviet units crossed the pre-war frontier into Volhynia and by 14 January had reached the eastern edge of the Pripet Marshes. In the eastern territories beyond the Curzon Line – which were to be incorporated into the USSR – Stalin was determined, where possible, to 'ethnically cleanse' the Poles from the area. Initially, in the first seven months of 1944, military progress inevitably dictated the shape and pace of this policy. In the area north of the Pripet Marshes, particularly in Nowogródek and Wilno districts (behind the German lines until July), Soviet partisans continued their policy of exterminating the AK. In Volhynia, Polesia and south-eastern Poland, which the Red Army began to occupy in January, different methods were used. Initially, until April, there was some military cooperation with the AK. However, once the Germans were defeated, the Russians began to move the Polish population westwards by forcefully enrolling AK and AL partisans into General Berling's army, which had been formed in Russia. This, according to information which reached London in May, was accompanied by compulsory recruitment of everyone fit for work, to man the supply brigades that accompanied the Red Army units westwards. 'The remaining population – children, the old and physically unfit' were 'being evacuated to the east on the same principle as in 1939–41'.

Berling's Army

Despite the departure to Poland of some 100,000 Poles from Russia with General Anders in 1942 (*see page 61*), there still remained hundreds of thousands of men in the USSR who could be formed into a new Polish army. By July 1943 a division was already in existence of some 14,380 men, and a month later it was expanded into a corps under General Berling. This force was given its first experience of battle at Lenino where, due to its inexperience, it suffered heavy casualties. It was then withdrawn to the Smolensk area to recuperate and complete its combat training. It was not until April that it was attached to General Rokossovsky's First Byelorussian Front. The significance of Berling's army was, of course, political not military: its entry into Poland in the baggage train of the Red Army was designed to create a force that could crush opposition to the creation of a Communist Poland.

The Political Failure of Operation *Tempest*, January–July 1944

Preparations for Operation *Tempest* started at the end of 1943, when all the soldiers of the AK in the eastern provinces were mobilized. Arms, ammunition, uniform and hospital equipment were gradually smuggled into the forests. The regiments, battalions and even divisions were given pre-war names and numbers. By the end of December, the AK's partisan groups in the east had grown into a substantial and formidable force.

The first contact made between the AK and Soviet troops was in Volhynia. In February, the local AK commander contacted the commander of a Soviet cavalry division near Luck, and they agreed that the officers commanding the Polish partisan detachments should disclose their identity to the Soviet forces in Ostróg, Równe, Przebraże, and several other areas. The Soviet commander readily conceded that he had been helped everywhere by the Polish Underground Army. On one occasion, Soviet troops were helped by AK units 'to find their bearings across the River Ikwa'. According to information that reached London, Polish partisan units known as the '44/63 Infantry Regiment' fought an engagement on 13 February with a 'mixed German–Ukrainian force' between the villages of Lubniki and Krczumek [*sic*] north of Włodzimierz Wołyński, which resulted in the withdrawal of the enemy, who suffered about twelve casualties. A Soviet partisan band offered assistance but this was declined on the grounds that the Polish commander thought he had the situation well in hand. The Bolsheviks apparently expressed their admiration for 'the fighting qualities of the Polish units'. Over a week later, near Włodzimierz Wołyński, a Polish unit fought a successful battle with an enemy 'mopping-up' formation, 'composed of a German battalion, several hundred Ukrainians and a regiment of Hungarians'. Once the Hungarians recognized who their opponents were they withdrew from the fighting. On 20 March AK units captured the town of Turzysk and took part in the battle for Kowel.

On 26 March the commander of the AK partisan units, which had now become the 27th Infantry Division, Lieutenant Colonel Kiwerski (alias 'Oliwa'), held a conference with General Stergerev, the GOC of the Soviet Army in the Kosel sector. Stergerev was given permission by his high command to cooperate with the AK under the following conditions:

Complete tactical subordination to the Soviet command.

The partisan forces were to become a regular army division and be given all the necessary equipment.

No partisan groups were to remain behind the Soviet lines.

The Russians recognized that this force 'was a Polish division taking orders from Warsaw and London'.

[NA, HS4/138]

Bór immediately radioed back his agreement in principle, but insisted on having the right to appoint senior officers from the rank of battalion commander upwards. Finally, Kiwerski was told:

In giving your answer to the Soviet command, you are to explain that your group is the first one which they have so far encountered within the territory of the Republic, and [as] their advance into Poland becomes deeper [...] they will encounter further Polish fighting units [...] similarly [...] part of the Underground Army. Looked at in this perspective, it is necessary that a basic settlement be arrived at between the Soviet Government and the Polish Government in London, which will make possible the harmonious prosecution of the war against Germany in Polish territory by the Soviet Union and Poland.

[NA, HS4/138]

The Polish Underground 1939–1947

If ever there was a Polish–Russian honeymoon this appeared to be it. The spirits of all those who hoped for cooperation between the Russian Army and the AK were raised. Mikołajczk and the British Foreign Office were particularly delighted, while a German report to the Governor of Lublin District commented with alarm on 20 April that 'news of cooperation of the AK with the Red Army spreads ever further'. However, it soon became clear that the Red Army front-line units were ready to cooperate with the AK on their own terms only in the execution of specific tasks. They had no compunction in deserting the Poles if the tide of battle turned against them. For example, Kiwerski's forces were cooperating with a Soviet cavalry division north-west of Włodzymierz when they were confronted on 9 April with a strong German counter-attack by the 'Viking' 5th SS Panzer Division and a German mountain brigade. The Poles and one Soviet cavalry regiment were left in the lurch by the main Russian force, which rapidly withdrew, and were encircled on the River Turia. After five days' fighting the units managed to break through the German lines and find temporary shelter in the forests near Szack, which lay between the German and Soviet front lines. From there, one column moved westwards to the Lublin area, while the other retreated to the Pripet Marshes.

Once the NKVD moved in, all cooperation ceased. Banaczyk, the Minister of the Interior of the Government-in-Exile, informed British officials on 7 April that Russian officers had already warned their AK counterparts that 'the NKVD would come later and they could not vouch for what they would do'. It did indeed turn up! In Volhynia it was headed by Polish Communist, political commissar and writer, 'a certain Mr Putrament', who at once issued orders that the Polish units should be disbanded and incorporated into either the Red Army or Berling's troops, and that those who resisted would be shot. Remnants of the 27th Infantry Division, sheltering in the Pripet Marshes, were disarmed by the Soviets and transferred to Kiev, while the officers disappeared into the depths of Russia.

This became the familiar pattern throughout the summer during the Soviet advance. On the Wilno front there was also initial cooperation between the AK and the Soviets. Bór informed London that 'on the night 7/8 July strong forces of the Underground Army (about one division) cooperating with the Soviet Army carried out an attack single-handedly against Wilno'. A week later 'a large proportion of the Wilno units, numbering three battalions and a platoon of artillery, cooperated with a Soviet division on the River Wilja, 30 miles north-west of Wilno'.

However, after the city's fall on 13 July, the AK Area Commander Colonel Krzyżanowski (or 'Wilk') feared that the Russians would liquidate the Underground Army units as soon as they had overcome difficulties 'connected with the exceptionally speedy advance'. A week later, he talked of 'increasing tension in Polish–Soviet relations' and asked for an international commission, or at least some British and American liaison officers, to be dropped by plane. On 17 July, together with his staff of thirty officers, he was asked to attend a conference with General Cherniakovsky, commander of the Third Byelorussian Front. None returned: they, too, were arrested and taken to the USSR.

A similar pattern occurred in Eastern Poland, where some 3,000 AK troops of the 5th Infantry Division played a crucial role in the capture of Lwów between 23 and 27 July. When the city fell, Marshal Koniev thanked the Poles for their 'brotherly cooperation', yet this did not stop the AK troops being forcibly disbanded and made to join either Berling's troops or the Red Army. The AK officers, despite their apparent willingness to join the former, were arrested and deported to the USSR, whence they never returned.

The SOE Intervenes, May 1944

The Polish Government-in-Exile, as it no longer had diplomatic relations with Moscow, looked to Britain to influence Stalin in an attempt to create a working relationship between the AK and the Red Army. As all its diplomatic initiatives urging military cooperation had failed, the Foreign Office turned to the SOE for help. To impress the Russians with the AK's military potential, the SOE lost no opportunity to supply the British Military Mission in Moscow with lists of the AK's achievements, ranging from sabotage to assassination and guerrilla activities. Sadly that failed to impress the Russians, as any Polish assistance in the overall military context of the Eastern front only was marginal, and Stalin had no interest in strengthening a force that was a rival to Berling's army. Similarly, SOE's suggestions of dispatching either a joint British–Polish VI Bureau mission or a purely SOE mission to Moscow, or, alternatively, of inviting a special Russian military mission to London, to coordinate joint Polish–Russian action also failed. The SOE's liaison mission in Moscow (SAM) made little progress in achieving any agreement or cooperation with the NKVD. On 17 May one of the mission's members dined with an NKVD official, who was code-named 'Greyman'. He broached the question of possible AK–Soviet cooperation with 'Greyman', but achieved nothing. He informed the SOE:

During friendly wrangle he [Greyman] made charge that SOE were not giving NKVD benefit of their Intelligence drawn from [the Polish] Secret Army concerning German dispositions etc. I challenged this and reminded him of our many offers [...] I suggested we should take a practical test, e.g. Take Red Army Corps or possible Divisional Front [in Eastern Poland]. Plan operation embracing [...] Operations would be planned by corps or division commanders. He would inform NKVD of his requirements and that SOE as intermediary would pass on instructions to Poles ...

[NA, HS4/138]

Apparently, 'Greyman' showed great interest but refused to start any planning without his superior, 'O's authority'. This authority was never to be granted!

Resistance Behind German Lines in the General Government, January–July 1944

As the Red Army tightened its grip on south-eastern Poland, AK and NSZ units had little option but to accept enrolment in Berling's forces or cross the Bug and vanish into the dense forests, which were ideal partisan country. Remnants of one Polish AK partisan division managed to cross the Bug on 9 June, where it formed the nucleus of one of the largest AK groups in the Parczew Forests. Two days later, according to German reports, an SS unit surprised an AK group of about thirty men crossing the Bug and shot an officer, whose diary revealed that it was one unit 'out of a Polish band consisting of several other sections', which were all attempting to move westwards over the river into the General Government. The diary contained notes about their plans, the direction they were taking, and contacts with other groups.

In the forests around Lublin and Zamość, in expectation of the Russian advance, the AK, the NSZ, BCh and the AL were already mobilizing their forces. German officials reported on 22 April that, in Puławy county, the AK's National Security Corps (PKB), which was trained to become the nucleus of a future police force, already had units in every commune (*Gemeinde*). In some villages it had already started to conscript young men. The ever-observant Klukowski noted in his diary in mid-April that 'our troops in the forest are on full alert. Training is in full swing; military

Campaign Chronicle

exercises, including shooting practice, are taking place'. The Germans consoled themselves that no general mobilization order had been issued, and 'that individual partisan bands were deciding to mobilize in order to recruit as many members for their own groups as possible'. Yet the AK was certainly preparing for the departure of the Germans and conducting large-scale manoeuvres. In July, the whole of the northern part of Chełm County was taken over by the Underground. The Germans again reported that 'all the roads were watched over by sentries and that peasants, who wished to go to the market at Włodawa, had to have passes issued by the local area AK commander'.

Increasingly, the emphasis throughout Poland was being shifted from underground work to guerrilla activity. At 'Reception Point' or 'Bastion' 319, in south-east Poland, Lieutenant Colonel Jaźwiźski (Commander of the Polish element at Brindisi) estimated in May that there was a force of some 10,000 men who were no longer living under conspiratorial conditions but functioning as 'an open guerrilla force'. In what Colonel Threlfall called 'a notable departure in our work to KENSAL [Poland] they were sent [...] some battledresses and boots'. On 19 May, five out of fourteen planes flying supplies to the AK from Italy headed for Bastion 319.

Neither was the AL idle. On 13 April the Germans reported that 'a number of officials from Warsaw had arrived in Lublin to recruit 'the young people of Lublin' for street fighting. Their training would begin after Easter in preparation for the arrival of the Red Army. With Operation *Bagration*, which aimed to clear the Germans out of Eastern Poland and Byelorussia, about to be unleashed on 22 June, the Russians showed great interest in the guerrilla groups between the Bug and Vistula. There was a big increase in parachute drops. Over 363 paratroopers were dropped by Soviet planes, amongst whom were the Communist Polish partisan leader Colonel Moshe Satanowski and the Russian General Baranowski. The PPR received orders from Warsaw to cooperate closely with the Russians, and in many areas (*Kreis* Radyn, for example) to recruit the various scattered Jewish bands, although there were cases of the anti-Semitism of individual AL commanders nullifying this order. In the Białobrzegi area one Russian-sponsored partisan group, led by a certain 'Serafin', numbered four units each of 120 men. According to German reports this group actually managed to shoot down a German plane. Two of the crew who parachuted out were then immediately put on a Russian plane and flown to Moscow.

The Polish Underground 1939–1947

At a meeting of the senior German officials of Lublin province on 8 July, SS *Oberstleutnant* Reindorf painted a bleak picture from the German point of view:

In August 1942 no partisan band contained more than 100 men; in March 1944 212 groups were observed, whose strength varied from 100 to 3,000. Our motorization has been completely overtaken: the bandits are quicker, more skilful, much better armed and, anyway, through an intimate knowledge of the area, always enjoy the advantage. In addition to this they have the full backing of the local population. It has been shown that a band has been able to cover a distance of 90 km in one day. For us such distances are impossible, our horses could not survive it.

[IWM, AL2583/1 (translated by the author)]

Why then, given that conditions were so favourable, was there no mass uprising in the Lublin area? The main reason lay in the bitter divisions between the AK, the NSZ and the AL: 'Only because of this are we still "masters of the situation",' stressed *SS-Gruppenführer und General-leutnant der Polizei* Jakob Sporrenberg. These divisions at times escalated into open fighting. At Grabówka on 2 July 1944 the Germans reported a bitter and bloody fight between an AL group under 'Cien' and a 'Nationalist' group under 'Chrestny'. Another clash between a 'Bolshevik band' about 500 strong, which was armed with machine guns and anti-tank rockets, and a 'Nationalist' group took place near Batorz. A few days later an AK band under one Jan Ociec actually managed to shoot Cien and some thirty supporters, losing sixteen men in the process. Many AK bands were penetrated by Communists. The Germans found, for example, that when they captured an AK unit near Sokół, not only did 'a long-sought-for terrorist' fall into their hands but also a PPR spy.

Such divisions enabled the Germans to launch in June two major counter-insurgency operations, *Sturmwind* 1 and 2, in the Biłgoraj Forest area, which was strategically important as it was traversed by two major railway lines. The Germans were able to assemble about 25,000 men composed of the best part of three *Wehrmacht* divisions, a Karpaty Kalmuc cavalry regiment, several police units and a bomber squadron. Their object was to encircle and eliminate the partisan bands, which amounted to some 5,000 combatants, in the forests of Lipsk and Janów. About 3,000 of these were enrolled in Soviet units, 560 in AL units (including at least 100 Jewish partisans), 570 in the AK and some 700 in the Peasant Battalions (BCh). *Sturmwind* 1 failed, as the great majority of the partisans were successfully able to break out of the German encirclement and escape to the Solska Forest.

Sturmwind 2 was more successful. The partisans were again encircled, this time in the Solska Forest. The Soviet and AL units cooperated closely under the command of the Soviet Jewish commander, Nikolai Prokopiuk, but the AK and the Peasant Battalions fought independently, although in the end, after severe losses, they did accept Prokopiuk's command. By 26 June several bands had been completely wiped out and the survivors, which the Germans assessed at 2,000–3,000, had little option but to flee. In one of the last surveys of the Lublin region on 15 July (before retreating westwards), the Germans, on the basis of information from prisoners, calculated that the following partisan bands (which predominantly belonged to the AL) had been encircled in the Solska forests:

The 'Rys' AL partisan group, which panicked but nevertheless managed to break through the encirclement in groups of three or four men.

A unit of the Peasant Battalions numbering about 500 men, the majority of whom were killed.

The 'Warsaw Brigade' of the PPR, which 'consisted of Poles, Jews and students', who had come by lorry from Warsaw, also suffered very severely.

The AL group 'Wanda Wasilewska', composed of 200 men from Lublin and Krasnik, was shattered, and from 21 June onwards had ceased all radio contacts.

The 'Henryk Dąbrowski' [unit] numbering about 300 Russians, Jews and a few Poles from the Puławy region.

The Kort unit, consisting mainly of 300 Russians.

[IWM, AL/2583/1 (translated by the author)]

The Red Army Crosses the Bug

On 20 July Soviet units crossed the River Bug, which the Russians officially recognized as the border between the USSR and 'ethnographic Poland'. A day later the Polish Committee of National Liberation (PKWN) was formed in Moscow. On 26 and 27 July its leaders signed two key agreements with the Soviet leadership. The first accepted the Curzon Line as Poland's new eastern frontier, while the second gave the Soviet military authorities virtually complete power during the duration of military hostilities over Polish territory 'liberated' by the Red Army. It agreed on the conscription of Polish manpower to join Berling's army, and to assist the Red Army by providing supplies and administrative help. As soon as hostilities were over, the PKWN would take over the running of the country. On 28 July the PKWN members were flown to Chełm, which had just been taken by the Russians.

As the Red Army advanced towards Lublin the AK followed instructions laid down in Operation *Tempest* and harried the retreating Germans. They captured seven towns in the Lublin district by themselves and assisted the Red Army to seize Lublin itself on 24 July. Out in the forests and the open countryside the roads were cut off by Soviet and AK units. Yet the same predictable pattern occurred. After a brief period of cordial relations, the AK's senior officers were arrested and taken into the depths of the USSR, while the junior officers and the rank and file were enlisted in Berling's army, unless they had managed to escape into the forests.

In Szczebrzeszyn, early on 26 July, Dr Klukowski waited patiently for the arrival of the AK, but initially only small groups of Russians appeared. At 8 a.m. a Russian officer appeared in the hospital, but, while he was talking, Dr Klukowski suddenly heard the cry:

'Our boys are coming!' I left everything and ran to see for myself. From the direction of Błonie a group of approximately twenty young men approached; all were armed, in uniform, with red scarves around their necks and white arm bands on their left sleeves. The people went wild. They were crying, shouting and throwing flowers.

[Klukowski, *Diaries from the Years of Occupation*, p. 353]

Sadly, within days, this joy was snuffed out and the NKVD began a fresh chapter of torture, arrests and fear.

Polish Resistance in Europe

Inevitably, Poland itself was the main focus of the resistance movement, but, organized by the Polish VI Bureau, the Interior Ministry in London and the SOE, the tentacles of the Polish resistance movement continued to spread throughout Occupied Europe. In Denmark, for instance, according to an agreement between the Polish Interior Ministry and the SOE, the subversive organization was to concentrate its main activities

Campaign Chronicle

amongst Polish soldiers in the *Wehrmacht* and workers in the *Todt* Organization, who were 'not to be encouraged to desert, but rather [. . .] by various ways and means to hold their compatriots together in secret cells, so that they may take active anti-German measures, as and when the occasion arises'.

In France, where there were nearly half a million immigrants (*see page 52*) as well as thousands of conscripted Poles in the *Wehrmacht* and the *Todt* Organization, a larger resistance movement existed. By the end of April it was calculated by the Polish authorities that there were approximately 3,200 Poles organized in cells, who would be able to assist the Allies after the D-Day landings. Until ordered to act, they were to spread propaganda, train combat groups, and supply information from specific areas, particularly the V-1 construction sites. Once the Allies invaded, the Poles fought in close cooperation with the *Maquis*. In the south of France, a Polish liaison officer, Captain Andrzej Fedro, was dropped on 25 August to organize Polish resistance behind German lines between Toulon and Cannes, following the Allied landings.

Hungary remained an important country for Polish Underground operations, and a small Polish VI Bureau group had been established in Budapest. Prince Andrew Saphia was General Bór's personal representative, whose task was to obtain Hungarian assistance for the Polish Underground Army. Radio information was sent to London whenever possible, and couriers continued to pass through. Hungary was also a source of arms purchases. A British agent, Lieutenant Colonel Howie, was able to arrange the clandestine dispatch of radio valves from the Phillips radio firm to Poland. He himself had a radio set installed in his flat early in 1944, which worked every two days until the German occupation on 19 March. Inevitably this made transmitting infinitely more difficult and 'extremely dangerous'. The Germans had radio detector vans (RDF), aeroplanes and civilian cars, which were on the spot three hours after a transmitter started working.

At the end of July, Prince Saphia and a Polish operator were transmitting from a house on the outskirts of Budapest when they found themselves surrounded and actually saw the *Gestapo* climbing over the walls of the house. They were preparing to fight it out, knowing that they would be killed, when, to their surprise, the Germans suddenly turned back. They learnt afterwards that the reason for this was that the officer commanding the Germans had suddenly noticed a large aerial on the house next door, and had assumed that his men were going to the wrong place! From late July 1944 onwards the Polish signals group enjoyed 'official connivance' by Admiral Horthy, the Regent of Hungary, and was actually allowed to contact London using the transmitter in the Royal Palace in Budapest, although this was rapidly discontinued under German pressure.

By late 1943 the Polish officers who had been planted in various Balkan States to establish courier lines were increasingly becoming rallying points for Polish deserters from the *Wehrmacht* and the *Todt* Organization. In March 1943 the War Office informed the VI Bureau that a large percentage of the German garrison in the region of Homolje, eastern Serbia, was comprised of Polish citizens. Understandably, the Germans distrusted their loyalty and only allowed them to retain weapons when on duty. British agents had ascertained that many were anxious to desert and join the guerrillas. In August 1943 a Polish officer was attached to the British Military Mission in Greece specifically to interrogate Polish deserters, many of whom had joined Yugoslav or Greek partisan bands, and to work out how their services could best be used. He was to investigate 'ways and means of using Poles in Greece for decisive action at the appropriate time'.

The Warsaw Uprising: the Decision to Revolt

The Poles had long had plans for an uprising once the Germans were in retreat and their grip on Poland irrevocably weakened. As far back as the winter of 1941, the Polish General Staff in London had drawn up ambitious plans for a national uprising involving the seizure of airfields and a large-scale airlift dropping both airborne forces and equipment (*see page 51*). At one stage there was even a plan for seizing 'the sea shore from Stettin to Königsberg' with the help of the Royal Navy and landing an Anglo-Polish expeditionary force. The problem with this scenario was that it assumed Poland would be liberated from the West. The original plan had stipulated that it would only occur if British Commonwealth forces were within six or seven days' striking distance of Poland. After Stalingrad and Kursk it was clear that it would be the Red Army that would enter Poland first and that Eastern Europe would become a Russian theatre of operations. Given this situation, the British chiefs of staff would only sanction the dropping by air of limited supplies for sabotage and guerrilla groups. The initial reaction on 7 March 1944 to this by Lieutenant Colonel Michał Protasewicz, the chief of VI Bureau, was optimistically to hope that the Chiefs of Staff would reconsider their decision in the near future. He also defiantly stated that:

Campaign Chronicle

No matter what decision was arrived at [...] and even though not one single further weapon was delivered to Poland by the Allies, the Secret Army, together with the people of Poland, would rise at the appropriate moment and attempt to take control of their country.

[NA, HS4/147]

The SOE had little doubt that the Poles meant what they said. Richard Truszkowski argued in a memorandum in July that this determination to revolt was 'an elemental force', which would have to be utilised 'to the best advantage of the Allied war effort', and suggested that a small SOE reconnaissance party should be sent to Poland on a fact-finding mission to examine local conditions and assess the strength of the AK. He saw considerable merit in encouraging a revolt in the Carpathians on both the Slovakian and Polish sides, as 'a liberated area based on this difficult terrain could be held successfully against an enemy possessing much superior equipment'. Four months earlier Lieutenant Colonel Perkins had come to the same conclusion. Writing on 8 March to Colonel Keswick (Director of the SOE's Mediterranean Group '43), who was working on plans to exploit the dissatisfaction in Hungary, Bulgaria and Romania, he observed that a Polish revolt 'would add that pinch of salt to bring out the true flavour of the goulash you are preparing'.

The Chiefs of Staff Committee on 20 May, however, remained unmoved by such prospects. While agreeing that only the Polish authorities were responsible for calling a general uprising, and that the timing should be left to the commander on the spot, they were adamant that, as the short summer nights would restrict air sorties to Poland, assistance could only be planned 'on the basis that the scale would be no greater than it is at present'. Consequently it advised that the Poles should concentrate on intensifying diversionary operations and sabotage. At an 'unofficial meeting' at the end of June or early July with General Tatar (alias 'Tabor'), the deputy Polish Chief of Staff, and Protasewicz, Perkins could only reiterate that the SOE 'were now powerless to do anything further about the increase in the effort to Poland' and that 'coordination of Polish plans with those of the Allies could only be effected in one direction, i.e. to the east'.

Tabor quickly grasped the situation and thanked Perkins 'for his clear and honest exposition of the situation as it stood today [...] the time for vague promise [...] was ended'. Given the lack of diplomatic cooperation between the Polish Government-in-Exile and Moscow, he appeared to be convinced that 'there must at present be continuation of activity at its present level'. General Sosnkowski's orders of 7 July reflect these facts. Bór was ordered to continue with the *Tempest* plan and to 'regulate the speed of action as the situation demands'. Ambiguously, however, Sosnkowski added:

> For political reasons, the Government would like to give the *Burza* action the character of an insurrection. My opinion is decidedly against representing it as such, so as not to misguide the lower commanders and local leaders.
>
> [Bór-Komorowski, p. 203]

By mid-July the Red Army had opened up the way to the west in a massive two-pronged attack. Units of the First Byelorussian Army Group from the Kovel sector, under Marshal Rokossovsky, had reached the Vistula by 25 July and established a bridgehead near Dęblin on 2 August, while the First Ukrainian Army Group had taken Lwów on 26 July and crossed the Vistula near Sandomierz two days later. The Fourth German Panzer Army had been routed in the Zamość sector, and its surviving units had been ordered on 22 July to regroup on the western bank of the Vistula. Already by this date the Germans were pulling out of Warsaw. The *Gestapo* was destroying documents and both the German Governor and the Mayor had fled, although the Governor was ordered to return on 27 July.

On 21 July Bór met with the chief and deputy chief of staff of the AK, and decided that the collapse of the German Army and advance of the Russians created the ideal situation for an uprising to enable the Underground to seize control of Warsaw. On 25 July Prime Minister Mikołajczyk and his Cabinet empowered him, despite Sosnkowski's reservations, 'to proclaim the insurrection at a moment when you will decide opportune'. That same day Bór ordered the state of alert 'for every eventuality' and radioed his government in London on the 26th that 'we are ready to fight for Warsaw at any moment'. In the meantime, the Russians were drawing nearer. Artillery could be heard with increasing frequency and Soviet patrols were probing the eastern suburbs. A major Russian attack on Warsaw seemed imminent.

On 29 July Bór met the General Commission of the Council of National Unity, which had been formed in January 1944 to represent the non-Communist political parties, and asked it two key questions: should the AK take control of the city before the Russians entered, and how long did the civil authorities need to establish themselves before the AK revealed themselves to the Russians? The first question received an affirmative response, while the answer to the second was 'twelve hours'. Two days later, on the 31st, Bór conferred with his two deputy commanders and Colonel Chruściel (alias 'Monter'), the head of the Warsaw region, while the Government Delegate Jankowski was waiting next door. Chruściel informed them that Soviet tanks were already approaching the suburb of Praga. On the basis of this information, Jankowski agreed that the AK could 'go ahead'. Bór then turned to Chruściel and said: 'Tomorrow at seventeen hundred hours precisely, you will start operations in Warsaw.' As Bór observed in his biography, 'the button had been pressed'.

And yet there were powerful dissenting voices. General Sosnkowski remained sceptical, foreseeing that the Russians would not come to the assistance of the Poles. Like General Anders, he believed that the rising could not succeed without outside help and would lead to pointless bloodshed. Sosnkowski also despairingly briefed Nowak, who was carrying messages from the Polish Government to Bór-Komorowski, that 'in terms of its effect on allied governments and public opinion' an uprising would literally be "a tempest in a teacup" '! A year later Bór told Nowak that if his information had come sooner, it would have been taken into account.

In reality, however, it is hard to see how the uprising could have been avoided. Much of the civilian population was restless and longing for revenge against the hated occupier. Ralph Smorczewski, who fought in Warsaw, described the atmosphere in the days preceding the uprising:

An eerie air of expectancy hung over the town. Pedestrian traffic was different, everybody seemed to hurry. There were hardly any Germans to be seen, except those guarding the entrances to their buildings, or in fast-moving motor cars or motorbikes tearing along the streets. One somehow felt that, however secret the Polish Army's preparations were, everybody knew that soon the town would rise against the occupiers. One had the impression the Germans knew it as well.

[Smorczewski, *Bridging the Gap*, pp. 140–1]

If Bór had not ordered the uprising, the Communists almost certainly would have done so. The Russians had already created the Polish Committee of National Liberation, which claimed to be the nucleus for a pro-Soviet Polish Government to be set up after the defeat of the Germans. The Kościuszko Radio in Moscow claimed on 16 July that the AL was conducting systematic military operations throughout Poland, and on 30 July actually issued a proclamation for an uprising:

> We shall not permit the Germans to make out of Warsaw a bulwark of resistance. The enemy in our capital should be defeated and annihilated with the speed of lightning. Thus we have to bend all our efforts to help the Allied Soviet armies in liberating our city.
>
> [Korbonski, *The Polish Underground State*, p. 172]

On 23 July Stalin himself informed Churchill in a telegram that the AL and General Berling's forces would liberate the city jointly. He dismissed the 'so-called Underground organizations', directed by the Polish Government in London, as 'ephemeral and of no consequence at all'.

Surely the known reservations of Britain and America should have dampened enthusiasm for the uprising, but there was a certain degree of optimism in Poland that once the uprising occurred the West would be bound to help. In London, Mikołajczyk – who was about to fly to Moscow for direct negotiations with Stalin – hoped that it would strengthen his hand, and that once he had secured an agreement over the future of Poland, Soviet aid would be forthcoming. Given the Soviet record in Volhynia, Wilno, Lwów and Lublin, there seemed little chance of the Poles establishing an independent government in Warsaw, but then optimists argued that if the Polish democrats were seen by the whole world to have recaptured Warsaw by themselves, would even Stalin risk the Grand Alliance by forcefully dislodging them? Anyway, as Norman Davies has pointed out, 'to do nothing was simply to invite a different form of disaster'. On 27 July Hitler had decided to turn Warsaw into a fortress, and that afternoon the Germans broadcast through megaphones an order calling on 100,000 men aged between seventeen and sixty-five years to report for fortification work. Passivity would only enable the Germans to turn Warsaw into a second Stalingrad.

The Outbreak of the Revolt: 1–5 August

As the runners were given their orders for the district leaders just before evening curfew on Monday 31 July, the latter did not receive them until Tuesday morning, and some not until just before 'W' or zero hour at 5 p.m. Consequently they had little time to mobilize their units, and hurried preparations had to be made. On the afternoon of 1 August, for instance, Ralph Smorczewski was en route to join friends at a bridge party in the southern outskirts of Warsaw when, at 5 p.m., he noticed that

> Clouds of smoke started appearing over various parts of Warsaw and almost immediately the rattle of machine-gun fire and hand-grenade explosions could be heard from the direction of Sadyba. The uprising had started and nobody had told us. The three of us ran down the street towards the sound of fighting [...] It was not long before we encountered one of the AK units. It consisted of ten to twelve men all surprisingly well armed. I was given a handgun and two hand grenades.
>
> [Smorczewski, IWM, 03/41/1]

Certain key personnel, like Adam Truszkowski – who would take on the role of English liaison officer and radio announcer in the event of an uprising – were mobilized several days before W hour. Truszkowski himself was called up on 26 July and had to report to Colonel Radwan's headquarters near Napoleon Square. From the moment the uprising broke out until the end he was attached to the official military transmitter (Błyskawica station), situated initially in a cellar in the headquarters of the PKO (the Polish Committee for Social Care). For the first few days the transmitter was unable to function because of the damp in the cellar.

On the evening of 1 August some 600 companies of AK troops began moving to their planned assembly points. The omens for their success were not good. There were serious gaps in the AK's Intelligence and a shortage of weapons, as many arms caches had been taken out of the city in preparation for a general uprising in the countryside. As the hours ticked by to W hour, it had also been impossible to keep preparations hidden from the Germans. There was a considerable amount of shooting from young, inexperienced members of the AK. For instance, around 1300 hours, several members of the AK Parasol Battalion rashly decided to throw Molotov cocktails at an SS guard post in Ochota, while in Żoliborz, a group of armed AL insurgents was discovered by German troops in the boiler room of a cooperative settlement and a firefight ensued in which twenty-one AL fighters were killed. By now the German security police were fully mobilized and tanks and armoured vehicles were patrolling the streets.

The Polish Underground 1939–1947

General Bór's own command post in the Kammler factory (in the Wola district) was an unfortunate choice, as it was dangerously close to an SS barracks. Inevitably, the SS noticed armed personnel inside the factory and for three hours laid siege to it until the *Kedyw* battalion, which had been assigned the duty of protecting the headquarters, arrived and drove off the Germans. Its troops managed to reach the headquarters from Okopowa Street by blasting their way through the walls of attics. The General's radio had also been damaged and it was not until noon on 2 August that he was able to contact London. In the city centre the AK successfully mobilized about 75 per cent of its troops, but these were poorly armed. For instance, in an example quoted by Professor Borodziej, for one unit of 901 soldiers in the Old Town there were only 103 grenades, 48 pistols, 8 automatic pistols, 9 rifles, 1 heavy and 2 light machine guns and probably 1,000 Molotov cocktails. In the suburbs, where the insurgents were potentially better armed, mobilization was painfully slow. By 3 August there were, altogether, some 30,000 fighters mobilized in Warsaw. The great majority were AK members but there were also small groups of AL and NSZ partisans. In the Old Town the AL was able to deploy some 300 men.

The initial Polish successes occurred in central Warsaw – the Old Town (Stare Miasto) and Wola – where there were relatively few German troops. In the evening of 1 August the city's tallest skyscraper, the Prudential building, was seized and the Polish national flag was hoisted at 8 p.m. The Labour Office, the former Czech Embassy and the Appellate Court were also seized, and in Stawki Street, north of the city centre, an SS warehouse full of uniforms and foodstuffs was captured. A significant success was the taking of the power station in Powiśle, where the workers had been making preparations for such an event since 1942. The Germans had reinforced the building, but were unaware that weapons and explosives had already been smuggled in. Just ten minutes after W Hour AK troops stunned the Germans by detonating explosives under the main building of the power station, By the following day they managed to secure the plant: twenty Germans were killed and seventy-eight taken prisoner, while the AK suffered forty-four casualties, seventeen of which were fatal.

There were, however, some serious setbacks. To enable supplies to be flown in from Italy, the AK attempted, unsuccessfully, to seize both the Okęcie and Bielany airports, and an attack on the *Luftwaffe* barracks to the south of the city centre was repulsed with heavy casualties. Similarly, the attempts to gain control of the two strategically important Vistula bridges – the Kiebedż and Poniatowski – also failed.

The uprising was greeted for the most part with initial enthusiasm. In the Old Town volunteers rushed forward to build barricades. In the Market Square a huge bonfire was lit to show the Russians on the other side of the river that the Old Town was in the hands of the insurgents. Nevertheless, the situation did take many locals by surprise – some people were caught out in the streets, separated from friends and family or indeed killed. Ralph Smorczewski's father, for example – returning from a music recital in the centre of the town – had almost reached the end of Śniadeckich Street when machine-gun fire and hand-grenade explosions forced him to seek shelter in the nearest doorway. He was let into the apartment and assumed he would soon be walking home, yet, as luck would have it, he was very near the barricade that divided the Polish and German sectors and was forced to remain in the flat until 4 October, not knowing which occupant would be killed next. Dr Damaszek Jacob, a Jew who had obtained an 'Aryan' birth certificate, was also caught out when, 'quite unexpectedly', at 18.30 hours, shooting began in the city; he did, however, manage to reach his own flat and within two hours was able to organize a first aid post there and, a few days later, a make-shift hospital in Pius Street.

The balance sheet for the first day of the uprising was bad for both the Poles and the Germans. The Germans had been forced to evacuate their forces from exposed bases, and their police headquarters in Mokotów was cut off from the Nazi Government quarter south of the Old Town. To hold Warsaw, the Germans urgently needed to reinforce their garrison and, above all, secure east–west communication through the city. The Poles, for their part, had failed to take key buildings and targets, and had suffered very high casualties. In one day these amounted to 10 per cent of the total number of AK troops mobilized. The Germans also managed to hang on – for the time being – to the central telephone exchange on Pius Street, which ensured the continued flow of German communications through telephone and teleprinter, while the Poles still had to rely on runners. On 2 August the rebels continued their offensive, and managed to liberate the whole of the Old Town, the city centre (Śródmieście), the working-class district of Wola and two districts situated on the banks of the Vistula – Powiśle and Czerniaków – although a fresh attempt to seize the northern aerodrome of Bielany failed.

The Germans were still unable to get to grips with the insurgency. General Stahel, commander of the city garrison, later observed that the

The Polish Underground 1939–1947

'German occupation [proved] helpless for street fighting with regard to tactics, leadership and human behaviour'. On 2 August, for instance, local SS commanders tried to smash through the Polish barricades in Wola with Tiger tanks lacking infantry support, in an attempt to clear a way to Bruhl Palace, where Stahel and his staff were surrounded. On the barricades at Karolkowa Street *Kedyw* troops armed with captured German *Panzerfäuste* and British-supplied PIATs managed to repulse the attack and even captured two Tigers. In his daily report, Stahel reported 'bloody losses' and reckoned that the Germans had lost some 500 men. The following day the Germans again employed armour, this time protected by a human shield of some fifty civilians lashed to the tanks, in order to free a route to the Poniatowski Bridge. They managed to break through to the bridge but, in their wake, the rebels rapidly rebuilt the barricades and closed up the corridor.

The German Counter-Offensive

So far the Poles had managed to hold the initiative. On balance, the mood was optimistic and their assumption was that the uprising would end rapidly in victory. However, by 4 August there were alarming signs that a ruthless German counter-attack was being prepared. On Himmler's orders a special anti-insurgent corps was formed under the command of *SS-Obergruppenführer* Erich von dem Bach, who was appointed Supreme Commander of all German forces in Warsaw. Once mobilized, it formed what Norman Davies has called 'a powerful if somewhat motley array', which consisted of:

- The SS Rona Brigade, recruited from the Russian National Liberation Army under Brigadeführer Kaminski.
- The SS Brigade commanded by *SS-Oberführer* Dirlewanger, which included the 3rd Azerbaijani Regiment.
- The 572nd and 580th Cossack Battalions.
- The 608th Special Defence Battalion.
- A militarized police battalion from Poznań.
- A *Luftwaffe* guard regiment.
- A reserve battalion of the Hermann Göring Panzer-Parachute Division, which was operating east of Warsaw.

[Davies, *Rising '44*, p. 252]

German reinforcements had been brought up by train to Błonie, 23 km west of Warsaw, on 3 August and were advancing towards the city.

Campaign Chronicle

Von dem Bach's instructions were not just to defeat the insurgents but, as he was to tell his Polish prosecutor at the Nuremberg trials:

- To shoot all rebels after their capture.
- To massacre non-belligerents indiscriminately.
- To raze the whole city of Warsaw.

His superior, Himmler, saw the uprising as a marvellous opportunity to destroy Warsaw forever, thereby extinguishing the capital of the nation 'that has blocked our way to the east for seven hundred years'.

Meanwhile, on the edge of Wola and Ochota, von dem Bach's chief of operations, *Gruppenführer* Heinz Reinefarth, began to amass his forces in preparation for a major counter-attack. According to information later relayed to Stockholm by the daughter of Colonel Alexander Björklund, a naturalized Pole and former Finnish Military Attaché in Warsaw, many Poles initially thought Reinefarth's men were members of the advancing Red Army, as so many of them spoke Russian. In Mochnaczka Street a workman told the inhabitants of one apartment 'that the Soviet Army was arriving on that day (4 August) at one o'clock in the afternoon' ...

Stores, medicines and so on were pulled out with the idea of organizing help for the wounded soldiers. At 12 o'clock units passed through the Mokotowski Fields firing machine-guns in the direction of the city. It appeared that they were Soviet troops. The people went down to the cellars, while awaiting the liberation of that part of the town. After ten minutes the front doors of the house were smashed in by rifle butts, and some kind of band burst into the apartments of our informant [...] They wore German uniforms, spoke in Russian and were completely drunk. They demobilized [*sic*] the room in five minutes, seizing everything that was of value. Not content with that, they beat up everyone else. They even wanted to kill our informant's child, but the assailant was persuaded [*sic*] from doing so with the aid of a bottle of vodka. The house dog was killed with a bayonet, after which everyone was taken out 'to be shot' [...] Machine-guns were fixed, and the command given to form threes, after which the entire multitude were suddenly pushed into Grojecka Street [...] The crowd of 15,000 people were driven along the burning street for about 4 kms between burning houses ...

[NA, HS/4148]

They ended up in the old vegetable market in Zieleniak, where they remained for five days with one glass of water for each person per day. After three days the unfortunate detainees were given two cows, 'which had been butchered before in a bestial manner'. Women gave birth, dying with their infants, and 'the worst scenes happened at night when women and young twelve-year-old girls were seized and assaulted'. Eventually the Polish detainees were sent to a camp in Grodzisk, although such was the chaos and lack of organization that many, possibly the majority, managed to escape.

By 5 August the Germans were ready to launch their counter-attack on Wola and Ochota. In Wola the worst atrocities of the German counter-insurgency campaign occurred on this day, when somewhere between 30,000 and 40,000 civilians were ruthlessly butchered. The Marie Curie Radium Institute was attacked and burnt down ward by ward, while the nurses, sisters and the sick were raped and murdered. In Ochota the death toll was considerably lower as the Kaminski Brigade was far more interested in plunder. Tens of thousands of refugees now streamed into the areas of the city the AK still controlled, which inevitably put a great strain on accommodation and food supplies. However, the news of the atrocities strengthened the links of the civil population with the Resistance, and made it clear that there was no alternative to fighting.

On 6 August the Germans tightened their grip on both Wola and Ochota. Armoured vehicles belonging to Dirlewanger's anti-partisan regiment managed, with the help of human shields, to break through AK defences along the Ektoralna Street and to liberate the trapped German garrisons in Saxon Gardens. The next morning they were able to evacuate Stahel from the Bruhl Palace. They were also successful in opening up a corridor through the centre of the city, which enabled them to re-establish contact with some of their besieged garrisons, but they still lacked the manpower to police the corridor securely and were only able to run armoured vehicles along it at full speed.

It took the Germans until 11 August to consolidate their hold over these two districts. Colonel Schmidt's Security Regiment met little difficulty in clearing the former ghetto area, but Major Reck's forces encountered stiff resistance from crack *Kedyw* units in the Jewish cemetery and in the north-western corner of Wola, which was not broken until 11 August. In Ochota AK units managed to eliminate a company of the RONA Brigade, together with its commander. However, when the Germans deployed pioneer troops, who used with devastating effect special demolition vehicles known as Goliaths to destroy the Wawelska redoubt in the Wawelska, Mianowskiego and Uniwersytecka Streets and the Kaliska redoubt in the buildings of the state-owned Tobacco Monopoly, AK rebels were forced to evacuate through tunnels that linked up with the sewers.

War in the Sewers

Increasingly the sewers were to play a key part in enabling messenger girls, couriers, convoys of wounded and transports of ammunition to move in relative safety under the German positions. Since the sewers were narrow, they could only be used as one-way routes. Consequently, as traffic increased, special timetables had to be devised and sent via London to the local commanders because their weak shortwave sets could not contact each other but were able to transmit to, and receive messages from, high-powered radio stations. The tunnels were, for security reasons, completely unlit. The air was foul and the semi-circular base was strewn with debris such as broken glass, even a superficial graze from which would cause septicaemia. To move at all, people used two sticks as supports and progress was made in short kangaroo-like jumps. In the German-occupied areas the manholes were left open so that hand grenades, mines and tins of gas could be thrown down by German troops. In some areas battles took place between German sappers and insurgents waist high in excrement. They fought at close quarters with grenades or hand-to-hand with knives, and if they had no weapons they drowned each other in the slime and excrement. At important crossing places in the sewers the Germans would also pour in petrol and set it alight. Bór painted a vivid and horrendous picture of the hell of the sewers, reminiscent of Dante's *Inferno*:

> the horror of the sewers was increased by the echo of moans and cries from the wounded and the hysterical laughter of those whose nerves had given way under the experience. The slightest sound was increased a hundredfold and repeated in an endless echo, which rolled along and could be heard miles away. The noises were truly terrible. It often happened that a whole convoy would be held up by the man in front who lost his nerve as he approached an open manhole in the German positions.

> [Bór-Komorowski, p. 302]

The Polish Underground 1939–1947

The Attack on the Old Town, 8–19 August

Von dem Bach was now determined to attack the Old Town and restore the German lines of communications across the railway and Kierbedź bridges in the city centre so that supplies from German-held areas on the right bank of the Vistula could reach the Ninth Army. His task was not, however, going to be easy. After their retreat from Wola and Ochota, the insurgents were pushed back into five main areas: Żoliborz, the Old Town, the city centre, Mokotów and Czerniaków. One advantage of this was that a smaller area was easier to defend. After the atrocities in Wola the AK was ready to fight to the last person, and during the first week of the uprising had rapidly adapted its tactics to urban warfare. The Intelligence Officer of the German Ninth Army observed that, while on the first days of the revolt they

> systematically held the streets under fire [...] as soon as the Germans appeared, the enemy now let the attacking raiding party, flame-throwers, and even tanks proceed to a certain place in order to annihilate them with well aimed sniper power. Soldiers and the wounded who returned from action reported that the fatal losses had been caused almost only by shots in the head [...] The firing ports [of the snipers] are half the size of bricks and most of them cannot be seen.
>
> [Quoted in Borodziej, *The Warsaw Uprising of 1944*, p. 99]

Although Dirlewanger's troops had launched probing attacks against the Old Town on 9 and 10 August, they had made little progress apart from seizing the ruins of the Royal Castle. On both the 11th and 12th they launched attacks from these ruins on the southern boundary of the Old Town, which again foundered amidst a hail of sniper fire and Molotov cocktails. The Poles were adept at retreating from the street barricades to the buildings, and then to the cellars or courtyards, nearby streets or even churches. As in Stalingrad, the battles were a series of small-scale fights for particular buildings, which were taken and retaken many times. This intense drama is only hinted at in an interpretation report of an aerial photograph, taken by an Allied plane on the 12th:

> Since Warsaw was last photographed on 15.6.44, all visible signs of normal life have disappeared; there is no road, rail or river traffic and a pall of smoke from fires which are still burning in the old city lies over the northern area.

Campaign Chronicle

Damage in the old city is severe, particularly in Districts VIII, XI and XII, where large areas have been completely gutted by fire [...] The newer parts of the city, including the suburbs, have not suffered nearly so heavily, and all the rail and road bridges across the Vistula remain intact.

Activity appears to be concentrated around the Central Railway Station. The cutting which carries the main lines westward has been completely blocked by three derailed wagons, which are piled up across it. In the streets around the station and extending from the racecourse in the south to District II in the north, barricades have been roughly thrown up and are improvised from rubble, vehicles and such-like. Several persons are moving about in the streets just north of the station, and this is the only place in the city where people can be seen. It is difficult to make any definite statement, but it is quite likely that 'incidents' are occurring in this locality.

Groups of M.T. [motor transport] are scattered about the city but the largest and most homogenous collection is seen in the courtyard of the Ministry of Education building, which is itself burning [...] Two small convoys are approaching the old city. One from the north moving southwards along the Marymoncka Road and another moving westwards along the Groconowska Road towards the port.

The bulk of rolling stock has gone from the rail yards and in the whole of the railway system around the city only one short length of trucks is seen moving [...] Warsaw/Bielany Airfield has been ploughed up and of the 73 aircraft seen in Warsaw/Okecie on 15.6.44, only 1 now remains, and that is an Fi 156 [Fieseler Storch].

[NA, HS4/156]

German attacks on the Old Town continued day after day, but after nearly a week of bitter fighting, they had still made little headway. Their armoured vehicles could not operate effectively in the narrow and confined streets of the old city, but slowly their preponderance in weapons and manpower began to prevail. From 17 to 23 August they attacked the Old Town from the air with Stukas and, to quote Sergeant John Ward, whose radio messages were the only direct contact the British Government had with Warsaw, 'their tactics are the same as those used in the liquidation of the ghetto, i.e. burning down street after street'.

While the morale of the Polish fighting units in the Old Town remained high, the civilian population's began to deteriorate. The cellars and shelters

The Polish Underground 1939–1947

were grossly overcrowded, often with no room to lie down, there was no adequate medical assistance for the sick, and the Germans had cut off the water supply on 14 August, making it virtually impossible to fight the fires. On 20 August Ward reported that 'on practically every piece of ground in Warsaw wells were being dug. The shortage of water is beginning to be serious.' Anaesthesia ran out that same day and doctors had to operate without narcotics.

By 21 August the rebels had suffered some 2,000 casualties, which was 30 per cent of their strength as of 8 August. Unless supplies and reinforcements could be dropped by Allied aircraft or the German siege broken, the Old Town and ultimately Warsaw would fall.

There were two unsuccessful attempts by AK forces to relieve the Old Town. In the night of 16/17 August an attempt to break through by reinforcements from the Kampinos Forest failed. A more ambitious plan was devised, which attempted to mobilize AK forces in the city centre and Żoliborz to make a pincer attack from both the north and south to relieve the Old Town. The Żoliborz units, reinforced by 650 partisans from the Kampinos Forest, attacked the Gdansk railway station (less than a kilometre north of the Old Town) in the night of 20/21 August, but failed to surprise the Germans and were mowed down by mortars, heavy machine guns and the armoured train *Panzerzug 75*. The next night a second attack took place by a force numbering almost 1,000 AK fighters from the Old Town and Żoliborz under the command of General Pełczyński, the chief of staff of the High Command, but again the Germans were able to repulse the attack with heavy casualties.

The Insurgents Retreat from the Old Town

The defeat of the attacks on the Gdansk railway station marked a turning point in the uprising. Both civilian and AK morale began to decline as it became clear that the Old Town could no longer be saved. On the night of 25/26 August the High Command withdrew through the sewers to the city centre. The Germans, in the meantime, continued to bombard the Old Town from the air, while on the ground they made two important breakthroughs. On the 26th they seized part of Kierbedź bridge and could not be dislodged. Two days later, with tanks and 'Goliaths', they finally destroyed Polish Resistance in the Polish Security Printing Works, the PWPW, which, with its massive concrete walls, was the key to the defence of the Old Town. The wounded and prisoners were shot in the basement. Over the next two days the Polish resistance in the old town was squeezed increasingly between Dirlewanger's troops, who had occupied the ruins of St John's Cathedral in the south, and Schmidt's troops in the north. Between them were caught some 2,000 AK soldiers and at least 35,000 civilians, who prayed in cellars and ruins for their survival or else made unsuccessful attempts to get to the sewers. To halt the growing panic, the AK's military police fired into the air and, to quote Borodziej, 'there were tussles, curses and threats'.

The situation was now hopeless. Colonel Karol Żiemski ('Wachnowski'), the commander of the Polish forces in the Old Town, decided to evacuate his best troops to the city centre, as ammunition stocks were nearly spent. As the wounded could not use the sewer system, Żiemski planned to create a corridor by a simultaneous attack from those units already evacuated to the city centre and those remaining still in the Old Town. The city centre units attacked as planned but the Old Town units – exhausted and decimated – were mobilized too late and the operation failed. Such an attempt two or three weeks earlier might have been more successful.

On 31 August Colonel Chruściel ordered a retreat of the surviving units and those wounded who could be moved through the sewers to the city centre. At 8 p.m. on 1 September their evacuation started. Two sewers were used: the main sewer, which was 6½ feet high and slightly over a mile long, where the sewage was knee deep; the second sewer was shorter but harder to negotiate because it was impossible to stand upright. Altogether, some 4,500 AK troops escaped. Captain Ryszard managed to lead eighty of his men, dressed in captured SS uniforms, right through the enemy lines to the city centre!

On 2 September, after an artillery barrage lasting several hours, the Germans reoccupied the Old City and shot some 7,000 wounded and civilians. The remainder were sent to the concentration camps or to the Reich for forced labour.

The City Centre, Mokotów and Żoliborz

The city centre was, except for a few islands of German resistance (the most important of which was the telephone company skyscraper, 'PAST'), in the hands of the insurgents. By 20 August there were some 23,000 AK troops in this sector, out of a total of 47,000 in the whole city. Compared to the bitter struggle in the Old Town, the combat here had been less intense. Even so, there were several important actions. On 15 August German Panzers attacked the western part of the centre to block a suspected attempt by the AK to relieve the Old Town, but this was repulsed with relatively heavy German casualties and seven tanks were reported destroyed or damaged. General Rohr did, however, achieve a considerable success with his battle group when he captured the Haberbusch brewery and a warehouse containing vital food supplies on 17 August. Two days later, his troops went on to seize the Technical University. Against this, however, the Poles seized the 'PAST' telephone company's skyscraper, which had been under siege since the beginning of the uprising, in a night attack. A Polish assault group managed to infiltrate its basement through an Underground passage unknown to the Germans. Attacked lethally at close quarters by grenades and flamethrowers, the Germans retreated to the upper storeys and surrendered the following morning. Arguably, the capture of this building, which, with its eleven storeys was one of the most prominent buildings in Warsaw, was the greatest psychological success of the uprising. The Polish flag was immediately hoisted over its roof. Rebel troops failed to retake the Technical University but did go on to take the local telephone exchange on Pius Street and the Police Headquarters in Krakówskie Przedmieście, which also necessitated flushing the Germans out of the ruins of Holy Cross Church. An account of this action was broadcast on the radio station 'Lightning' on 24 August:

> Reinforcements for the Germans came from the Holy Cross Church. It was necessary to fight for the Church. The Holy Virgin Chapel had to be taken by grenades. The Germans were beaten to their knees there. At the same time the ring around the Police HQ was tightened. There the Germans had six machine-guns with which they swept all our positions with fire, and the road of retreat was cut off. We shot the Germans like rabbits. Through the open door the Germans shot salvos from guns, all around houses were burning. Our fire defence and the civilian population immediately went into action. About noon the first group of German prisoners showed themselves. Finally it was over. One of the prisoners said 'Lieutenant Kutscher fled like a crazy person, he got a bullet in the stomach and was taken to hospital.' About thirty Germans were taken prisoner. Joy showed on all faces that the Holy Cross Church was hit with artillery fire and still carried the eloquent inscription 'sursum corda' ['lift up your hearts'].
>
> [NA, HS4/156]

Sadly, however, these successes did not change the overall situation in the Old Town.

In Mokotów the rebels' position was greatly strengthened by access to the Kabaty Forest, the nearness of farms and market gardens that could provide food, and also by the fact that the area immediately south of Warsaw was occupied by the Hungarian 5th Division, which had refused to participate in crushing the uprising. In theory, it should have been relatively simple to funnel in reinforcements from Southern Poland, but AK units from Radom and Kielce, which numbered some 5,000 troops, were unable to break through the German military dispositions and reach Warsaw, and consequently decided to pull back. To the east and south-east, Russian troops disarmed and imprisoned any AK partisans heading for Warsaw. Nevertheless, some 400 reinforcements were able to slip through to Mokotów from the nearby Kabaty Forest and bring the total numbers in the southern section up to 3,000, 10 per cent of whom were women.

During the nights of 26–28 August attempts were made to break through to the city centre but were halted by German forces in the barracks near Łazienki Park. On the 29th the Germans felt strong enough to take the offensive in Mokotów. The insurgents were forced out of the village of Sadyba and in their flight across the fields to Dolny Mokotów were mowed down by machine-guns.

Żoliborz also remained a relatively quiet area, where the insurgents had access to the Kampinos Forest to the north. They were lucky that, until 30 August, this sector was patrolled by the 12th Hungarian Infantry Division, which, like the 5th Division, refused to move against the Poles. The local AK units participated in the coordinated attack on the Gdansk railway station on 20 August (*see above*), but after being driven back with heavy casualties played no further role in relieving the Old Town. At the end of the month they were reinforced by some 800 soldiers who managed to escape the Old Town through the sewers, and it was not until mid-September that the Germans turned their attention towards them.

Attitude of the Soviet Union

The Warsaw Uprising was initially sanctioned on the assumption of Soviet military assistance. The point-blank refusal of this until September condemned the whole operation to a most bloody failure. The reasons for Stalin's decisions cannot be constructed from the Soviet archives because the key documents are missing. For instance, in one series of documents entitled 'Before the Eyes of the Kremlin', there is 'a gaping hole' between 29 July and 21 August 1941, and in what one would imagine to be the key collection, 'Stalin and the Warsaw Uprising', there are no Soviet sources

The Polish Underground 1939–1947

from 8 August to 16 September. And so, to quote Professor Borodziej, 'we find ourselves in that state of knowledge where the more or less logical reasoning of the historian must replace information from sources'.

Militarily, by the end of July the Russians did indeed seem poised to take Warsaw. The Eighth Guards Army had established a bridgehead across the Vistula at Magnuszew, while the Second Tank Army – which was heading north-west for Warsaw – had, on 27 July, routed the German 73rd Infantry Regiment at Garwolin. On 31 July the Second Tank Army was in the outskirts of Warsaw, and Soviet leaflets signed by Molotov were dropped, urging the people of Warsaw to rise up. A German counter-attack, however, halted the advance and pushed the Soviet III Tank Corps out of Wołomin and forced it to retreat some 20 miles eastwards. This was hardly a major defeat, but it did delay the immediate capture of Warsaw, and gave Stalin a pause to reconsider the situation. On the 5th General Rokossovsky told Stalin that he wanted to resume the advance on Warsaw within five days but this was rejected – and here we do not know whether it was by Stalin personally. Instead, the new plan delayed the attack until 25 August, which was, of course, disastrous news for the insurgents. In his memoirs, Bór recalled his reaction when he could no longer hear Soviet artillery across the Vistula in the early hours of 4 August:

> After four hours sleep, I awoke suddenly with a vague feeling of apprehension, which I could not at first analyse [...] I leaned over the balcony, from where I could usually hear the artillery from the east. After listening for a couple of minutes, I realized the cause of my apprehension. The sounds across the Vistula had ceased.
>
> [Bór-Komorowski, p. 237]

This was indeed bad news, but there was still a possibility that Prime Minister Mikołajczyk, who had flown to Moscow for talks, might be able to appease Stalin and so gain Soviet assistance for Warsaw. He had a friendly, if non-committal, meeting with him on 3 August and then, on the 6th and 7th, had discussions with the PKWN leaders on the future government of Poland. The PKWN demanded control of fourteen ministries, while offering the London Government-in-Exile only four. Mikołajczyk agreed to present this to his Cabinet for discussion, and in his final meeting with Stalin was promised Soviet military assistance for the Warsaw insurgents. Yet Stalin was probably still buying time or keeping his options open. By 16 August he had made up his mind and told Churchill that the Warsaw campaign was 'a foolish adventure' and that, consequently, the Soviet High Command 'could bear no direct or indirect responsibility for it'. The key reason for this was, to quote the American Ambassador in Moscow, 'ruthless political calculations'. Stalin wanted the AK and the supporters of the London Government destroyed, so that opposition to the PKWN would be eliminated. Effectively, this was the death warrant for the uprising.

Help from the Western Allies: Too Little and Too Late

On 29 July General Tatar (alias Tabor) presented Gubbins with Poland's shopping list for Allied assistance:

1. Immediate increase of stores and dropping operations in the area of Warsaw.
2. Bombing of airfields near Warsaw.
3. Polish Mustang wings to operate from these airfields once taken by the AK.
4. Despatch of the Polish Parachute Brigade.
5. Recognition of the Polish Secret Army as an Allied military force and so covered by the Geneva Convention.
6. Despatch of an Allied mission to Warsaw.

[NA, HS4/317]

The Joint Planning Staff considered these requests and on 30 July recommended that, with the exception of the 5th point, they should all be turned down. Even this ran into considerable diplomatic problems with the Foreign Office, as it argued that a unilateral declaration by Britain would infringe on Soviet control in a 'Soviet operational theatre'. Instead, the War Cabinet suggested on 11 August that the Soviet Government should be persuaded to issue a general declaration 'pointing out that all organized forces in Poland fighting against the Germans are regarded by the Soviet Government as having full belligerent status'. This initiative met with little success and it was only on 29 August that the British and Americans issued a unilateral declaration recognizing the AK as part of the Polish armed forces.

The outbreak of the uprising on 1 August did have an immediate impact on British views. Under pressure from Churchill, to whom the Polish Government had made 'the most earnest appeal', the Chiefs of Staff signalled to the British Mission in Moscow ('30 Mission') to pass on Polish requests for ammunition supplies. At the same time they also contacted the Mediterranean Allied Air Force and impressed on Air Marshal Slessor the immediate urgency of responding to Polish requests for assistance. On 3 August the weather made operations impossible anyway but, after due analysis of the proposed operation, General Wilson, Supreme Allied Commander of the Mediterranean, and Air Marshal Slessor the following day 'reluctantly came to the conclusion that it was not a practical proposition even if the weather permits':

> Halifaxes and Liberators would have to proceed north of Zagreb in daylight and on the return journey the same would apply. With the moon at the full we are likely to suffer considerable losses en route and dropping off supplies from a low altitude over a built-up area, which is bound to have a reasonable scale of ack ack and machine-gun defences, is likely to result in very few aircraft getting through. Much of the material which we would drop would certainly get into the wrong hands.

> [NA, HS4/148]

They also asked what impact 'a fiasco such as this' would have upon the Russians, adding: 'it might be as well to imagine our views if the situation were reversed and the Russians attempted to support a resistance group in Florence'.

In fact, dropping operations did take place on the following night, 4/5 August. The planes that were supposed to have flown to Warsaw were diverted, dropping to other targets in Poland. One of the dropping zones was only some 15 km north-west of Warsaw, and two Halifaxes piloted by Poles disobeyed orders and dropped twelve containers with arms over Wola, which fell into the insurgents' hands. Four planes, however, failed to return and two crash-landed on return.

As a result of this, all further flights during the current moon period were again banned, on the basis that the planes were too vulnerable to the German radar and night-fighter belt protecting the Silesian industrial area. 'The position, therefore,' as Lieutenant Colonel Threlfall, Commander of Base 139 in Brindisi, dryly remarked, 'was that at the time of Poland's greatest need not only was help to Warsaw refused but all support of the Secret Army cancelled'. The reaction to this by the Poles was understandable. President Raczkiewicz immediately wrote to Churchill, who forwarded his communication to the Chiefs of Staff. On 6 August Bór sent an angry message, stressing how Polish forces had assisted Britain since 1940 despite themselves receiving no assistance in 1939. It ended on a peremptory note: 'We do not ask for equipment – we demand it.'

Despite the ominous silence from the Russian guns, the Poles also attempted to contact Moscow. On 8 August Captain Kalugin – an escaped Soviet POW – tried to get into contact with both Stalin and General Rokossovsky by way of the Polish radio in Warsaw, which could only transmit messages to Moscow by way of London. He informed the USSR that

> in spite of the heroism of the Army and the entire Warsaw popula-
> tion, there are still needs, who [*sic*] if made good would permit a
> speedier victory over our common foe. These needs are: automatic
> arms, ammunition, grenades, anti-tank weapons.
>
> [NA, HS4/157]

There then followed a list of dropping places within the city. After Stalin's apparent offers of help to Mikołajczyk on 9 August, the Chiefs of Staff believed that Stalin had accepted responsibility for supplying the rebels. So, briefly, it seems, did the GOC Warsaw, who actually drew up plans for receiving a Russian liaison officer in the Kampinos Forest and communicated them to London on 10 August.

In the night of 8/9 August three aircraft flew to Warsaw from Brindisi and successfully dropped supplies on the southern region of the city, and three Halifaxes and two Liberators flew out the following night. The Halifaxes were briefed to drop to the receptions in the Kampinos Wood, where there were 3,000 men without arms and the two Liberators were to head for Napoleon Square in the city. The Halifaxes were successful but one Liberator suffered engine trouble and could not take off. The remaining Liberator found Napoleon Square under a dense pall of smoke so also dropped its load over the Kampinos Wood. All flights were cancelled to Poland on 10 and 11 August because of bad weather, but in the night of 12/13 August, 28 Liberators were sent to drop material directly over the city, although only 11 of the sorties were successful.

Inevitably, these small token drops were grossly inadequate and London continued to be inundated with demands for further flights. The Polish Government-in-Exile was informed by the Warsaw Command on 11 August that 'the soldiers and population of the capital look in vain at the skies waiting for help from the Allies [...] They feel surprised, deceived and begin to revile.' That same day, the Deputy Polish Prime Minister wrote to Churchill, who was in Italy, informing him that Warsaw would fall if there was not a more effective airlift involving at least 200 aircraft. The joint pressure of the Poles and the SOE resulted in a re-examination of the whole problem and the allocation of two extra squadrons of Liberators. Between 12 and 17 August ninety-three planes set off for Warsaw: seventeen failed to return and three crash-landed. On the 17th further flights to Warsaw were stopped in view of these high losses, although flights to the rest of Poland continued. Then, on 20 August, the Poles managed to gain permission for 1586 Flight to continue to fly to dropping points on Warsaw and its environs, but the losses were heavy and on the 27th all flights were again halted.

A new directive was issued to Air Vice-Marshal Elliot, giving priority 'to such Polish targets other than Warsaw [...] without incurring a wastage rate above normal'. Balkan Air Force interpreted this to mean that both Warsaw and the Kampinos Forest were ruled out. However, Elliot was persuaded by the extreme need for supplies in the Old Town to relax this rule. Seven planes with Polish crews were permitted to fly on 1 September to dropping points in the Kampinos Forest and the Kielce area. If this mission was a success, the Polish Flight would be able to fly to Warsaw the following night using a new dropping device invented by SOE, which enabled aircraft to keep above the level of short-range AA fire. Unfortunately, four out of seven of these planes were lost and operations were again suspended, but on 10 September a further mission of twenty aircraft took off for Warsaw. Five planes failed to return: one crash-landed over Yugoslavia and four went missing over Poland. Only five of the planes managed to find the correct dropping targets because of the huge cloud of dense smoke hanging over Warsaw. On the 13th two Polish aircraft reached Warsaw, and on the 21st the last supply mission was flown to Warsaw from Italy by five South African planes, which dropped supplies over the Kampinos Forest.

The minimum needed each night to keep Warsaw fighting was ninety containers or seven planes each night. It was a rare occurrence when this happened, but the Polish Chief of Staff in London informed SOE on 21 August that, even though Warsaw had not received this minimum over the past fortnight, 'no matter how small the deliveries they will be of great value and will enable the garrison to hold out'. On the ground in Warsaw, the paucity of flights from Italy caused great disappointment and growing anger with the West. For instance, an 'Appeal of the Women of Poland to Anglo-Saxon Women', dated 28 August, reminded their 'sisters' in the West that 'the community was accustomed to believe in the honesty of the Anglo-Saxon nations, it believed that with these nations behind words go acts, and that behind promises comes fulfilment'. A week earlier, on 20 August, the GOC Warsaw angrily informed London that 'There were no drops on or around Warsaw since the night of 16/17. You do not even bother to explain why not. We are astounded by your indifference and your English phlegm'. Such remarks were understandable. Of course it was too little too late, but nevertheless it did represent a considerable effort in blood and resources. The total tonnage dropped for August was 97.71, but, in terms of Warsaw's needs, this was a drop in the bucket! Ironically, as Robert Forczyk has pointed out, on the nights of 26 and 29 August two raids – each involving over 170 Lancaster bombers – took place against Königsberg, which was in fact some 45 miles further from the bomber bases in Lincolnshire than Warsaw. Königsberg was not a military target and was well within the Russian sphere of operations. Undoubtedly these two raids show that the RAF had the ability to operate in strength over Central Poland and, if this had been used to supply Warsaw, Forczyk is right to argue that 'the AK might have received enough arms to blunt the German attacks'.

Nevertheless, Norman Davies has called the Warsaw Airlift one of the 'great unsung sagas of the Second World War'. Warsaw was some 815 miles from Brindisi. The planes were not escorted by fighters and could only defend themselves with their own guns. There was a *Luftwaffe* night-fighter training centre near Kraków, visibility over Warsaw was badly hampered by a dense pall of smoke, and the planes had to make the approach run at 150 feet at the limited speed of 125 miles. On the way back they would frequently run into electric storms over the Alps. The extreme hazards of the flight are recalled by Henry Lloyd-Lyne, who flew with 178 Squadron. On the night of 13/14 August twenty-four Liberators took off

about 8 o'clock, and of course we had to fly over enemy territory practically the whole of the way. Didn't have a lot of trouble; met up with one Messerschmitt 109, but he didn't even bother to attack [. . .] Then the Canadian pilot, Flying Officer Dougie Mac Rae said to me, 'There should be a river visible,' and I said, 'Yes there is,' and he said, 'That's the Vistula.' Navigating that far and coming spot bang right over the Vistula, I thought was great. Then Doug had to turn to fly up the Vistula, those were the briefing instructions, and it wasn't more than a few minutes passed by, fairly quickly, we could see what was ahead of us, and it was nothing but a huge pall of smoke. In between you'd get red glows that were obviously fires, and that was all we could see of Warsaw. We had to fly up and pass over three bridges and turn to port after the third bridge, that was said to bring us to Pryziński Square, where Polish females fighting in the Home Army would be holding hurricane lamps in the form of a cross, and that's where we were supposed to drop the supplies.

The canisters were in the bomb bay, just like bombs. I think it was 12 × 500 bomb canisters. At about the second bridge the anti-aircraft fire was really intensive, and this was the moment that saved my life [...] Doug came over the intercom and he said, 'Lloyd, go back to the beam guns; you'll be able to help silence the ground fire and be more advantage there than dropping the supplies. I'll get Gordon [the navigator] to nip down and drop the supplies when we are over the target.' So with that I got up immediately, never thinking for one moment I wasn't going to be back there again, left my parachute, and went back onto the beam guns, opened up both starboard and port apertures, stuck the guns out and started to fire at the ground. I can also of course hear and realise that the mid-upper gunner and the rear gunner are also firing a hell of a lot onto the ground [...] and I could see that the outer port engine was on fire [...] it wasn't long before the port inner was on fire as well, in fact the whole wing looked to be on fire [...] the anti-aircraft shells were coming through the bottom of the aircraft and going out through the top. I likened them then, and still do, to cricket balls that were on fire ...

[H. Lloyd-Lyne, IWM, 97/23/1]

Astonishingly, the plane managed to reach the dropping zone and actually dropped the supplies before crashing in a 'wooded area'. Lloyd-Lyne was the only member of the crew to survive, probably because the explosion of one of the plane's fuel tanks threw him clear. He was found by the Germans on a small island in a lake in Paderewski Park and taken to an army medical centre.

September: Hanging On
On 2 September Bór issued the following message for the Government-in-Exile in London:

Campaign Chronicle

The loss of Stare Miasto/Old Town has made a serious breach in our defence system. I reckon with increased enemy pressure on other districts aiming at successive liquidation of our resistance.

I have decided to continue the defence of Warsaw to the utmost.

We have food until 7 September, bread until 5 September, ammunition nearly exhausted, how long it will last depends on the intensity of fighting.

Morale of troops good, civilians suffer from lack of food, water, accommodation, clothing and diseases. Their morale is lowering and depends on hope for speedy ending of fight or increase of assistance.

Possibility of further resistance depends not only on our endurance but above all on supplies from you or successes of Soviet armies in our streets.

[NA, HS4/156]

Initially, it did not seem that much more help was forthcoming. Mikołajczyk's urgent request for the dispatch of the Polish Independent Parachute Brigade to Warsaw was again met with refusal from the British Chiefs of Staff on the understandable grounds that this would lead to devastating losses of both men and planes. They pointed out on 9 September that 'few of the men dropped would land uninjured in the parts of the city held by the Home Army'.

In the meantime the Germans, increasingly worried that the Russians would renew their advance and occupy Praga – from where they would be able to cross the Vistula – attacked the riverside suburb of Powiśle and had, by 6 September, forced the insurgents to withdraw. There followed the usual brutal shooting of prisoners and wounded, which set off a mass exodus into the city centre, and led to increasing desperation and depression amongst the civil population. The Germans then began to attack the eastern part of the city centre, and took the Central station and the Polonia Hotel but failed, after two days of intense fighting, to cut the insurgents' north–south communication corridor. Dirlewanger's SS regiment and Reck's *Kampfgruppe*, after a massive air and artillery bombardment, managed to push back the insurgents along Nowy Świat towards Napoleon Square.

The very real possibility of surrender now hung in the air. On 8 September Bór accepted von dem Bach's offer of a two-hour truce on the western sector of the front line, so that civilians could be evacuated. He radioed to the Government-in-Exile that only immediate bombing of

The Polish Underground 1939–1947

German positions and the dispatch of supplies by the Allies could save Warsaw. He was informed, in reply, that the chances of such operations were virtually nil and that, therefore, he was authorized to surrender if the AK leadership and the Government Delegate so decided. Meanwhile, General Rohr sent the Polish High Command conditions for surrender, which guaranteed that the Home Army would receive combatant rights as POWs and the civilian population would be evacuated to safety. On the 9th Bór even got as far as drafting a letter of surrender but the message was never dispatched since, for the first time for five weeks, Soviet fighter planes were seen above Warsaw, and the following day artillery fire was heard from Praga, where the Soviets had commenced their attack against the German IV SS Panzerkorps. By 14 September all the key German positions east of the Vistula had been overrun and the Germans assumed that Soviet troops would cross the river. The Poles still held the Czerniaków district, which would form an invaluable bridge-head on the west bank. To eliminate this now became a priority for the Germans. On 11 September Dirlewanger's troops managed to sever the corridor linking the city centre with Czerniaków, which, by the following day, was completely cut off.

However, the Red Army did not attempt a large-scale river crossing. At most, the Soviets were prepared to take only token actions, possibly to appease the Western Allies. Limited airdrops of food and equipment took place after 14 September but much of the equipment was damaged because parachutes were not used. Similarly, only very limited radio contact functioned between the Warsaw command and General Rokossovsky's headquarters. In the night of 15/16 September soldiers from the 3rd Infantry Division of the Polish People's Army (Berling's Army) attempted to cross the Vistula in small boats and join up with the surviving AK troops of the Radosław Group, who were still holding a small enclave on the left bank. The first wave was relatively successful but the second wave ran into concentrated fire from the Germans. The Soviet barrage of smoke bombs only helped reveal where the boats were. Further reinforcements crossed the Vistula on the nights of 17/18 and 18/19 September, and a few more units landed in Marymount, north of Żoliborz. Altogether, the total number of Berling's troops to land on both bridgeheads was about 1,500 men – but they suffered some 5,000 casualties whilst trying to cross the Vistula. The troops themselves were of poor quality. The great majority were Polish peasants conscripted unwillingly from the Lublin region in July, and who had scarcely any military training, unless they had fought in September 1939. Dumped into the intense fighting in Czerniaków, they proved, in many cases, to be unreliable and even useless. In the end, each 'Berlinger' was twinned with an AK soldier who, if necessary, would use the former's weapons.

The crossing of Berling's troops made the Germans even more determined to crush the bridgeheads as soon as possible. They pressed on with remorseless attacks from the north, west, and south, wearing down Lieutenant Colonel Masurkiewicz's (alias 'Radosław') forces. On 19 September he decided to withdraw the last 200 troops through the sewers. One platoon of the Zośka Battalion, under Captain Bielous (alias 'Jerzy'), continued to defend a small group of houses until 23 September, in the hope that, even now, Soviet troops would land, but this was to prove a will o' the wisp. Despite pleas for ammunition, food and above all troops, the military efforts of the Soviets were confined to artillery fire on the German positions. The Russians promised to send pontoons to pick up Bielous's troops, but these never materialized. In the end, with about sixty troops, Bielous attempted to break through to the AK positions in the centre of the city, but only Bielous himself, two soldiers and a messenger girl made it.

Five days before the final rout of Berling's troops and the fall of Czerniaków occurred Warsaw's one last moment of hope. Stalin had at last agreed, on 10 September, that American planes could supply Warsaw and then land on bases in Poltava, but the operation was constantly postponed until the 18th when, in fine autumn weather, 110 bombers took off. They filled the skies over Warsaw and dropped just under 1,300 containers from between 14,000 and 16,000 feet in bombing formation. Initially they were greeted with great enthusiasm, but depression rapidly followed exhilaration:

> We had a splendid exhibition of Allied air power – but the majority of the containers fell beyond our lines, on the very places which a week or ten days before had been held by the Home Army. The vast crowd of people who had been shouting and cheering bowed their heads and returned to their cellars [...] had the 1,800 [*sic*] containers been dropped in the first days of the rising [...] the whole of Warsaw would undoubtedly have been freed of the enemy.
>
> [Bór-Komorowski, p. 350]

A report reaching London shortly after the drop stated 228 containers were collected by the insurgents while, according to the estimates of the Polish commander, at least a hundred more had probably fallen into Polish hands, either military or civilian.

The massive American sortie of 18 September was only of marginal assistance. It did not prevent the fall of Czerniaków, and von dem Bach was able to launch an attack on Mokotów on the 24th. As the Germans had come to the conclusion that a Russian attack across the Vistula was not imminent, his forces were reinforced by the 19th Panzer Division and a part of the Hermann Göring Parachute-Panzer Regiment. As usual, the AK units fought tenaciously, but sheer force overwhelmed them and on the 27th the whole of Mokotów was at last occupied by the Germans. The 2,000 Polish insurgents captured were given POW status.

Two days later, on the 29th, the Germans launched a massive attack on Żoliborz from the south with artillery and tank support. Again they were tenaciously opposed but, on the first day, despite the arrival of a few anti-tank weapons from the Red Army across the Vistula, the Germans managed to occupy nearly half the district. Colonel Chruściel made contact with troops of the Polish People's Army across the river and was assured that, at 11 a.m. on the 30th, pontoons, together with artillery and air cover, would be provided so that his troops could cross to the right bank of the river. While they were attempting to break through the German positions to the river, he received news that the rescue was postponed until 7 p.m. To stop further bloodshed, as negotiations were about to begin with the Germans, Bór ordered the survivors to surrender.

Surrender

With the fall of Czerniaków and Mokotów, the Germans had essentially won the Battle of Warsaw and were in position to crush the remaining insurgent pockets with overwhelming strength. Food supplies were exhausted and the population was near starvation. Adequate help was not to be expected from either the Western Allies or the Russians. There was, therefore, little option but to surrender. On the 27th von dem Bach had already proposed surrender negotiations. After discussions with the surviving senior AK officers and the Delegate, who all gave their consent to negotiations, Bór sent envoys to the Germans, asking for clarification of their proposals. Von dem Bach, who wished to bring the fighting to a conclusion as soon as possible, in reply proposed evacuation of the civilian population and the granting of POW combatant rights to the Home Army. On the 30th Polish Red Cross emissaries signed a ceasefire agreement with the Germans with effect from 5.30 a.m. on 1 October to 6.30 a.m. on 2 October, to enable the evacuation of the civil population

Campaign Chronicle

to take place, although initially very few availed themselves of this opportunity. On 2 October the Poles signed the surrender document and the fighting ceased at 9 p.m. The Germans had agreed to treat all AK and AL soldiers who had fought in Warsaw as POWs and to deal humanely with the civilians, although all would have to leave the city.

The last messages coming from Warsaw were defiant and more unrelenting towards the Russians than to the Germans. Bór, in his final order of the day, stated on 3 October:

> The capitulation of the capital does not signify that we have made peace with the Germans, and Poland, which has fought the Germans during five years of occupation, will not today, even after this brave defeat, being in so unenviable a situation, cease to fight. The demands of Moscow were worse than surrender to the enemy. We would rather die than agree to these conditions. The Soviets wanted to deport us and destroy us in the same way as the 10,000 victims of Katyń.
>
> [NA, HS4/156]

The *Biuletyn Informacyny* stressed that the AK surrendered as 'the best army in the world' and appealed to Poles:

> Do not believe those who say that with the fall of Warsaw the heart of the Polish nation is broken. This is only a transient failure, which will soon pass, and Warsaw will rise again as of old, as before 1939. Goodbye fellow countrymen. Do not think badly of us.
>
> [NA, HS4/156]

General Chruściel defended the surrender to his soldiers:

> We had two alternatives – Siberia or a POW camp, and after long and anxious thought, we selected the second. Every one of you will understand that the fall of Germany is certain, and may be expected any moment, and we shall then be free, while on the other hand people rarely, if ever, return from Siberia.
>
> [NA, HS4/156]

Further west, near Kraków, Major Dziura-Dziurski observed, when his partisans heard the news of Warsaw's capitulation, 'anger and determination in their faces. Had an order been issued to march against the

165

Anglo-American Allies, it would not have surprised me if all or most of them had marched!'

In Warsaw the military evacuation took from 3 to 5 October. The Home Army units marched off in long columns to the entry points in the German lines:

> They were all wearing their red-and-white brassards and their White Eagle badges. The men had their weapons shouldered – anything from captured *Panzerfausts* to sten guns, rifles and revolvers. The women were carrying their first-aid kits, postbags and radio equipment. They were nearly all overpoweringly, sensationally, young.
>
> [Davies, *Rising '44*, p. 437]

The columns then marched on to Ozarów station, where they were entrained and sent to prisoner-of-war camps in Germany. Bór and Chruściel were taken under very tight security to Berlin and thence to Oflag 73 in Langwasser, near Nuremberg. In February 1945 they were moved to Colditz.

Some 500,000 civilians were also forced to leave the city and walk to the transit camp at Pruszków. One of the evacuees compared 'our Polish exodus' to the exile of the Jews from Egypt. Most of the civilians remained in the area of the General Government, but some 90,000 were conscripted for forced labour and another 60,000 – in violation of the surrender terms – were sent to concentration camps.

They left behind them a shattered city, where at least 15,000 AK soldiers and probably 200,000 civilians had died. The German losses were about 16,000 dead and 9,000 wounded. While Warsaw capitulated, the Red Army looked on in silence. As Norman Davies has observed, 'the largest army in the world pretended not to be there'. In fact, although locked in bitter conflict with the *Wehrmacht* elsewhere, here, on the Vistula, 'the two armies were acting in silent, unwritten connivance'.

The Civilian Population During the Uprising

The uprising cannot be considered from a purely military angle. The mood of the people inevitably impacted on the morale of the insurgents, and in the final analysis they could not have continued to fight without the tacit support of the people. The crucial aim of the uprising was to ensure that a free civil Polish administration of the city was in place before the Russians entered. To achieve this the uprising would have to be rapid and successful. The failure to seize the whole city meant that Warsaw was divided up initially into disconnected and uncoordinated fragments. In the first few days it was the AK that provided the administration. It was not until 9 August that regional delegates were appointed to administer those parts of Warsaw still in the insurgents' hands. At the lowest level, there were the block and house commanders and their elected committees, on whose work the effectiveness of the administration was essentially dependent. Their duties included organizing air-raid precautions and a fire-fighting service, ensuring adequate supplies of water and sand, as well as finding accommodation for refugees from other areas of the city and checking on food supplies for the people for whom they were responsible. Instructions, orders and information were communicated to the civil population through the house and block committees, posters, newspapers and the civilian radio station, Polskie Radio Warszawa. A limited field post was delivered by boy scouts.

The main task of the civil administration was to keep the city infrastructure functioning as well as possible and for as long as possible, which was equally vital both to the military and public interest. As long as the power station in Powiśle was in Polish hands there was sufficient electricity to supply insurgent Warsaw. When it fell on 5 September, accumulators had to be built and charged by petrol engines for supplying hospitals, workshops for the AK, and lights in the sewer tunnels. The supply of water also posed great problems, once the Germans took the municipal waterworks on Filtrowa Street on 14 August, thereby cutting off the city's central water supply. To overcome this, wells were dug, often by German POWs. The most intractable problem facing the civil population of Warsaw was hunger, although this was alleviated by soup kitchens and, in Mokotów, by the availability of allotments and vegetable gardens.

The outbreak of the rising was generally greeted with enthusiasm, and this almost certainly played a role in persuading the insurgents to continue fighting even after they had failed in the first few days to take the city. By mid-August, with no prospect of a decisive breakthrough, the initial euphoria had cooled, but thanks to the civil administration and the ability to improvise, the inhabitants of Warsaw appeared to grow used to the daily struggle for survival. However, with the fall of the Old Town and Powiśle in early September, morale reached crisis point and almost certainly persuaded Bór to consider capitulation. The evacuation arranged by the Polish Red Cross, with German permission, on 8 September was a safety valve, in that it enabled some 6,000 of the most demoralized members of the population of the Śródmieście (city centre) to quit. With the renewal of Soviet military activity on the opposite bank of the Vistula and the American airdrop of 18 September, there was a marked upsurge in morale, but this was shortlived and, inevitably, morale declined again sharply until the surrender.

Joanna Hanson, in her book *The Civilian Population and the Warsaw Uprising of 1944*, argues that the refusal of the inhabitants to leave Warsaw did not necessarily mean that they totally supported the uprising. Essentially, given the cruelty of the Germans, 'the choice for the citizens [...] was between staying in the city, which although a risk to life at least kept them among their own people in a small piece of "Free Poland", and leaving the city to an unknown fate'. This of course played a key role in prolonging the uprising and stopped its political opponents and critics from leaving. It is also worth stressing that the bond between soldier and civilian was very close, as many families had a son, husband or father fighting and often the soldiers fought in the vicinity of their own homes.

The Three Polands, October 1944

As Richard Lukas observed, the 'Warsaw Uprising doomed the Poles in the capital to defeat and destroyed the heart of the political and military institutions of the Polish Underground'. Although the AK survived for another three months, it was so weakened that it could no longer seriously influence the course of Polish politics or indeed military events. Bór, just before he surrendered to the Germans, appointed his chief of staff, General Okulicki, to be his successor as Commander of the Home Army. He had been parachuted into Poland from Italy only a few months before and the *Gestapo* knew nothing of his existence. To avoid captivity he and his staff officers left Warsaw individually.

By October 1944 Poland was effectively divided into three distinct areas, each administered by different authorities. East of the Bug was the area claimed by the Soviet Union in September 1939 and now once again integrated into the USSR. Between the Bug and the Vistula there was a provisional authority – the Polish Committee of National Liberation (PKWN) based in Lublin – although in reality power lay with the Soviet occupying forces, who had direct control over both the army and the security forces. West of the Vistula lay what remained of the General Government and the annexed territories still under German control.

Campaign Chronicle

East of the Bug there was little scope for resistance against the Soviet occupying forces. As Stalin considered this Soviet territory, the population was subject to Soviet laws. Political activists from the parties that supported the Underground State were rapidly arrested, as were any AK soldiers betrayed by informers. The AK commander of the Wilno district reported to the Polish Government in London on 22 August that the Soviets, were 'carrying out a hostile policy of extermination [...] Several thousand men had already been deported for labour to Russia.' Another report from the Lwów district on 11 September revealed that in Złoczów women between the ages of eighteen and twenty-five were being recruited for work in the Donatesk coalfield, and that virtually all AK members seized by the Soviets were deported to camps in the USSR.

Opposition to the Polish Committee of National Liberation

Once the members of the PKWN arrived in Chełm, they assumed the powers of a government, thereby completely overriding the delegacy and the structures that had been in place since 1940. They were, however, subject to General Nicolai Bulganin, who was appointed the Soviet plenipotentiary for the liberated Polish territories. The security service was composed of a Soviet-trained special battalion and new units of the citizens' militia, which was formed of ex-AL members, and the police. Stanisław Radkiewicz, who was later to become Minister for Public Security, was put in charge of internal security. Over the next few months the PKWN had only very limited success in establishing its control over the Soviet-occupied territories, as its writ did not run outside the towns. Initially, Gomulka and other leaders of the Communist Underground movement continued to talk of cooperation with the AK and the 'democratic wing' of the London Government, but in practice this proved elusive. On 15 August, for example, the PKWN announced conscription for all eligible males, but the AK advised its members to avoid registration.

In September an Allied mission, under the command of Colonel Sanders, visited the V-2 site at Blizna. Despite his Soviet minders, Sanders was able to gain some interesting impressions of the PKWN regime in the Lublin area. In the forward areas he found relations between the Red Army and the population surprisingly good, but in the back areas there was 'a very noticeable atmosphere of distrust' towards the Russians, and in Lublin itself a 'whole company' of the NKVD was seen marching down the street. Nevertheless, Sanders was able to make some contact with the Polish population. He gathered that conscription was particularly unpopular, as the officers of the new Polish People's Army were all Russian. Some of the conscripts were quartered in Majdanek concentration camp, part of which had been converted to barracks. He was also told that they were poorly fed and were 'virtually prisoners', as they were not allowed passes into Lublin:

> Everywhere we went (except in the forward areas) there were posters with portraits and short descriptions of the nine or ten chief members of the Lublin Committee. Other posters dealt with conscription, giving up of wireless sets, giving up of arms and payment of social insurance instalments. In addition, all along the roads, there were numerous billboards with slogans in Russian and Polish, such as 'Long Live the Red Army!' and 'Glory to our Great Leader Stalin!'

> [NA, HS4/146]

There was even some lingering faith in help from the Western Allies. Sanders heard a story from his American colleagues about an American plane that had made a forced landing near Lublin. The crew marched into town to be immediately surrounded by Poles who shouted, 'Thank God you have come. Please free us from the Russians!' Tragically, nothing, of course, could have been further from the truth. Consequently, faced by the impotence of the Western Allies in Poland, what could the Poles do? In Janów County it appears, according to Marek Chodakiewicz, that 'initially the non collaborationists rather successfully adjusted their *modus vivendi* to the challenges of the new occupation'. The AK and its allies simply reverted to the tactics of early 1940. All partisan units were disbanded, members of the Underground were again ordered to spread propaganda, gather Intelligence, set up safe houses and infiltrate the local administration, the army and police. Dr Klukowski confided to his diary that 'our entire organization is going underground once again and we are beginning a new period of conspiracy'. In Szczebrzeszyn, the local Home Army inspector, 'Adam', went into hiding and only appeared from time to time to attend secret conferences in safe houses, while in Janów County the district doctor and the head of the draft board were both members of the AK. Many other former members of the Underground volunteered for work in the local administration and in the village councils. However, the leadership of the Independentists was adamant that its members should avoid being drafted into the army, boycott the

Communist Party, and attempt to block forced-food deliveries from the farms to the Red Army and PKWN.

In August 1944 remaining above ground or marching to Warsaw to assist the uprising was not an option for AK members once the front had rolled on. The escaped British POW Sergeant Rofe personally witnessed, in August, a group of 600 Poles from the Lwów area marching through the town of Grodziska en route for Warsaw. They were stopped by a small group of Russian soldiers who ordered them to go no further. When they disregarded this and proceeded, they were surrounded by a much stronger force of tanks and cavalry. The unit was disarmed, the men ordered to join the Polish People's Army, and the officers arrested. The other ranks rapidly deserted and were hiding in the countryside when Rofe last saw them, and he was doubtful whether food stocks in the villages were sufficient to feed the population.

Klukowski's diary gives an illuminating account of day-to-day life in 'Lublin Poland'. It chronicles both passive and active resistance, as well as the relentless pressure exerted by the NKVD. In August he reported that in the Lublin area the Home Army organization was 'falling apart' and that its members were scattered throughout the region, working in the fields, helping with the harvest, or else doing nothing. However, on 24 August in Zamość Major 'Wacław' – the Commanding Officer of the 9th Infantry Regiment and AK District Inspector – decided to disobey the order issued by the PKWN to register for conscription into the People's Army of Poland, and immediately began to reorganize the local AK units to go and fight in Warsaw. At the same time he issued a statement of loyalty to the Soviet Army, stressing the desire to fight jointly against the German enemy. The details of this decision were then taken for approval to the Commandant of the Home Army in Lublin with a request for a rapid reply, but a decision could not be taken until all the inspectors from Lublin province were present. Given the scale of NKVD activity, such a meeting was increasingly difficult to organize. Every day Klukowski received news of key members of the Underground either being arrested or betrayed to the NKVD. Consequently, in Szczebrzeszyn, the Underground decided at a meeting at the end of August not to organize any new combat units but to concentrate instead on educating the people and organizing a common front against Communism, while still keeping in close touch with all Home Army personnel, so they could be mobilized at short notice. But maintaining contact was not easy. The AK officers, even if they escaped arrest by the NKVD, had little control over their former units. To survive they had to remain in hiding and were often so well hidden that it was virtually impossible to contact them. Many units could only survive by robbery and intimidation. At the end of December 1944 the Home Army was 'virtually non-existent' in the Biłgoraj district and the former Peasant Battalions were rallying to the PKWN en masse.

The NKVD also attempted – not always successfully – to prevent former members of the Underground State from playing any role in local politics or administration. Initially, in Zamość a local banker, Antoni Wiacek (or 'Janusz Sandomierski' as he was known in the Underground), presided over the meetings of the county officials. His deputy, Judge Witoszka (who had the Underground name of 'Marek'), and several other key officials were all loyal to the London Government. Their agenda ranged from rebuilding the county's administration to reorganizing its social and economic life. Reopening the schools and the appointment of teachers was a particularly important task. Under pressure from the NKVD, Wiacek was forced to resign on 3 August in favour of one Dubiel, a member of the Polish Workers' Party. At a stroke this made the situation in the Zamość region much more hazardous for the supporters of the London Government. In Lublin, too, the representative of the London Government was dismissed, but Biłgoraj and Hrubieszów were temporarily taken over by units of the AK and the administration firmly put into the hands of the supporters of the London Government.

It was clearly a confused period of transition. The NKVD was hardly going to accept the presence of those loyal to London in leading positions. In his diary, Klukowski recorded on 20 August that the 'Soviets were slowly widening their influence'. Dubiel, accompanied by a Russian colonel, toured the region inspecting the Communes, and in Szczebrzeszyn the Soviet Commandant took control of the administration. The NKVD requisitioned rooms in the Zamoyski chateau and showed great interest in the cellars – most likely, as Klukowski observed, for use as a future prison.

The Soviet/PKWN takeover of the Lublin area did not go unchallenged. On 7 October, for instance, the AK achieved a spectacular success when it sprang some twenty prisoners from the Zamość jail without killing a single jailor, and also leaving the real criminals and Germans still behind bars. However, by November 1944 constant NKVD raids and betrayals had virtually broken the remaining AK forces, while fear and exhaustion were alienating the population. As an escape from the daily terror, growing numbers of young men were joining the Polish People's Army. By December 1944 Soviet-occupied Poland – despite the still-unrepressed 'banditry' – was becoming increasingly Sovietized. The press had been taken over by the Communists. Factories, offices and the public utilities were in the course of nationalization, and the break-up of the big landed estates was accelerated. To most Poles under the Lublin Government there seemed little difference between the Soviet and German occupation.

The Re-establishment of the Underground State in the General Government

The Government Delegate, the Cabinet, the Council of National Unity and the Delegacy departments, which had all been based in Warsaw, were not committed to surrender by the terms of the capitulation of 2 October. They therefore did not need to disclose themselves to the Germans and were able to escape in the mass exodus from Warsaw. Some leaders, to avoid detection, attached themselves to the Central Welfare Council or the Polish Red Cross, while others sought anonymity in the mass of the fleeing population. In the final days of the uprising, the Department for Internal Affairs had drawn up plans for locating key officials either in Kraków or the small towns along the electric suburban railway line, such Pruszków and Grodzisk. The areas along this line rapidly became packed with refugees, but after the hell of Warsaw, it seemed almost a paradise. Stefan Korboński, Head of the Directorate for Civil Resistance, recalled years later:

> We were having regular meals, and we lived in houses equipped with intact windows and electric light. Water, too, was plentiful, and we spent hours on end in the bathrooms. What with clean beds, we felt as if we were in paradise. The rising was gradually receding in our memories like a terrible but splendid dream. The Germans were everywhere but they were unable to control the wanderings of the populace of a great city.
>
> [Korboński, *Fighting Warsaw*, p. 40]

On 18 October the Government Delegate, Jankowski, issued a proclamation declaring that 'the Home Cabinet and Council of National Unity have left Warsaw [...] to continue to carry on their constitutional duties outside the capital'. It also formally dissolved various ad hoc administrative bodies that had sprung up outside Warsaw during the siege, in the belief that the whole Underground leadership would perish in the uprising. The most immediate problem facing the Delegacy was the fate of the hundreds of thousands expelled from Warsaw. In practice there was little that could be done apart from appealing to the people in the General Government to come to the aid of the homeless and generously share their accommodation with them. Similarly, appeals were made to the Germans not to plunder and destroy what was left of Warsaw, but these fell on deaf ears and by December Warsaw was reduced to a desert of rubble. It was vital to re-establish radio contact with London and the individual areas of AK commands (inspectorates). Several transmitters, including 'the American beauty', had been buried in hiding places beneath the rubble in Warsaw, while others were placed in a coffin in a cemetery. When attempts to construct a transmitter failed, a boy was sent back to retrieve the 'American beauty', which he managed to smuggle out of Warsaw despite German checks. Put to the test, it functioned perfectly and was able to make contact with London.

The Underground Government was rapidly re-established. Most of its staff were located along the suburban electric railway, which the *Gestapo* nicknamed 'Little London'. Within a few days contact was established with the Government Delegate, Jankowski, and the High Command of the AK based 'somewhere on the Częstochowa–Kraków line'. Within a couple of weeks, three key departments had managed to recreate their organizations, find new hiding places for their work and gather most of their staff together. The Department of Press and Information was once again able to issue the government's official paper, the *Republic*, while the Department for Labour and Social Welfare began to channel through the Polish Red Cross and the Central Welfare Council money for assisting evacuees and hospitals. The Department for Internal Affairs had also been resurrected and made contact with both the military authorities and civil districts.

The first conference held between the military and civil leaders of the Resistance was held in November in Piotrków Trybunalski, in the monastery that had originally sheltered the members of the National Government during the rebellion of 1863. The three departmental directors each gave progress reports on their departments, but the meeting was a melancholy affair, which was primarily given over to a review of the international situation, the inevitability of the Soviet occupation, and the crisis within the Polish Government-in-Exile in London, where Prime Minister Mikołajczyk was about to resign (*see page 175*). The decision was taken to oppose any territorial concessions to the USSR and to continue the struggle. When Korboński retired to sleep in one of the monastery's cells, 'thoughts', as he later wrote in his memoirs, 'chased through [his] mind, each more gloomy than the one before. One wave of enemies was receding, another was advancing.'

The Moscow Conference, October 1944

In October 1944 Churchill again attempted to find a solution to the Polish question. He persuaded Stalin to agree to Mikołajczyk joining him for talks in Moscow in October. The Polish Premier was ready to go, provided that the Conference took note of the memorandum issued by the Polish Council of Ministers in London on 29 August 1944. The essence of this was that the PPR and the four parties represented in the London Government should each be given an equal share in a new Polish Government to be formed in Warsaw after the defeat of Germany. In foreign affairs the aim was to negotiate a durable Polish–Soviet alliance, but the final Polish eastern frontier could only be decided by a 'Constitutional Diet in accordance with democratic principles'.

Mikołajczyk brushed aside Churchill's suggestion that a compromise between the demands of the PKWN and the London Government was possible and stuck to the power-sharing proposals in his memorandum. Stalin refused point-blank to see the PKWN effectively marginalized, and at the same time insisted that the Curzon Line be recognized as Poland's future eastern frontier. Under pressure from Churchill, Mikołajczyk realized that the Curzon Line would have to be accepted, although he did not immediately concede this. More lethal still was Stalin's demand for the fusion of the legitimate London Government with the PKWN. This meant, in Mikołajczyk's words, that Poland's independence would effectively 'be effaced by the rule of agents of the Comintern in Poland'. He concluded accurately that the Polish Government was expected to 'commit suicide of its own volition'. Consequently, much to Churchill's annoyance, he rejected Stalin's invitation to Poland to participate in the new government. Nevertheless, once back in London, he stressed to his Cabinet the inevitability of recognizing the Curzon Line. When this was rejected, he resigned and was replaced by Tomasz Arciszewski, who, despite being a Socialist, was utterly opposed to doing a deal with Stalin, and the London Government became increasingly marginalized.

The AK's Attempt to Re-group, October 1944–January 1945

Okulicki left Warsaw on 3 October disguised as a civilian and escaped from a convoy bound for Germany. He managed to arrive safely at the District Headquarters at Radom and eventually set up his headquarters in Częstochowa. His work was initially hampered by the refusal of the Government-in-Exile to approve his appointment, as he was too closely identified with Sosnkowski but, on the insistence of the Government Delegate, Jankowski, it relented and recognized him as Commander of the Home Army.

After the fall of Warsaw, the Home Army in the General Government found itself in deep crisis. The AK units that had been mobilized during the uprising were sent underground again, as there were not enough weapons and munitions to keep them fully mobilized. In December Okulicki sent a pessimistic dispatch to London:

> Many provincial units, and in particular those which were operating in the Kampinos Forest, have been destroyed, while the soldiers of these units have taken shelter in the area on their own or in small groups. In the desperate situation in which these people find themselves, there lies the danger of the transformation of these small groups into common plundering bands or of their defection to the People's Army.
>
> [Quoted in Krystina Kersten, *The Establishment of Communist Rule in Poland*, p. 114]

On 26 October Okulicki issued his 'Guidelines for activity during the winter period 1944/45'. He recognized that the AK needed time to recuperate and regroup. He cancelled *Tempest* and the original instructions that the AK should disclose their identities to the advancing Red Army. He also stressed the importance of consolidating all military organizations under the AK and 'preparing for the worst' by adapting the resistance organization so that it could 'last out a possible Soviet occupation'. The instructions from London in November were less clear and appeared to be an attempt to square the circle: the AK was to continue the struggle against the Germans but to avoid actions that would provoke German repression. To the advancing Red Army, the Government-in-Exile thought that 'partial, even minimal disclosure [of AK units] would be useful as before'. As the historian Krystina Kersten observed, this 'plan was in all respects half-cocked and unrealistic'.

Supply and Liaison

The weakness of the AK was exacerbated by the reluctance of Britain and America to risk flying supply sorties over General-Government territory. The Polish Government and the acting head of the Polish Army, General

Tatar, exerted constant pressure on the SOE and the Air Ministry to resume flights both from Italy and Britain. Selborne, Gubbins and the members of the Polish Section of the SOE were sympathetic. Lord Selborne wrote in October to the Air Minister, Sir Archibald Sinclair, heartily supporting the proposal 'because it is our bounden duty to help this army of such proven gallantry'. Lieutenant Colonel Threlfall (Commander of SOE 'Force 139' in Italy) reported on 5 October that the meteorological officer of 334 Wing had forecast that in the late autumn/ early winter quarter there would be only twelve nights with suitable flying conditions. Provided, therefore, that thirty planes flew on each of those nights from Brindisi, it would be possible to supply AK units around Radom, Piotrków and Kraków with the minimum equipment for their operations. Mediterranean Allied air forces did agree to make available thirty aircraft, but in October and November there were only eight sorties flown, dropping a mere 10 tons. This was partly because of poor weather, but more importantly the Red Army had advanced to within 100 miles of Budapest, and Stalin resolutely refused to allow Allied planes to fly over Soviet-occupied territory. The alternative route, via Denmark, was deemed to be too great a risk for British pilots because of the strength of German fighter forces, although the Poles were free to risk such flights. This elicited from Lieutenant Colonel Perkins on 20 November a scathing comment:

> The RAF have [...] refused to operate British aircraft in view of a report that 'nearly all aircraft reported flak and one saw [a] night fighter'. This does not surprise us very much for we have always understood that this is what one expected to meet if one flies over enemy territory.
>
> [NA, HS4/156]

Perkins was also bitterly critical of the ruling that only Poles could risk these dangers, observing that it was 'intolerable that the Poles should be asked to undertake greater risks than our own men'.

Dispatch of the British Military Mission to Poland

After the fall of Warsaw the British Government had virtually no reliable information about Poland and decided at last to send liaison officers. The government may well have been prompted into this action by rumours of the imminent evacuation of Sergeant John Ward in November, who had, in effect, acted as an unofficial liaison officer in Warsaw during the uprising. His telegrams were almost the only information the British Government had received from Warsaw and consequently attracted considerable attention. According to Perkins, when the FO heard that Ward was leaving Poland, 'they threw up their hands in horror. Quietly paced up and down their marble corridors and decided that Corporal [sic] Ward must be replaced by fully-fledged Portman [British] observers.' The Poles were informed of this decision in early November. Besides acting as conduits for information, Perkins told Tatar and three of his colleagues on 1 November that he hoped they would also be able to act 'as shields if, and when, the Red Army penetrates more deeply into Poland'. Tabor welcomed the decision, which he had persistently advocated since 1940. However, given the 'rather delicate' situation at the headquarters of the Home Army, which was being reorganized, he cautioned that the area commanders needed first to be forewarned of this decision.

In fact, because of political developments within the Government-in-Exile in London, it was not until 28 December that a mission reached Poland. The replacement of Mikołajczyk by Arciszewski on 24 November appalled both the Foreign Office and the British Cabinet, which reckoned that this would make a settlement over the Russo–Polish border and the future of Poland even more difficult to achieve. On 25 November the British Government stopped all flights to Poland and introduced censorship on the communications of the Government-in-Exile with Poland. The British Military Mission, which was at last on the way to Poland, was halted in Italy. As Anthony Eden pointed out to Churchill on 4 December:

> Our original intention to send them was based on the assumption that they would be attached to an army under Monsieur Mikołajczyk's control. The Polish Underground is now controlled by a Government in whose political attitude we have no confidence, and the presence of British liaison officers in Poland might well prove a source of embarrassment to us. The Russians would also wonder why we had waited until the emergence of a less friendly Government before making this marked gesture of support for the Home Army.
>
> [NA, HS4/318]

General Tabor was officially informed of this by Perkins on 30 November. In reply, on 5 December, he did not mince his words. He pointed out that the Home Army would be deprived of ammunition, arms, W/T equipment, medical supplies and money. The ban would also stop military specialists such as W/T operators and staff officers being parachuted into Poland, while sensitive messages carried by couriers would have to cease. Finally, censorship of all radio correspondence would cause long and potentially dangerous delays 'with the field'. All this, Tabor pointed out, would 'inflict damage both moral and material, the extent of which can hardly be exaggerated', and would effectively lead to the dislocation and ultimately the dissolution of the whole Underground movement.

These arguments were endorsed emphatically by SOE, who argued that the actual people of Poland were 'well aware of the necessity and desirability of establishing an understanding with the Russians' and that both the Émigré Government and more especially the Lublin Committee were out of touch with public opinion.

On 20 December a meeting chaired by Churchill decided that 'the carrying of supplies, including money, to German-occupied Poland should be continued but not to areas near the Russian lines'. Three days later the Polish Ambassador was informed of this decision and also told that the dispatch of the British liaison team, still waiting in Bari, could now go ahead. However, the British Government did insist that all communications with Russian-occupied Poland should cease and that communications between the Government-in-Exile and German-occupied Poland should still be submitted for censorship by the British before dispatch. The British Military Mission, under the command of Colonel Hudson, was at last dropped in Poland on 28 December, some 30 miles north of Katowice. After this, the Foreign Office vetoed any more dropping of supplies in view of the impending Yalta Conference.

Intelligence, Sabotage and Guerrilla War in the General Government, October 1944–January 1945

A considerable number of AK troops still remained west of the Vistula in the German-occupied areas. According to information given to the SOE in December, the following forces were mobilized:

Radom:	429 Full platoons, 29 Cadre platoons
Kraków:	487 [Full platoons], 185 [Cadre platoons]
Silesia:	145 [Full platoons], 502 [Cadre platoons]
Łódź:	105 [Full platoons], 300 [Cadre platoons]
Pomerania:	32 [Full platoons, 395 [Cadre platoons]

[NA, HS4/247]

The Polish Underground 1939–1947

Altogether there were between 100,000 and 150,000 men still mobilized. The full platoons contained between fifty and seventy men, while the cadre platoons had about twenty-five or thirty men each.

Sabotage and guerrilla activities continued in these areas and, as the Germans stripped the countryside bare in preparation for their eventual retreat, Home Army forces continued to harry them with considerable success. However, as they were suffering from lack of equipment, secure bases and deficiencies in manpower, head-on confrontations and prolonged battles with the Germans were avoided. Actions were confined to general sabotage, and elimination of the security forces and collaborators. Information reaching London in October revealed, for example, that in the Kraków and Silesian areas a military train had been derailed and a prison attacked, liberating a considerable number of prisoners. Also in December another telegram from the Tarnów region, just behind the German front line, reported further AK activity, involving the blowing-up of bridges, the annihilation of the *Gestapo* in Tarnów town and the destruction of a German artillery battery.

Inevitably this provoked German counter-insurgency operations in an attempt to stabilize the area behind the front line before the Soviet offensive took place. In the Radom District, for example, three German battalions attacked Home Army forces in the woods near the village of Krzepin on 27 October. Ralph Smorczewski – now a deputy platoon commander in a battalion in the much-depleted 7th Silesian Division – remembered how his platoon was initially taken by surprise:

> The morning dawned like so many others, except that the wind was howling and the rain was beating at the windows of the small village house where our troops had spent the night. We all slept on the straw, spread on the floor in the only big room in the house. There was still time before the roll call so we all enjoyed a few more minutes rest while the farmer's wife, who was already up, lit the fire in the stove and began preparing our breakfast. Suddenly, above the noise of the wind, the rain and the crackling of the fire, occasional louder bangs and thuds could be heard. One of our men with better hearing said that he could hear the sound of battle. Mark thought it was water boiling on the stove. I sent one of my men outside. He was back in a split second shouting: 'machine-gun fire and grenade explosions on both ends of the village. We are surrounded!'

> [Smorczewski, *Bridging the Gap*, p. 168]

Campaign Chronicle

Smorczewski managed to get his troops outside and take up position with the second company at the edge of the woods. The Germans launched a ferocious attack on the position, forcing the partisans into retreat, but they were saved by an unexpected attack on their left flank by a strong detachment from Smorczewski's battalion, which forced them to surrender. The Germans were a mixed bunch: mostly SS men, police and soldiers. Amongst them was the SS commander of the battalion:

> That night our platoon was ordered to report to the regimental headquarters. We found Major 'Roztoka' and his staff in a small clearing in the forest. In front of him were the prisoners, their hands tied behind their backs, all of them SS and police. They were to be executed and our platoon [was] to carry out the order [...] The Germans were led a short distance into the woods, where a trench had been dug previously, and shot in the backs of their heads. All soldiers and non-commissioned officers were released and escorted to the edge of the woods.

> [Smorczewski, *Bridging the Gap*, p. 170]

AK units were still capable of limited military successes but shortage of supplies and weapons and continued German pressure took their toll. After their success at Krzepin the Silesian Division was encircled in the Włoszczowa Woods, and the only way the regiment could escape was by disbanding and letting the individual partisans fend for themselves.

When the British Military Mission landed in Poland at the end of December, it reported several instances of AK units being disbanded. One AK officer in the North Silesian Inspectorate, who was in command of an 'offensive unit', had been carrying out small-scale raids and sabotage across the border into the Reich, but had been forced back into the General Government, and had to disband his unit because of winter conditions and lack of supplies. On a larger scale, the 25th Infantry Regiment, which had fought its way out of German encirclement near Łódź, had been 'almost entirely demobilized except for one detachment'. A similar fate befell the 7th Polish Division, commanded by Colonel 'Wojek'. After engaging in several skirmishes with the Germans – one of which resulted in seventy of them being killed and over a hundred taken prisoner – it was split up in early December and its personnel sent home to await further orders.

The Polish Underground 1939–1947

The AL and NSZ

The AL had relatively few units west of the Vistula. When the front line stabilized, AL and Soviet partisan units attempted to cross the river and move into Soviet-held territory. Reports reached London in October that units of the AL and Soviet paratroops (who had been dropped in August and September) were forcing their way through to the Soviet side. During the night of 26/27 September about 8,000 got through to the Janowiec bridgehead. Those units that remained were primarily used by the Red Army and PKWN for Intelligence purposes. According to AK sources they were poorly trained and their officers often drunk, and consequently were easily rounded up by the Germans. John Ward reported that every night during his stay in a village near Kielce, AL bands raided the local farms and took whatever they needed. Around 12 December he himself, with an AK lieutenant, was stopped in the woods near Krzepin by a band of twenty members of the People's Army: 'After some discussion they decided not to shoot us, but they robbed us of our overcoats, boots, money, etc.'

The NSZ broke away from the AK in November 1944 and merged a few months later with another Nationalist group, 'NOW', to form the National Military Union (NZW). It was an implacable enemy of the AL, as it had decided (particularly after the uprising) that its main enemies were the Russians and the Polish Communists. It was debatable to what extent it was ready to collaborate with the Germans. The most prominent NSZ unit in the autumn and early winter of 1944 was the Holy Cross Brigade in the Kielce District, which numbered some 1,000 men. General Okulicki informed the British Military Mission that the Germans did not consider the NSZ a 'menace', but actual collaboration was confined to the higher levels. There were also contradictory rumours of a fierce fight between the Germans and the Holy Cross Brigade and the death of its commander, Colonel Szacki ('Bohun-Dąbrowski'). Okulicki was at a loss to know the truth of these rumours but according to the Military Mission, 'two suppositions were given as to the reason for this. Firstly that Bohun [...] had refused a German demand to form a Polish legion. Alternatively, there were many AK sympathizers among the NSZ [who] deliberately provoked this German attack to clear the NSZ from charges of collaboration.'

Soviet Advance, January 1945

On 12 January the Soviet assault towards the River Oder and ultimately Germany began. In the night of the 13th Colonel Hudson heard heavy gunfire in the east, which continued throughout the night. By the 15th Soviet forces had taken Kielce and Soviet tanks were in Włoszczowa. On the night of the 16th the British Military Mission moved yet again to a safe house populated by young scions of the landed gentry and their friends from Warsaw, as well the Deputy Inspector of the Częstochowa inspectorate. The evening was a melancholy affair, as Hudson recorded in the official diary:

> Among the Poles present many rumours were circulating about the proximity of the Russians, and it was generally felt that this would be the last night of the world they had known for the last six years. Although it meant liberation from the Germans, it was also the beginning of a new uncertainty for Poland, and in particular for people of their class. Our hostess and some of the other guests decided to leave for the north immediately.
>
> [NA, HS4/249]

At midnight the Mission left for a small peasant cottage and was able to send off a batch of telegrams to London against the background noise of 'the continuous roar of transport on the main road to the north and also a great deal of machine-gun fire'. After revealing themselves to a local AL political leader, they decided to notify the Russians of their presence, as the Red Army was well west of their location. By the night of the 19th it had already reached Kraków and Łódź, and the ruins of Warsaw had been taken two days earlier, while the Second Byelorussian Front, commanded by Marshal Rokossovsky, was advancing across East Prussia and Northern Poland. On 31 January 1945 Red Army troops crossed the Oder, a mere 50 miles from Berlin. Apart from a few German pockets, the whole of Poland was now in Soviet hands.

There was no widespread repetition of Operation *Tempest*. On 19 November 1944 the Council of National Unity and the Home Council of Ministers flatly told Mikołajczyk that 'after the battle for Warsaw, *Tempest* will have no political impact. It makes no difference to us whatsoever that some locality which will become known because of our further bleeding will thereby be occupied by the Soviets a half day sooner.' Colonel Hudson certainly received the impression from his AK contacts that 'no steps had been taken to mobilize the territorial units of the AK and that nothing was being done to harass the Germans'. The Government-in-Exile agreed on 17 January that key personnel of the

The Polish Underground 1939–1947

Underground State and the political parties should not reveal themselves to the Russians. Their withdrawal to the west was admissible, provided that provision was made for establishing some sort of substitute secret underground organization. Similarly, officers and soldiers especially sought by the NKVD were permitted to withdraw westwards, provided their units were not left without commanders and had accomplished their 'assignments'. Nevertheless, a few limited actions did take place against the Germans at the start of the Russian advance. Some units played a role in mopping up the Germans in Kraków, and in Radom AK troops of the 72nd Regiment, in close cooperation with the Red Army, actually killed and wounded some 200 Germans, but the Poles were then surrounded by Soviet troops – probably NKVD – and shot before they could retire.

There was, of course, no question that the writ of the London Government-in-Exile would be recognized or the AK tolerated by the Red Army. Stalin had made that very clear by pointedly recognizing the Lublin Committee (PKWN) as the new Provisional Government of Poland (RTRP) on 5 January. The Poles west of the Vistula now experienced what their countrymen in the east had already suffered at the hands of the Red Army. Reports from British POWs and former Underground political and military sources in Poland all spoke of looting, raping, stealing and requisitioning. Apparently there had been an order that Poland should be spared the full horrors of Soviet plundering, but any initial restraint soon broke down. John Ward witnessed the arrival of the Russians at Raszków around 18 January 1945:

> The first Russian forces were a tank corps, and both officers and men were very drunk. On arrival they proceeded to act as though they were masters of the earth. Within a few days the Russians had raped every female in the district over 14 years of age [...] They appeared to beat Polish men without provocation and some were shot. All livestock on the farms in the district were stolen and taken to other villages where they were exchanged for vodka.

[NA, HS4/256]

The Russians ruthlessly worked to eliminate the AK and other potential opponents. All reports coming from Poland were in agreement on the rapid action taken by the NKVD, which, as in Eastern Poland, appeared immediately in the areas liberated by the Soviet forces. In Kraków, for example, by 21 January NKVD personnel were already busy reading reports and collecting information. They then began arresting AK members, magistrates and the more prosperous farmers, who were to be eliminated as a class.

Continuing the War Against Germany Outside Poland

A few Intelligence reports from Poland were still dispatched to the VI Bureau in London in late January, but once the Red Army occupied Poland the underground war against Germany within Poland ceased. In a meeting with members of the VI Bureau and SOE on 24 January, Lieutenant Colonel Perkins stated categorically that the British would support any action against the Germans but could not support any organization in Russian-occupied Poland. Outside Poland, on the other hand, there was certainly still work to be done. In Northern Italy and Norway there were thousands of Poles in the *Wehrmacht* who could easily be persuaded to desert as the Germans no longer had the chance to penalize their families in Poland. Colonel Utnik of the VI Bureau also reported that the courier Jan Nowak had recently arrived with informa tion that the leaders of the Underground might try to operate from German territory, where there were some 3 million Polish workers. Indeed, in November 1944 the SOE and a specially created Polish Special Operations Office had planned to infiltrate Polish agents into Germany from Poland, Western Europe, Switzerland, Sweden and Denmark in what was called Operation *Dunstable*. Their task was to make themselves known to Polish workers and create cells for future action. In January 1945 five agents were sent into Germany and some forty more were being trained, but the war ended before Operation *Dunstable* could really take off.

Aftermath

Although the AK, and what might be called the 'Independentist groups' in Poland, appeared to have swapped one enemy for another in the spring of 1945, the situation was very different from October 1939. The Big Three at the Yalta Conference agreed both to create a provisional government in Poland, which, after consultations in Moscow, would include 'democratic leaders from Poland itself and from Poles abroad', and eventually to the holding of 'free and unfettered elections'. In the meantime, the PKWN, the Polish National Committee, would remain in power.

The problems it faced were enormous. It had to rebuild the administration, re-establish government, revive the Polish economy and assimilate those German territories that were to be ceded to the Polish state. To survive and neutralize its enemies, the PKWN had initially relied on the Red Army and the NKVD, but by early spring 1945 the Soviet Army was moving westwards to Germany, leaving only small cadres of the NKVD and lightly manned garrisons in Poland.

Dissolution of the AK and the Emergence of NIE

After the collapse of German power in Poland, what options had the Underground State? Against the USSR it no longer had the backing of the USA and Great Britain. The British, as we have seen, were adamant that the Underground should not support guerrilla attacks on Soviet troops. Consequently, all supplies were abruptly cut off. On 19 January General Okulicki disbanded the AK, but his order was ambiguous about the future. It stated that, 'We do not want to fight the Soviets, but we will never agree to live except in an entirely sovereign, independent, justly governed Polish state.'

Aftermath

With a much reduced staff, he then withdrew to build up the NIE organization, which Bór had envisaged back in November 1943 (*see page 109*). In many ways, NIE was eventually intended to become, in Norman Davies' words, the 'Home Army Mark II'. General Emil Fieldorf, the Commander of the *Kedyw*, was appointed as its chief. His task was to create a General Staff rather than a mass organization and collect together a cadre of men of proven organizational and leadership abilities, who would draw up plans for future resistance against the Soviet occupation and its 'Quisling' Government, the PKWN. Korboński observed that its structure could be compared to the 'ferroconcrete construction of a building that would have walls and interiors added at the proper moment'.

Flight and Concealment

What did the Soviet occupation of Poland entail for the soldiers of the Home Army? Many units had already been disbanded in the winter of 1944/45, but some – especially in the great forest regions in the Lublin area – sought to evade arrest, certain torture, deportation or death at the hands of the NKVD by once again becoming 'forest people'. A few of the more fortunate managed to escape to Italy and Western Europe.

The NSZ Holy Cross Mountain Brigade (Świętokrzyska) retreated westwards to Polish Silesia in January 1945 and remained hidden in the forests until March. To escape the NKVD and the PKWN security forces, the brigade moved on to Galatz in German Upper Silesia. There its commander was able to negotiate with the German Army a safe conduct through the German lines. Later, according to an article on 30 July 1945 in the *News Chronicle*, the Chief Intelligence Officer of the Brigade told one of its journalists that they had been invited by the Germans in the last months of the war to form a Polish Legion to fight the Russians, but this was rejected as the Polish Government in London had not yet declared war on Russia. Nevertheless, they promised to fight the Russians 'when Britain, America and Poland joined hands to start a war on Russia, which they expected soon'. The Brigade eventually reached the Boehmerwald, some 35 miles from Pilsen. The other NSZ/NZW units remaining in Poland were ordered to dissolve, and as many of the personnel as possible to move westwards to escape the Russians.

In the spring and summer of 1945 it was possible in the general chaos of post-war Europe to escape over the Polish frontier into Czechoslovakia or the British and American Zones in Germany. For many, this was the only way to escape the NKVD and the *gulag*. For others it was a way to join up with the Polish forces in Italy under General Anders. Ralph Smorczewski, for instance, managed to reach Italy via Austria and Bavaria, where he joined the II Polish Corps.

The SOE strongly championed the cause of its former agents, who had been parachuted into Poland from Britain and, rather than fall into NKVD hands, now wished to return. Many of these men, on their way out of Poland, passed through Pilsen, where the senior British officer was Lieutenant Colonel Perkins of the SOE. On 27 June, when three agents reported to him requesting a safe passage to the West, he immediately cabled London for permission, but in the event of a refusal he was ready to give them papers certifying that they were members of the Polish Parachute Brigade who had been captured in Holland and were now returning to their units after looking in vain for their families in Poland. In August he urged Gubbins to take up the case of Peter Czer, who had been another of SOE's Polish agents and commander of the AK in the Lublin area. Perkins stressed that he felt most strongly on this point: 'We must, repeat must, honour our debts or lose every vestige of respect in Central Europe.'

A few Poles were able to pass themselves off as British POWs and were able to join the transports to Odessa, where British and Empire troops were being repatriated to Britain by boat. Jan Cias (*see pages 103–4*), for instance, was directed by former AK contacts to the British Repatriation Commission in Lublin in March 1945. According to the account he gave in London on 21 April 1945:

> He gave his name and particulars and when soon afterwards a New Zealand Major Croft came in, the doors were locked, and Cias told his story. Then he was promised further assistance and the Major gave him his own trousers and put on his dress ones. A jerkin was also found for him and Cias was given new particulars, which he was left in the room to learn by heart. He was given the name of a killed POW [...] of the Cameron Highlanders [...] captured at St Valerie in June 1940.
>
> [NA, HS4/21]

With the help of a British POW, who had been a member of the AK, he was registered at the Red Cross and then passed the interview at the Russian headquarters without being discovered. He reached Odessa on 22 March and arrived back at Gourock on 17 April. Another person smuggled out of Lublin to Odessa in a POW transport was a 68-year-old

Aftermath

Scottish woman, Miss Jane Walker, who had arrived in Poland before the war as a teacher and married a Pole. As she had helped numerous British POWs find shelter and safety and had been a member of the AK, she was, understandably, in the words of Flight Sergeant Mcphail, 'afraid to stay behind as many of the Underground had disappeared and not been heard of again. As she was an old lady of 68, we decided to take her with us . . .'

End of the Underground State, March–June 1945

On 6 March the Government Delegate Jankowski, General Okulicki and the Party leaders received letters inviting them to meet Colonel General Ivanov, who represented the Soviet Commander of the First Byelorussian Front. It emerged after preliminary discussions that the Russians wished to discuss how the parties would surface from the Underground State and adapt themselves to the new situation in Poland. Although there was deep scepticism about the intentions of the Russians, mainstream Polish politicians desperately hoped this showed that the Soviets were ready to come to an agreement that would pacify Poland. In fact this was a triumph of wishful thinking. There were two meetings just outside Warsaw at Pruszków, which resulted in the arrest of sixteen leaders of the Underground State, including Okulicki and Jankowski. They were speedily whisked away to Moscow and incarcerated in the Lubyanka. Only on 4 May were the Western Allies informed of their arrest. They were charged on 21 June with conducting diversions behind Soviet lines and given sentences varying from ten years to four months. Only three were acquitted. As Stefan Korboński later observed, 'the curtain fell on the tragic spectacle, whose staging bore the imprint of Stalin's perfidious hand'.

The arrests destroyed the leadership of the Underground State. However, on the initiative of the head of the Directorate of Civil Resistance, Stefan Korboński, the leaders of the parties, which had previously been represented on the Council of National Unity, met on 7, 16 and 24 April, and decided to maintain the Underground State as the key to regaining Polish independence in defiance of the PKWN. Its administration was streamlined, the Council of National Unity was reconstructed, and only the departments of Finance, Internal Affairs, Labour and Welfare and Press and Information were retained.

Although the Home Army had been nominally dissolved in January, Colonel Rzepecki was appointed Delegate for the Armed Forces in Poland. The NIE organization was wound up by the orders of General Anders (the new commander-in-chief of Polish forces), as it had been penetrated

189

by the NKVD and many staff arrested. Rzepecki had to a tread a tight-rope between overt opposition and passive resistance. There was to be no retaliation for the arrest of the sixteen Underground leaders but, on the other hand, Rzepecki's duties involved the following tasks:

To keep headquarters in London informed about the situation in Poland;

To eliminate individuals who constitute a threat to Polish society and the Underground;

To cooperate with headquarters in the transfer of mail, money, necessary materials, and specialists to Poland;

To undermine the morale of the soldiers of the People's Army and persuade them to desert.

[Kersten, p. 141]

The Underground State limped on until the end of June. It accepted the Yalta decision on the creation of a broad-based Provisional Government of National Unity, but pressed for the release of the sixteen arrested leaders and the holding of elections under conditions of complete freedom as soon as possible. It attempted, as best it could, to keep radio contact with London and to deal with the problems arising both from the Polish annexation of East German territory and the remorseless Russian pressure on the Poles to quit the land east of the Curzon Line. It advised Poles still living there not to move voluntarily, since a Polish presence in those territories was vital to refute Soviet claims. The Underground State was seriously weakened when the Peasant Party (PSL) withdrew its members from the Delegacy on 29 May, on the grounds that the London Government was no longer representative of the Polish people. Finally, with the formation of the Provisional Government of National Unity, which Mikołajczyk had agreed to join as vice-premier, and the arrival of the government's leaders in Warsaw on 27 June, it wound itself up. In its 'Testament of Fighting Poland' the Council of National Unity pointed out that

the establishment of the new Government, and its recognition by the Western powers, puts an end to the possibility of a lawful Underground resistance. The problem now arising is that of an open struggle of the democratic parties in Poland to achieve the national goals and the realization of their programmes.

[Korboński, *Polish Underground State*, p. 237]

Aftermath

On 6 August Colonel Rzepecki dissolved the Delegacy for the Armed Forces, but replaced it a month later with a new organization: 'Freedom and Independence – WiN' (*see below*).

The Revolt of April–July 1945

By the end of the war the Polish economy was in ruins. The population had declined from 35 to 24 million. Some 65 per cent of factories and refineries were destroyed. The bigger cities such as Warsaw, Gdansk (Danzig) and Wrocław (Breslau) were heaps of rubble. Food supplies were also inadequate as the Soviet and Polish Armies had priority in the allocation of food, which was forcibly collected from the countryside. This inevitably led to strikes and industrial unrest, particularly in Silesia. If these had coalesced with the armed insurrection in the countryside, pacification without major military operations would have been impossible. To avert this, the government took drastic action to provide adequate rations in the cities. In mid-July in Warsaw, for instance, when the PPR Committee learned that there were only sufficient flour supplies for two days, flour was immediately brought in from the country and famine averted. In this way the authorities were just about able to keep the lid on political protest. The Communists found cities such as Gdansk and Wrocław – which had just been annexed from Germany – much easier to control because the large number of homeless and impoverished refugees who had flooded in from the east to replace the pre-war German population were unable to form a cohesive opposition. However, clandestine organizations were still active, particularly in Kraków. A British diplomat, who had visited the city in August, noted that nearly all the students 'are said to be in opposition to the Government and many hold extreme right-wing views'. On two of the evenings he was in the city he also saw 'Poles being marched to prison by the Polish Security Police with a detachment of Soviet NKVD following behind'.

It was in the countryside, particularly in the vast wooded areas of Kielce and Lublin province, where, as under the German occupation, partisan resistance was at its strongest. Looking back, a Communist historian later wrote that 'the year 1945 was the hardest period in the history of the region of Lublin'. In the spring of 1945 what was in effect a full-blown insurrection broke out in Lublin province, which reduced Communist control to the larger towns and cities. The removal of the bulk of Soviet forces westwards in January and the spring weather facilitated the revolt, but it was fuelled principally by the record of the Soviet occupation. One Underground fighter baldly remarked that 'there would have been no Underground had there been no arrests of AK soldiers, who revealed themselves to the Soviets in August 1944'. Their reservations about the Soviets were, of course, amply confirmed by the arrest of the sixteen in March.

By the spring of 1945 the bulk of the partisans, who had been members of the AK, had now fragmented into separate bands. They were only very loosely linked to the Delegacy for the Armed Forces and its successor, WiN. However, they could draw on the tacit support of the PSL, the Polish Peasants' Party, which was founded in August 1945, as well as the Church itself.

After visiting a training camp near Zamość in June 1945, Dr Klukowski mused on the hardened character of the insurgents:

> They are ready to act, fanatics of a kind, ready to fight out solutions to problems, people of dulled sensitivity towards the acts of violence they command [...] At the same time they are people willing to sacrifice, risking their lives, being pursued, persecuted and searched, without a home of their own for years [...] They have but one aim in view, the final victory in which they believe fanatically.

> [Klukowski, *Red Shadow*, pp. 78–9]

In the summer of 1945 it seemed as if this – in the countryside at least – was within their grasp.

The tactics of the partisans were similar to those used against the Germans: anti-Bolshevik posters were put up; assassinations of Communist officials, Polish militia commanders and informers regularly carried out; and confiscated crops stolen from the official collecting places. Prisons and police posts were also frequently attacked. The town of Janów was seized and thirty political prisoners released, while on 22 June the NSZ/NZW destroyed a police station in Zakrzówek, and by the end of the month there were only three police outposts left in Janów county, out of the seventeen set up in the autumn of 1944. Elsewhere in rural Poland, the picture was the same. On 4/5 August about 250 men equipped with seven lorries occupied Kielce and then stormed the jail, releasing some 376 prisoners. A month later a similar operation occurred in Radom. It was, to quote Chodakiewicz, 'a grassroots re-enactment of Operation *Tempest*'. Through assassination and intimidation, PPR council leaders and government officials were driven out of office. Grudgingly, but only temporarily – as time was to show – the Communist authorities had to tolerate the appointment of 'Independentists' or members of the Polish Peasants' Party (PSL) to local government positions.

Both the militia, the army and the security services of the Provisional Government had also been penetrated by ex-AK men. A summary of reports for the British authorities on conditions in Poland from 11 January– 1 May 1945 stressed that there were 'an unknown number of Home Army men' serving in the People's Army, 'some having joined to get a livelihood, but a large number has done so with the purpose of penetration for patriotic motives'. Inevitably the successes of the partisans demoralized the young conscripts who made up the bulk of the personnel. On 5 May, for instance, Klukowski recorded in his diary that news of the destruction of militia posts was pouring in from all sides and that 'some militia men do not wait to be disarmed [. . .] Not only individual soldiers but entire detachments are deserting, some to the forest, some to go home.' Even the officers of the new army proved unreliable. A British diplomat happened to meet in the foyer of the Bolshoi Theatre on 30 May 1945 two young Polish officers, who had been sent to Moscow for an officers' training course. Meeting the following day at Sokolniki Park, where he hoped they would be safe from the NKVD spies, they poured out their hearts to him about the state of Poland. One of them observed that the Poles were not a free people: 'they feel like birds in a cage, constantly teased by the hand of a bully and in danger of death at any moment'. He also made very clear that the real government of Poland was in London not Warsaw.

In July, Russian troops and units of the Polish People's Army attempted to fight back against the insurgency using the same methods as the Nazis. Agents provocateur and security police were disguised as partisans and large 'anti-bandit' sweeps were launched across the countryside. On 1 September Klukowski observed that the Underground fighters were going through extremely troubled times: 'They are constantly tracked, they don't have any place to spend even one night in peace.' In July several key members of the former AK were arrested, including the delegates of Białystok, Kielce and the Central region. Nevertheless, in the wake of these sweeps and arrests, the partisans again came out of the woods and re-established their control over the countryside.

Creation of the Provisional Government of National Unity and the First Amnesty

The political situation in Poland was also ambiguous and at times seemed to offer a war-weary people some glimmerings of hope that through compromise a democratic government might be possible after all. In June

The Polish Underground 1939–1947

1945, after talks in Moscow, the Provisional Government of National Unity was at last set up with Mikołajczk as one of the deputy prime ministers. The Communists and their political allies filled seventeen out of the twenty-one ministerial posts and significantly controlled the key ministries of Security, Defence, Justice, Information and Propaganda and Foreign Affairs. On 21 August 1945 an amnesty of one month was granted to all insurgents, who handed in their arms and came out of hiding. However, those who 'performed the highest leadership functions' were specifically excluded. The deadline was extended at the end of September to 15 October. The Peasant Battalions, the Boy Scouts (under the leadership of Aleksander Kamińsky) and probably about 5,000 ex-AK members decided to reveal themselves.

To adapt to this situation, Colonel Rzepecki created a new organization known as the Association of Freedom and Independence (WiN). Its task was to organize the remaining ex-AK partisan units into a political pressure group, which would focus on the coming election and combat the PPR through political rather than military weapons. It accepted that war would not break out between the West and the USSR and that, consequently, all decisions concerning Poland's future could only be made in Poland. Over the coming months it forged close links with the PSL, which seemed to be the only force capable of stopping Communism. Inevitably, WiN was viewed with extreme suspicion by the PPR and the Russians, as it defined its aim as being

> to force through the introduction in Poland of democratic principles in the Western European meaning of the term [...] the first step in attaining our basic aim is to force the carrying out of honest and democratic elections to the Legislative Diet.

Thus it was no surprise that in November its leaders were arrested and considerable sums of money seized. Through interrogation, which, of course, involved torture, the NKVD was able to discover its links to the PSL.

The end of the amnesty led to further arrests and violence. Many of Mikołajczk's key supporters were arrested and killed one by one. Władysław Kojder, president of the PSL in the Przeworsk area and a member of the party's pre-war Supreme Council, was murdered in suspicious circumstances in September and his body only found in May 1947. Similarly, Bolesław Ścibiorek, the general secretary of the Polish Peasant Party in Łódź, was shot dead on 6 December. According to the

Aftermath

account given to the British Ambassador, the security authorities had actually come to arrest him at six in the evening, but, as he was not in, they returned at ten, locked his daughter in her bedroom, and shot him in the bathroom.

Food quota deliveries remained a burning issue and continued to alienate the peasantry. In many of the smaller towns the oppression, extortion and injustice – combined with the sheer inefficiency and corruption of the authorities – led to violent protests and subsequent vicious crackdowns. The British Ambassador reported on 17 December that in Grójec, a small town some 30 miles south of Warsaw, the local population had attacked the headquarters of the security authorities and killed several of the principal officials. In retaliation the security authorities arrested without warning the Director of the Agricultural Cooperative, the Director of the Court of First Instance, the head of the local secondary school and a peasant named Sikorski. They were driven out in the country and then shot. Later, obituaries were published in the main Warsaw newspaper, *Życie Warszawy*, lamenting their tragic death. However, Sikorski had only been wounded, and after the car had driven away, he crawled out of the shallow grave in which the bodies had been buried. He was able to reach a neighbouring house, where he was clothed and cared for. About a week later he travelled to Warsaw to make a disposition before a 'reliable' (non-Communist) judge and to be interviewed by senior members of the PSL. Mikołajczyk, supported by Władysław Kiernik, the Minister for Public Administration, then seized the chance to raise the whole issue in the Cabinet on 11 December. Apparently, this so enraged Berman – the Communist vice-minister in the Prime Minister's office and the driving intellect of the PPR – that he was, according to accounts reaching the British Ambassador, 'literally stifled by his own rage in trying to reply and foamed at the mouth, apparently behaving like a complete animal'. The upshot of the discussion was that, in the future, any political murder would be investigated by an inter-party committee, but in practice this changed little.

In November the High Command of the NSZ/NZW was almost eliminated when its officers were arrested for the alleged mass murder of the inhabitants of the village of Wierzchowiny. When the trial started in February, there were several embarrassing hiccups for the authorities. The British Embassy was told that three of the accused refused to admit the validity of the statements they had made to the security authorities under interrogation, as 'they had been so beaten on the body and on the soles of the feet and even on the face with rubber truncheons that they had agreed to make any declarations required in order to save their lives'. The judge was reported as having 'shrugged his shoulders in despair'.

The murders, arrests and show trials increased political tensions and ensured that Underground resistance continued and that hatred towards the PPR increased. Although there is little direct evidence of coordinated action between the PSL and the partisans in rural Poland, the latter undoubtedly shielded the former and enabled the PSL to campaign politically. Assassinations of officials and government supporters from the autumn of 1945 until well into 1946 ran at about 200 a month. The spring witnessed a new upsurge in activities. On 14 March Klukowski reckoned that 'there is every indication that the "forest" will come alive with the arrival of warmer days'.

Support for the Underground from Poles Abroad

During the Underground struggle against the Germans, assistance from Britain was crucial, even though it was meagre enough. By 1945 such assistance could no longer be expected as Soviet Russia was still seen as an ally by the British Government, which was determined to back the agreement made at Yalta for a provisional Polish government and an early election. On 11 May the Combined Chiefs of Staff ordered Eisenhower as Supreme Commander in Western Europe to stop any transfer of equipment for sabotage and Intelligence activities to Poland, and on 19 June the SOE's Polish section was closed. On 2 July all powers and diplomatic privileges were withdrawn from the former Government-in-Exile. Despite this, a certain amount of money and supplies – particularly radios and weapons – continued to find their way across the borders into Poland. These came mainly from sources in the Polish II Corps in Italy under General Anders and from the former Government-in-Exile in London, as well as from occupied Germany, the Pilsen area of Czechoslovakia, and Brussels, where, according to a report in the Communist paper *Le Drapeau Rouge*, a 'new type of general staff had been installed under the title of Conseil Polonais de Belgique'. In September the Provisional Government in Poland claimed that, from listening in to illegal radio transmissions, it had evidence that Polish Underground couriers were being instructed to get in touch with either the commanders of the 1st Armoured Division at Meppen or the Polish Parachute Brigade at Bergen Bruck, or else with the Polish camp at Murnau or the Military Mission at Frankfurt on Main.

As late as December 1944 the Government-in-Exile had managed to send considerable sums in dollars, *złoty* and German marks to the AK.

Aftermath

When air operations from Italy to Poland ceased, $5 million dollars were still in Polish hands and instructions were issued to return the money to Britain. Over $3 million dollars were dispatched and the rest actually boxed up ready to be taken back to London by a draft of Polish troops. However, instructions were received from the Polish Headquarters to transfer the money to the Polish Wireless School in Rome. A British Treasury memorandum in October observed balefully that 'nothing has since been heard of the present whereabouts of these dollar funds'. It was only in 1952 that it emerged the Polish Army had in fact set some of this money aside to buy a series of safe houses to train agents to infiltrate Poland.

As in the fight against Nazi Germany, radios were of crucial importance to the Underground, both to communicate with Poles abroad and to transmit instructions and news to the home population. In May 1945 there were at least two clandestine broadcasting stations in Poland called 'Wyzwolenie' (Liberation) and 'Wolność' (Freedom). Clandestine radio contact between England and Poland continued at least up to December 1945. Under the 1942 Anglo-Polish Agreement, the Poles provided their own staff for the production in Stanmore of W/T equipment for operations in Poland. Gubbins conceded to Cavendish-Bentinck, the British Ambassador elect for Warsaw, on 18 May that 'we are not entirely clear about the use to which the Poles nowadays put or intend to put the W/T equipment manufactured at this station', but the SOE were reluctant to stop delivery to the Poles because they were also manufacturing equipment for clandestine British operations in the Far East.

In September the Polish Provisional Government protested to the British Government about illegal radio transmissions from London, and provided a list of sixteen operators arrested in Poland in August and full details of transmissions and call signs of radio stations in both Poland and London. From the identification numbers it could be proved that they had been manufactured in Stanmore. There were Polish radio stations both at Chipperfield, near King's Langley, and at Conington, north of Cambridge. Both were supposed to be transferred to the Royal Signals Corps, under the control of the War Office, on 30 September, but MI6 reported in December that they were still under Polish military control. Conington was being dismantled by Polish personnel but there was no indication of where the material was going!

There were other Polish transmitting stations in Italy. The British Radio Security Service discovered one situated somewhere between Rome and Naples and another in the neighbourhood of Calcarno in north-east

Italy, which had links with outstations in Istanbul, Jerusalem, Athens, Cairo, Angora, Teheran, Baghdad and Lisbon. In Rome a station was located in a large block of flats and probably run by Colonel Hańcza, who was the Commander of the Polish Wireless School. Possibly in an effort to pre-empt the British, in October Anders ordered the Polish Field Security Service to close this station and arrest the colonel, who was, however, found dead in his flat by the Polish Military Police. When Allied Forces HQ asked for a report on the incident, Anders raised British suspicions by refusing, arguing that this was a purely Polish domestic affair. To what extent Hańcza was a convenient scapegoat to divert further Allied action is hard to determine. Efforts reminiscent of the Germans in occupied Poland continued to be used by the British to pinpoint the Rome transmission station. In November a search party was installed under suitable cover in a flat in the block where the transmissions were taking place, but even then it was technically difficult to get a precise fix because the radio was receiving rather than sending messages. According to a Foreign Office report in December, 'at least one raid' was made, but the station was still not found. In February 1946 another illicit wireless set was traced to the basement of the (London) Polish Legation to the Holy See in the Vatican City.

As between the years 1939 and 1944, couriers continued to play a key role in communications, carrying information, money and sometimes weapons. In the days of German-occupied Europe, the routes of couriers into Poland were circuitous and could take weeks. Now, in the summer of 1945, with Allied control of Italy, the British and American Zones in Germany and Austria, and American troops in Pilsen, it was relatively easy to slip in and out of Poland. The Czech border south of Dresden was a major crossing point for couriers and political refugees from Poland.

The NSZ Brigade, which had managed to escape from Poland in the rear of the German retreat to the Boehmerwald, some 35 miles from Pilsen (*see page 182*), was, according to the journalist Stefan Litauer of the *News Chronicle*, 'the HQ of intensive activity in Poland', from where 'secret couriers go and arrive'. This may have been an exaggeration but it was true that the NSZ in Poland began to rebuild its organization in the spring. British contacts also confirmed that the brigade had become a collecting place for families and couriers. When it was moved on to Bavaria (in the American Zone in Germany) in early August, largely as a result of British efforts, Perkins, who had been appointed acting British Consul, informed London that they were 'incensed, for my action broke their short courier route up to the Polish frontier, a route over which many hundreds of their friends were moving from Poland to the British and American Zones and several of their agents back into Poland'. An indication of the sort of material the couriers were carrying came at the end of the month, when the Americans caught two couriers coming from Poland carrying microfilm addressed to a Colonel Radwand-Pfeiffer, a name that was almost certainly an alias. Radkiewicz, the Polish Minister of Public Security, produced a considerable amount of evidence in February 1946 purporting to show close links between WiN and the Polish General Staff in London, and the NSZ and General Anders' staff in Italy. While some of the details were undoubtedly falsified, there was no doubt that such links did exist.

General Anders and the Former Polish Government-in-Exile

The Polish Army and the former Government-in-Exile, by its very existence, remained a threat to the Provisional Government. By 1946 Polish exile leaders and opinion formers were already looking into the future and claiming to be the leaders of the alternative Poland. In a lecture in Scotland, one of the leaders of the pre-war Socialist party (and former Minister of Information in the Government-in-Exile), Professor Pragier, stressed that the mere existence of the Polish Armed Forces abroad 'constitute a most eloquent protest to the world against what is now being done to Poland'. He also addressed himself to the whole Polish Diaspora in the West and called upon it 'to maintain ideological solidarity' and realize that the 'problem of Poland is not settled yet [...] nor is the world war finished, although hostilities ceased and the world fronts changed'.

It is difficult to assess what impact Anders and the former London Government still had on the Polish people. Certainly, for the two young Polish lieutenants whom a British diplomat met in Moscow in June 1945, the words 'Polish Government' and 'Poles in England' seemed synonymous. There is also some evidence from Dr Klukowski's diaries that Anders and the former London Government still had some resonance inside Poland. In a political meeting organized by the PPR in Szczebrzeszyn on Sunday, 14 April 1946, a speaker was interrupted by the cry 'long live the London Government'. Three months later the town was woken up at eleven o'clock at night by a band of some twenty men, who, after they had beaten up a particularly unpopular Communist, paraded around the town firing their guns and singing 'Anders will win'.

With the withdrawal of British recognition from the Government-in-Exile in July 1945, control over Polish troops was theoretically transferred to the War Office. In Italy, however, where there were some 110,000 Polish troops in the II Corps, the War Office exercised only nominal control and, in the words of a Foreign Office memorandum, Anders enjoyed the position of 'commander of an independent Allied army'. Anders, having been sent to Siberia by the Russians in 1939, had no illusions about Soviet Russia and was one of the most implacable foes of the Soviet occupation of Poland. In fact, he was sure that a war between the West and the USSR was imminent. He was, therefore, able to exploit his status as the victor of Monte Cassino to encourage both active and passive resistance to the PPR and the Russians. That is not to say he was quite the Machiavellian figure described by the Polish Communist press, but it would be fair to say that his known antipathy to the USSR encouraged some of his officers to receive and send couriers and W/T messages to Poland. The majority of his officers also came from Eastern Poland and shared his antipathy towards the Bolsheviks. In many ways the II Corps became a beacon for former AK men fleeing Poland and increased in size, despite the repatriation of some 14,000 men. In Barletta a DP [Displaced Persons] camp had been set up where disaffected Poles who had escaped Poland by Underground channels were assembled. Mikołajczyk confirmed this when he told the British Ambassador on 12 February that he believed that several thousand individuals had left the country during the past six months to join General Anders' army.

Anders arguably created a 'state within a state' in Italy. Through the Army welfare services he was able to take charge of all propaganda amongst his troops. The Corps' two daily newspapers, as well as what the *Manchester Guardian* in a report of 24 January 1946 called 'innumerable pamphlets', were violently anti-Communist. The Provisional Government's new Polish Ambassador in Rome, Professor Kot – who had been in Sikorski's Cabinet (*see page 47*) – complained that the soldiers' letters from Poland were intercepted and censored. Kot was convinced that over half the men in reality wanted to go home but were prevented from doing so. Allegedly, Anders had agents watching the Polish Embassy day and night to identify any Polish soldiers daring to approach the building.

Inevitably, Anders was subjected to sustained and vitriolic abuse from Warsaw. He was accused of being a fascist and systematically murdering his opponents, a view accepted by some left-wing British papers and MPs. One Polish Communist paper, the *Głos Ludu*, on 5 April claimed, for example, that there was a hospital in Egypt where 'difficult' people were incarcerated by Anders' agents and from which 'nobody ever leaves'. To the British, despite his brilliant war record, he was a political dinosaur

Aftermath

who could not come to terms with modern, 'proletarianized' Poland. In their eyes, his hostility to Russia threatened to torpedo the possibility of a Mikołajczyk government, which, as Orme Sargeant, the Permanent Under-Secretary of the Foreign Office, observed on 31 January 1946, would be a 'non-starter if good relations with Russia were not a main plank in his platform'. Mikołajczyk shared this view and told the British Ambassador that Anders' agents had been instrumental in causing reprisals by the security forces because they had urged the peasants not to surrender their quotas of agricultural produce to the authorities. He made it very clear that the sooner Anders' forces were dissolved the better. Following this advice from both Poland and his own Foreign Office, the Prime Minister, Clement Attlee, invited the Polish commanders to London on 15 March and informed them that their men would soon be demobilized with the option of either remaining in Britain or the Commonwealth or returning home.

A month earlier Anders had rejected outright the accusation that he was encouraging sabotage in Poland and pointed out that, while there were no obstacles being put in the way of any of his soldiers returning to Poland,

> feeling as I do, I could not justify myself in my conscience if I were to exhort anyone under my command to return under prevailing conditions when I am not, myself, prepared to do likewise.

> [NA, FO371/56464]

To what extent Anders actually encouraged the Underground in Poland is difficult to say. On 21 April Cavendish-Bentinck reported to the Foreign Office that he had 'repeatedly' asked the Vice-Minister for Foreign Affairs and other members of the Polish Government to provide him with conclusive evidence of the contacts between 'terrorist organizations' in Poland and General Anders' army, but they had failed to do so, and he came to the conclusion that the evidence they did provide would not stand close examination.

The complexity of attempting to unravel the multifarious threads of the Underground movement is shown by a communication from the British Embassy in Rome on 11 March 1946. Apparently, the senior officer named Pulczyński, whom Mikołajczyk had accused of being the organizer of these clandestine activities, was in reality Major General Pełczyński, Bór's chief of staff in Warsaw, who, after his liberation from a German POW camp, had gone to London. There he had resumed Underground activities and had sent a courier to Italy, who had been arrested.

It was only in December that he visited Italy to see his wife, who was herself involved in some political intrigue with former Polish diplomats in Rome. He also approached Anders with the hope of getting a staff post in the Corps, but was rejected, possibly because of his role in the Warsaw Uprising, of which Anders disapproved.

The Referendum and the General Election, 1946–1947

Given the strength of the Peasants' Party (PSL) in the countryside, there was every hope amongst its supporters and allies that it would win an outright majority. The pro-Soviet parties, the PPS and PPR, therefore decided in March 1946 to postpone the election, but nevertheless contrive to gain a popular mandate by holding a referendum on three proposals, which they hoped the Poles would support. These were land reform and nationalization, a single chamber legislature and Poland's new western border with Germany. Despite the continuing unrest in the countryside, it was significant that the PPR felt strong enough to hold the referendum on 30 June. The PSL was aware that the referendum was, in fact, principally directed against itself, but advised its voters to vote 'no' to the first two questions and 'yes' to the last.

In the late winter and early spring major security operations were launched in the countryside. In February the Internal Security Corps and some 10,000 troops carried out a sweep in Białystok, Warsaw and Lublin provinces, detaining some 6,000 suspects of whom over 300 were shot. On 29 March a State Security Commission was set up with branches in the provinces, and well over 150,000 militia men and soldiers were deployed in Eastern Poland. In Kielce province some 1,600 suspects were arrested in an operation between 12 and 15 April. PSL activists were particularly targeted and whole villages were razed to the ground; the most notorious example was at Walwolnica in Puławy County, where the security forces behaved as ruthlessly as the Germans had. In tandem with the terror, propaganda brigades were formed and military units that had been used to help the peasants bring in the harvest were trained to develop friendly relations with the rural population. The propaganda brigades fanned out across the country and distributed newspapers and leaflets. Good speakers were recruited and voters were to be beguiled by military bands and theatre troupes.

Yet the Underground was by no means crushed. The PPR did indeed control the upper ranks of the security forces, but still could not rely on the loyalty of the lower ranks. Klukowski's diaries for this period continue to record incidents of former AK units springing prisoners from

Aftermath

jail and liquidating militia posts, but there are also many references to police action. On 19 June he reported that 'alarming information of numerous arrests is coming from all directions. Chaos, disorganization and problems are escalating.' In Biłgoraj on 22 June he noticed soldiers setting up machine-guns on the sidewalks to protect the polling booths, yet he was puzzled by the fact that, on the lawn in front of the command post, they had laid out small red-and-white stones forming the words 'God, Honour, Fatherland'.

On the 24th Klukowski himself was arrested for a few days but was let out just before the referendum. His description of that day in Szczebrzeszyn casts an interesting light on political reality in Poland at that time:

> telephone poles and walls are plastered with handbills: 'Vote 3 times "Yes".' There was a propaganda meeting in the market place, where people clearly expressed their feelings. They interrupted the speakers, laughed at them and whistled. In places hand-made posters with the words 'Bolshevik Referendum' with a caricature of Stalin [...] At the bottom of every poster someone had written, 'Death penalty for tearing it down' or 'I am watching you'.

> [Klukowski, *Red Shadow*, p. 120]

The referendum results were falsified by the authorities and officially the public were told that 68 per cent had indeed voted '3 times "Yes",' yet documents released forty years later showed that only 29 per cent had done so. In reality, the results were a defeat for both the PPR and its opponents. The PPR realized that despite massive pressure, the majority of Poles did not support them, while their opponents, in the face of military pressure and the falsification of the referendum, increasingly became convinced that resistance was useless.

The decks were now cleared for the election. When Bierut, one of the leading Polish Communists, visited Stalin in early September 1946, Stalin effectively gave the green light for the destruction of the PSL. The elections were scheduled for 19 January 1947. During the months before the elections, 162 PSL candidates and thousands of activists and party members were arrested. Its electoral structure was smashed. British and American protests were brushed aside by the Provisional Government and the peasantry subjected to intensive propaganda by the newly created Military Protection Propaganda Group (GOP). In most places force and the threat of force were constantly present. The elections on 19 January took place in an atmosphere of anxiety and intimidation. Officially, 80.1 per cent voted for the Democratic Bloc, while the PSL only won some 6.9 per cent. Clearly these results were rigged. Both Mikołajczyk and the Western ambassadors complained, but it was too late to alter the course of developments. The way was open for the creation of a one-party Stalinist state.

Assessment

On 22 February 1947 another amnesty was granted to the Underground. Altogether, according to government figures, 55,000 members gave themselves up and surrendered some 13,883 weapons. Some partisan activity still continued in the north-eastern provinces, but the partisans were relentlessly harassed by government troops and increasingly lost the support of the local population. The fate of the remaining 'forest people' was summed up by Korboński when 'a lad from the woods' talked frankly about the hopelessness of further opposition and asked his advice about whether he and his comrades should give themselves up:

> In place of the burning desire to fight and unceasing harassment of the opponent, there are depressing escapes from raids and night-time wandering around forest tracks. Instead of open doors, at each shack, house, and lodging, gates are closed, and there are requests to try further on, because there will be arrests and repression. Instead of air drops of weapons and supplies – old shot-out junk and meagre amounts of ammunition treated as if it were gold. And on top of that hunger, the lack of sleep and horrible fatigue, which cannot be shaken off, predominates.
>
> [Quoted in Kersten, p. 363]

The PPR leaders were uneasily aware that it was only Soviet bayonets and exhaustion that enabled them to rule Poland. As the Cold War intensified, the tempo of arrests inside Poland increased. When the amnesty expired, political repression was ruthlessly applied. Its aim was not just to destroy the remaining Underground structures, but also to create a psychosis of fear in order to paralyse the will to resist.

The election 'victory' had enabled the Communists to establish a general monopoly of power – a one-party state. In name only the old institutions remained in place, but real power was now located in the Party's Politburo, and subject to direct Soviet control. Marshal Rokossovsky, a

Aftermath

Russian Pole who had served both the Tsar and his Bolshevik successors, was appointed Vice-Premier and Minister of Defence. In October 1947, to save him from arrest and execution, Mikołajczyk had to be brought out of Poland. He was hidden in an American Embassy truck and driven to Gdynia, where he was smuggled onboard a British ship. In June 1948 even Gomułka was replaced as General Secretary and confined to house arrest for his 'national Bolshevism'.

By the end of 1947 the wheel appeared to have turned a full circle. Poland was once again under the control of a foreign power. As Norman Davies points out, 'middle-aged people born and reared in Warsaw or Wilno in Tsarist days experienced a strong sensation of the déjà vu', as Stalinism established its grip on Poland. Was there any way the Poles could have escaped this fate or was it, as in Greek tragedy, inevitable?

Poland had been most secure in the days of the Polish–Lithuanian Commonwealth in the seventeenth century, long before the emergence of the Russian and German empires. The fragile state created in 1919 bore little resemblance to the Commonwealth, and was only made possible by the simultaneous collapse of the powers that had partitioned Poland in 1815: Austria, Russia and Prussia-Germany. To counter a Russian revival, Piłsudski invaded the Ukraine in an attempt to ensure that Poland's borderlands remained free of Russian control. Yet his very success in achieving this intensified the enmity the USSR felt towards Poland. Similarly, in the West, the award to Poland of West Prussia and the Danzig Corridor and the coalfields in Upper Silesia made détente with Germany hard to achieve. Consequently, with the revival of German power and the growing strength of the USSR under Stalin after 1933, Poland was faced with a dual threat. Poland might, perhaps, for a time have survived as a satellite under Nazi Germany, but at the very least this would have meant the end of her independence. Alternatively, a military pact with the USSR might have been possible but again at the risk to Polish independence, as the Russians would have insisted on stationing troops within Polish territory. Instead, the Poles chose to accept the will o' the wisp of the Anglo-French guarantee.

The disastrous war of September 1939 exposed as wishful thinking the belief that the Western powers would come to the rescue of Poland by attacking Germany across the Rhine. The Soviet–German pact and the subsequent partition of Poland between the USSR and Germany emphasized with brutal clarity that Poland had two enemies. The initial organization of the Underground reflected this reality. The only hope was that Germany, as in 1918, would be defeated in the West and that

The Polish Underground 1939–1947

Russia might then be induced to withdraw either peacefully or through a successful insurgency back into her pre-1939 borders. The fall of France made the former possibility less likely, while the German invasion of Russia led to the Sikorski–Maisky Pact and, temporarily at least, the prospect of Soviet–Polish cooperation.

The German invasion of Russia also gave greater strategic importance to the role the Polish resistance could play, as Poland now straddled Germany's lines of communication. Increasingly, the most effective work done by the Home Army was sabotage, intelligence and the undermining of German morale through propaganda. The Polish resistance developed into the most effective in occupied Europe, with not only an Underground army but also an Underground State that provided an alternative structure for the Polish people within the oppressive and brutal General Government. By 1943 the AK was pinning down a large number of German and Axis troops.

Yet Soviet–Polish distrust never vanished. The revelations at Katyń showed all too clearly the real intentions of the USSR towards an independent Poland. Once the German Army was forced onto the defensive by its defeats at Stalingrad and Kursk, Stalin's long-term aims towards Poland again surfaced, and the Home Army was increasingly seen as a barrier in the way of establishing a Communist Poland. In essence, Stalin was waging a war on two fronts in Poland: against both the retreating Germans, and the AK and the traditional Polish elite. In vain did the Poles look to Britain and America to put pressure on Stalin, as neither power was willing to alienate the USSR and run the risk of rupturing the Grand Alliance. Consequently, the *Tempest* operations and, above all, the Warsaw Uprising were doomed to failure.

When the Germans were finally driven out of Poland, for all but the small minority of convinced Communists little but the enemy appeared to change. In the eastern provinces the Poles were deported into the USSR or else forcibly moved westwards. In the rest of Poland the PKWN relied on the NKVD, which was probably more ruthless and effective than the *Gestapo*, to enforce order and weed out dissidents. Once again, ex-AK and NZW groups retired into the forests, but, deprived of supplies and facing constant counter-insurgency operations, they had little long-term chance of success. The faked election results of 19 January 1947 opened the way for a Stalinist regime.

Was the heroic and unique Polish Resistance – like so much in modern Polish history – quixotic, courageous, but ultimately doomed? Of course, it is true that it proved a formidable instrument against the Germans, until

Aftermath

its back was broken by the defeat of the Warsaw Uprising, through what was unspoken and unacknowledged cooperation between the Germans and Russians. As the Russians intended, the Underground never recovered from that defeat, and failed to re-establish a free and independent post-war Poland. The officer class and the landed gentry, who had played such a key part in the Resistance, were eliminated or, at the very least, dispossessed. Henceforth it was to be the industrial workers who were to challenge the Communist regime in 1956, 1970, 1976 and in the end most effectively with the creation of the Solidarity Movement in 1980.

The courage, stubbornness and sheer bloody-mindedness of the Polish Resistance was, however, never forgotten by the Russians. Stalin attempted to crush it with terror, but his successors were more cautious. This was shown, for example, by the events in Poznań in 1956, when the workers in the ZISPO Locomotive Factory rioted and demanded 'bread and freedom' and the departure of the Russians. This led to a palace revolution in the Polish Communist Party and the restoration to power of Gomułka. Khrushchev initially considered using the Red Army to tighten Russia's grip on Poland, but drew back, observing that 'finding a reason now for armed conflict would be very easy, but finding a way to put an end to such a conflict would be hard'. The persistent rumours that the Polish Army, in the event of an invasion by the Red Army, was prepared to invade East Germany to destroy Soviet power in Central Europe may well also have played a part in this consideration!

Stalinism gave way to Gomulka's National Communism in 1956, which made Poland the most independent of the Soviet satellite states until the military coup of December 1981, but it was not until the collapse of Communism in the USSR that a genuinely democratic Poland would emerge in 1989/90.

Appendices

---••—•((•))•—••---

Appendix I: Chronology of Major Events

1772–95
Polish state ceases to exist after being partitioned between Prussia, Austria and Russia.

1815
Congress of Vienna partitions Poland once more between Russia, Prussia and Austria.

1914–18
First World War.

1917
Russian revolution.

1919
Creation of Polish Second Republic by Treaty of Versailles.

1919–21
First Polish–Russian war.

1926
Marshal Piłsudski seizes power in Poland.

1933
Hitler comes to power in January and German rearmament begins.

Appendices

1939

31 March:	Provisional British guarantee of Poland.
April:	Polish General Staff draws up plans for partisan and guerrilla warfare.
23 August:	Nazi–Soviet Non-Aggression Pact signed by Ribbentrop and Molotov.
1 September:	War begins at 14:15 hours with German dive-bomber attack on the Tczew Bridge.
3 September:	Britain and France declare war on Germany.
4 September:	Polish Army Modlin retires behind the Vistula. RAF attacks German fleet at Wilhelmshaven.
17 September:	Soviet troops cross Polish border. Polish Government flees to Romania.
27 September:	Warsaw surrenders. Tokarzewski given command of Polish Underground.
28 September:	Soviet–German Agreement on Poland's eastern frontiers.
October:	SZP (Service for Poland's Victory) formed.
2 October:	Polish Government-in-Exile, headed by General Sikorski, meets in Paris.
5 October:	Failure of plot to assassinate Hitler in Warsaw.
16 October:	Formation of General Government announced.
22 October:	'Plebiscite' held in Russian-occupied Poland to endorse full Sovietization.

1940

January:	SZP replaced by ZWZ (Union of Armed Struggle), under the command of General Rowecki.
5 March:	Stalin approves plan to execute 25,421 Polish officers and NCOs.
February:	Political Coordinating Committee of ZWZ created.
30 April:	Major Henryk Dobrzański's (alias 'Hubal') partisan group destroyed by the Germans.
June:	Over 3,000 of the Polish intellectual elite shot in Palmiry Forest.
21 June:	Franco–German Armistice.
19 July:	Sikorski forms new government in London.
22 July:	British SOE formed to assist and coordinate resistance forces in occupied territory.
December:	Office of Government Delegate for Poland created.

The Polish Underground 1939–1947

1941

January–May:	First Polish plan for national insurrection.
February 15:	First British flight to Poland to drop agents and supplies.
March:	British Treasury agrees to supply $100,000 and RM 20,000,000 to Polish Underground.
7 March:	Igo Sym assassinated.
May:	Polish Minorities Section have agents in France, South America, North Africa and Denmark.
22 June:	German invasion of USSR.
30 July:	Sikorski–Maisky Pact.
11 August:	General Anders released from prison in the USSR.
September:	Stalin presses for open revolt in Poland.
December 3–4:	Sikorski–Stalin talks.

1942

January:	People's Guard (GL) formed.
19 February:	ZWZ changes name to AK (Armia Krajowa or 'Home Army').
February:	AK plans diversionary operations behind German lines.
May:	Central Staff for Partisan Warfare set up in Moscow.
June:	About 250 Underground papers had appeared in circulation since occupation.
August:	'Anglo-Polish Society' assists escaped British POWs.
August:	*Gestapo* smashes Polish Intelligence operation in Warsaw.
August:	*Angelica* Organization in France now consists of about 5,000 agents.
27/28 March–8/9 April:	Twenty-two agents and some supplies dropped in Poland by RAF.
November:	Jan Karski briefs Eden and American Ambassador on the Holocaust.
12 November:	Himmler announces that Zamość County is to be first German colony in Poland.

1943

31 January:	German Sixth Army surrenders at Stalingrad.
February:	SOE estimate a presence of 10,000 Communist partisans in Eastern Poland.

Appendices

13 April:	Bodies of 4,321 Polish officers discovered at Katyń.
19 April:	Warsaw Ghetto uprising begins.
25 April:	Stalin breaks off relations with Sikorski Government and recognizes Union of Polish Patriots.
30 June:	*Gestapo* arrest Rowecki.
1 July:	Bór-Komorowski appointed commander of AK.
4 July:	Sikorski dies in plane accident at Gibraltar.
July–August:	Soviets defeat Germans at Battle of Kursk.
November:	Teheran Conference.
November:	Orders issued for Polish Underground Operation *Burza (Tempest)*.
18 December:	First attempt to fly supplies to Poland from RAF base at Brindisi.

1944

January:	GL absorbed into AL (People's Army).
January:	AK sets up *Antyk* to place Communists and fellow travellers in Poland under surveillance.
3–4 January:	Red Army crosses Polish pre-war border into Volhynia.
1 February:	SS Major-General Kutschera assassinated by Polish Underground.
6–9 April:	Operation *Jula*.
22 May:	AK retrieve V-2 rocket near Sarnacki.
6 June:	Western Allies land in Normandy.
June:	Operations *Sturmwind* I and II.
20 July:	Soviet units cross the Bug.
24 July:	Fall of Lublin.
25 July:	Operation *Wildhorn* III.
27 July:	Fall of Lwów.
28 July:	PKWN flown to Chełm.
1 August:	Warsaw Uprising breaks out.
4 August:	German reinforcements sent to Warsaw.
4/5 August:	Start of RAF supply flights to Warsaw.
8 August:	Major German attack on the Old Town begins.
15 August:	PKWN announces conscription to Polish People's Army.
16 August:	Germans seize filtration plant.
1–2 September:	Insurgents evacuate Old Town.
11 September:	Soviet forces resume offensive.

The Polish Underground 1939–1947

15 September:	Units of the Polish People's Army cross the Vistula to Czerniaków.
18 September:	US bombers fly supply mission.
23–29 September:	Germans break resistance in remaining pockets in Warsaw.
2 October:	Insurgents capitulate.
18 October:	Jankowski announces that the Underground State will carry on.
26 October:	Operation *Tempest* cancelled.
24 November:	Mikołajczyk resigns as Prime Minister of Polish Government-in-Exile.
28 December:	British Military Mission lands in Poland.

1945

5 January:	Stalin recognizes PKWN as Polish Provisional Government.
12 January:	Red Army reopens offensive in Central Poland.
19 January:	AK disbanded.
4–11 February:	Yalta Conference.
5 February:	Red Army crosses the Oder.
27–28 February:	Arrest of sixteen Polish Underground leaders.
April:	Reconstruction of the Council of National Unity.
April:	Widespread unrest against Communist control breaks out.
11 May:	All supplies to Polish Underground halted by Britain and USA.
June:	Establishment of the Provisional Government of National Unity.
2 July:	Britain withdraws all diplomatic recognition from the Polish Government-in-Exile.
August:	Formation of WiN (Association of Freedom and Resistance) by Colonel Rzepecki.
November:	NSZ/NZW leaders arrested.

1946

15 March:	Polish commanders in Western Europe informed that their men would be demobilized with option of return to Poland or to remain within Britain or the Commonwealth.

Appendices

February–April: Major security sweeps aimed at 'Independentists' by Polish Provisional Government.

30 June: Referendum on economic and constitutional reform as well as approval of annexation of Germany's eastern territories.

1947

19 January: General election resulting in fraudulent Communist victory.

22 February: Second Amnesty declared by Communist authorities for Underground resistance fighters.

October: To avoid imprisonment and death, Mikołajczyk escapes from Poland in a British ship.

Appendix II: Biographies of Key Figures

Lieutenant General Władysław Anders (1892–1970)

Served as a cavalry officer in the Russian Army in the First World War. In 1939 he was Commander of the Nowogródzka Cavalry Brigade, which was attached to Army Modlin. On 11 September he was given command of an independent operational unit, Group Anders. He was taken prisoner by Soviet forces near the Hungarian frontier at the end of September 1939 and imprisoned in Lwów, before being transferred to the Lubyanka jail in Moscow. He was released after the German attack on the USSR in 1941 and given responsibility for forming a new Polish corps composed of thousands of Poles imprisoned in the USSR. This force, known as 'Anders' Army', eventually regrouped in the Middle East as the II Polish Corps under ultimate British control. It played a key role in capturing Monte Cassino in 1944. For understandable reasons, Anders was fiercely anti-Bolshevik. In Italy in 1945–46 his Corps attracted many dissidents and refugees. He died in London in 1970.

Erich von dem Bach (1899–1972)

Nazi Party member of the Reichstag and a member of the SS, in which he reached the rank of *SS-Obergruppenführer*. He was appointed Commissioner for the Strengthening of Germandom in Silesia in November 1939. Two years later he became Commander of anti-partisan units on the Central Eastern front. In July 1943 his command was extended to cover all anti-partisan actions in Belgium, Belarus, France, the General Government, the Netherlands, Norway, Ukraine, Yugoslavia and parts of the Białystok area, although in practice his activities remained confined to Belarus, Eastern Poland and the Russian borderlands. On 2 August 1944 he took command of all troops fighting against the Warsaw insurgents. After more than two months of heavy fighting, which resulted in the destruction of Warsaw, he crushed the uprising and was awarded the Knight's Cross of the Iron Cross (*Ritterkreuz*) by the Nazi regime. In early 1945 he commanded the X *SS Armeekorps*, but this was annihilated in a matter of days. After the war he was arrested and died in prison in Munich.

General Zygmunt Berling (1896–1980)

Gifted soldier of Jewish extraction, promoted to lieutenant colonel in 1930. Berling retired from active service in June 1939 and did not fight in the September campaign. He was arrested by the NKVD in Wilno, but was not executed at Katyń because he consented to cooperate with the USSR. In August 1941 he was released from prison and became Chief of Staff of the reconstituted 5th Infantry Division, and then the Commander of the temporary camp for Polish soldiers in Krasnowodsk. During the evacuation of the Polish corps under Anders, Berling deserted to join the Red Army and for this was sentenced to death *in absentia* by a court martial set up by Anders. Berling was appointed the commander first of the 1st Tadeusz Kościuszko Infantry Division, and then of the Polish People's Army in the USSR in March 1944. This latter force moved into Poland in July, but by January 1945 Berling had been removed from its command and transferred to the War Academy in Moscow. He returned to Poland in 1947, where he organized and directed the Academy of General Staff and retired in 1953.

Major Henryk Dobrzański ('Hubal') (1887–1940)

Fought in Piłsudski's legions in the First World War. He became a professional soldier and an Olympic equestrian rider. In September 1939 he was Deputy Commander of the 110th Reserve Cavalry Regiment, which was to become involved in heavy fighting at Grodno with the Red Army. After the capitulation of Warsaw, with a band of about fifty men he waged a guerrilla war in the Kielce area, but was captured and executed by the Germans on 30 April 1940.

Hans Frank (1900–1946)

Had been Nazi Minister of Justice in Bavaria, and then, in 1934, Reich Minister without Portfolio. He was Governor-General of German-

Appendices

occupied Poland 1939–1945 and was sentenced to death by the Allies at the Nuremberg trials. He was executed on 1 October 1946.

Major General Sir Colin Gubbins (1896–1976)

Became an expert in irregular warfare. His initial experience of this was gained as a member of General Ironside's staff in Russia in 1919 and then in Ireland, 1920–1921. Gubbins served as the military member on the International Commission in the Sudetenland. From 1935 to 1940 he was a staff officer at the War Office and wrote manuals on irregular warfare, which were later sent to the Polish Underground movement. He was Chief of Staff to the British Military Mission to Poland in September 1939. In November 1940 Gubbins was seconded to the SOE as Director for Operations for Western and Central Europe, and appointed its chief in September 1943. He retired in 1946 and became managing director of a carpet and textile manufacturers.

Stanisław Jankowski (1882–1953)

Chief Government Delegate of the Underground State, 1943–45. He was arrested by the NKVD on 27 March 1945, sentenced in the Trial of the Sixteen, and murdered in a Soviet prison.

Lance Corporal Ron Jeffery (1917–2002)

Was captured in 1940 near Doullens and ended up in a German POW camp near Łódź. He escaped and joined the AK in Warsaw. Before the war he had been a business manager, and already spoke German and French. He learnt Polish and served as a courier travelling to Vienna, Prague, Budapest, Berlin and Hamburg. He also took part in executions of Nazi collaborators and traitors sentenced by special Underground courts. In early 1944 he escaped to Britain via Sweden, bringing invaluable information about the Polish Underground. After the war he settled in New Zealand.

Sir Howard Kennard (1878–1955)

Had served as a diplomat in various positions in Teheran, Washington, Havana and Tangier. He was Minister Plenipotentiary in Yugoslavia and, before moving to Warsaw, Ambassador first in Stockholm and then in Berne. He represented the British Government in Warsaw from 1935 to 1939, where he proved a highly effective ambassador, whose dispatches have become important historical documents. He was highly critical of the Polish occupation of Teschen but as supportive of the Polish Government as London permitted during the period March–September 1939. He accompanied the Polish Government to Romania and then to Angers and finally London with Sikorski's Government-in-Exile. He retired in 1941.

Zygmunt Klukowski (1885–1959)

Was a medical doctor, Superintendant of Szczebrzeszyn hospital, local historian and book collector. His books *Diaries from the Years of Occupation, 1939–44* and *Red Shadow: A Physician's Memoir of the Soviet Occupation of Eastern Poland, 1944–1956* contain invaluable eyewitness accounts for these years.

General Count Tadeusz Komorowski, alias 'Bór' (1895–1966)

Took part in the September campaign and then helped set up an Underground group in the Kraków area. In July 1941 he became deputy commander of the ZWZ/AK and its commander in March 1943. He is best known for ordering the disastrous but heroic Warsaw Uprising to start on 1 August 1944. After two months of fighting, the Polish forces surrendered and Bór was interned as a POW in Germany. After the war he remained in London. His memoirs, *The Secret Army*, are an important historical source.

Stefan Korboński (1901–1989)

Fought in the Polish–Soviet war and took part in the attempt by the Poles to seize Silesia from the Germans in 1921. After graduating from university he practised law and joined the (Polish) People's Party. In 1936 he became the Party's chairman for the Białystok *Voivodship*. He fought in the September campaign and managed to escape from the Soviet zone to reach German-occupied Poland, where he became one of the leaders of the illegal People's Party, as well as playing an active role in the SZP/ZWZ. In April 1941 he became head of the Directorate of Civil Struggle, and in December 1942 the chief of the Directorate of Civil Resistance. During the Warsaw Uprising he briefly became the head of the Department of Internal Affairs. In March 1945, after Jankowski's arrest by the NKVD, Korboński became the last Government Delegate, but in June he too was arrested. On his release he became an active member of the PSL, but after the 1947 election fled Poland for the USA.

Stanisław Kot (1885–1975)

Was a Professor of History at the Jagiellonian University in Kraków, but in September 1933 he was dismissed by the *Sanacja* Government for his

Appendices

defence of academic liberty. In September 1939 he escaped to France and served in the Polish Government-in-Exile, initially as Minister of Internal Affairs. After the Sikorski–Maisky Pact of July 1941 he was appointed Polish Ambassador to the Soviet Union in Moscow until 1942. He then served as Minister of State for a year in the Middle East, and later as Minister of Information (Press and of the Propaganda Department) in both the Sikorski and Mikołajczyk governments. He accepted the post of Polish Ambassador to Rome (1945 to 1947) under the Provisional Government of National Unity, but resigned and returned to Britain in 1947 for fear of arrest in Poland.

Franz Kutschera (1904–1944)

Was appointed an *SS-Brigadeführer* in 1940 and then, in 1942, *General-major* of the police. He was a fanatical and successful opponent of the Underground and consequently was appointed to the command of the SS and police in the Mogilev district of the USSR from April to September 1943. He was then transferred to Warsaw, where he was assassinated by the AK on 1 February 1944.

Stanisław Mikołajczyk (1896–1980)

Was originally a peasant farmer from near Posnań. He went into politics in 1937 and became President of the PSL. He fought in the September campaign as a private, but after the fall of Warsaw escaped to Hungary, and thence to Paris. In 1941 he became Minister of the Interior in the Government-in-Exile, and, when Sikorski was killed in a plane crash in July 1943, Prime Minister. He resigned in November 1944 because of disagreements with his Cabinet over his readiness to recognize the Curzon Line. In June 1945 he joined the new Provisional Government of National Unity in Poland, becoming one of two Deputy Prime Ministers. He revived the PSL, but the rigged election of January 1947 gave the party just 28 seats as opposed to 394 Communist seats. In October, to avoid arrest and death, he fled to Britain.

General Leopold Okulicki (1898–1946)

Joined the SZP after the fall of Warsaw in 1939 and became Commander of the Underground organization in Lwów, where he was arrested by the NKVD. Released after the Sikorski–Maiski Pact, he joined the Polish corps in Russia under Anders' command. After serving as Commanding Officer of the Polish 7th Infantry Division, he was parachuted into occupied Poland, where he became General Bór's deputy and successor.

The Polish Underground 1939–1947

After the capitulation of the Warsaw Uprising, he moved to Kraków and reorganized the Home Army, which he dissolved on 19 January 1945. In March he was arrested by the NKVD and sentenced to ten years' imprisonment, but in December 1946 was murdered in prison.

Joseph Retinger (1888–1960)
Adviser to the Sikorski Government in London. In 1944 he was parachuted into occupied Poland to talk with leading political figures and deliver money to the Polish Underground. After the war he became a leading advocate of European unification and helped found both the European Movement and the Council of Europe.

Stefan Rowecki, alias 'Grot' (1895–1944)
After the September campaign, Rowecki managed to evade capture and returned to Warsaw where, in October, he became one of the senior officers of the SZP. In January 1940 he was appointed commander of the ZWZ (later the AK). On 30 June 1943 he was betrayed by *Gestapo* agents within the AK, arrested in Warsaw and sent to Berlin, where he was interrogated by leading Nazis, including Himmler, and offered the prospect of forming an anti-Bolshevik alliance with the Germans, which he rejected. He was executed in August 1944 in Sachsenhausen.

Lord Roundell Selborne (1887–1971)
Had occupied government posts in the Conservative governments of the 1920s. He was appointed Minister of Economic Warfare from 1942 to 1945, which made him responsible for the Special Operations Executive (SOE). After the war he went into business.

General Władysław Sikorski (1881–1943)
Fought in the Polish Legions in the First World War. In 1922–1923 he was Prime Minister and then, in 1922–1924, minister of military affairs. After Piłsudski's coup Sikorski fell from favour, and it was only after the defeat of Poland that he became Prime Minister of the Government-in-Exile and Commander-in-Chief of the Armed Forces. In April 1943 Stalin broke off relations with the government because Sikorski demanded that the International Red Cross should investigate the Katyń massacre. In July Sikorski was killed in a plane crash at Gibraltar.

General Kasimierz Sosnkowski (1885–1968)
Commanded an Operational Group in the September campaign, and then was Deputy Commander of the Polish armed forces in exile, 1939–1943.

Appendices

From 1943 to 1944 he was Commander-in-Chief. He was dismissed on 30 September 1944.

Stefan Starzyński (1893–?1943)
Politician, economist, writer, statesman and Lord Mayor of Warsaw before and during the Siege of Warsaw in 1939. After the fall of the city on 27 September 1939, he initially remained as mayor and actively supported the resistance by providing it with thousands of blank ID cards, birth registry forms and passports. He was arrested by the *Gestapo* and imprisoned in Pawiak jail. He probably died in Dachau in 1943.

SS-Brigadeführer Jürgen Stroop (1895–1952)
Joined the SS and the NSDAP in 1932 and served on the Eastern front, 1941–1943. Historically, his most prominent role was the suppression of the Warsaw Ghetto Uprising, April–May 1943, which cost the lives of over 50,000 people. He was executed for war crimes in Poland in 1952.

Władysław Studnicki (1867–1953)
A Polish politician and publicist, who throughout his life had been pro-German. In October 1939 he wrote to the Germans suggesting rearming the Polish Army, which would then fight the USSR in alliance with the *Wehrmacht*. In January 1940 he appealed to the German Government to moderate its occupation policy but he was ignored and later imprisoned by the Germans.

General Stanisław Tatar, alias 'Tabor' (1896–1980)
Joined the ZWZ/AK and was on its General Staff, where he did the planning for Operation *Tempest*. In 1944 he was transferred to London, to become Deputy Chief of the General Staff. In 1945 he became the Commander of Artillery of the I Polish Corps in the United Kingdom, and when it was disbanded, he settled in the UK. In 1947 he organized the transfer of Polish gold reserves in the UK back to Poland, where the government had promised to use it to help ex-servicemen. In fact it disappeared without trace. Tatar returned to Poland in 1949 but was arrested in 1951. He was released in 1956.

General Michał Tokarzewski-Karaszewicz (1893–1964)
Served as the commander of the Operational Group of the 'Armia Pomorze' during the September campaign and fought in the Battle of Bzura. He was the second-in-command to General Juliusz Rómmel,

The Polish Underground 1939–1947

during the defence of Warsaw. On 27 September he founded the SZP and was its Commander-in-Chief until December 1939, when he was transferred to Lwów. He was arrested by the NKVD in March 1940. He was released in August 1941 and served as the second-in-command of the Polish Army in the Middle East. After the war he remained in exile in England.

Sergeant John Ward (1919–1995)

Was a wireless operator in a Fairey Battle bomber, which was shot down on 10 May 1940 over Holland. He was initially hospitalized and then sent to various POW camps. He managed to escape, and with the help of Polish Underground networks made his way to Warsaw, where he assisted the AK by monitoring BBC broadcasts and constructing wireless receivers and transmitters. He also acquired Polish, albeit with a 'strong foreign accent'. During the Warsaw Uprising he fought on the barricades and, as the only Englishman in Warsaw with the right skills, was also able to transmit invaluable information to the British Government. He escaped from Warsaw in October 1944 to join AK troops in the Kielce area. He was interrogated in January 1945 and then again in March by the Russians about the Polish Resistance, but in the end he was repatriated via Odessa. After the war he never mentioned his heroic exploits in Poland.

Sir Peter Wilkinson (1914–2000)

Was commissioned into the Royal Fusiliers in 1935. He was a member of the British Military Mission in Poland in September 1939, and went on to join No. 4 Military Mission in Paris from where, in early 1940, he was sent to Hungary to assist the Polish Underground. After the fall of France he joined the SOE. He was sent to Crete and, after a period back in London, to Yugoslavia. After the Second World War he pursued a diplomatic career.

Appendix III: Glossary and Abbreviations

AA	Anti-aircraft Artillery
Abwehr	German military Intelligence
AK	*Armia Krajowa* (Home Army)
AL	*Armia Ludowa* (People's Army)
BCh	*Bataliony Chłopskie* (Peasants' Battalions)

Appendices

II Bureau	2nd Bureau of the Polish General Staff, responsible for Intelligence
VI Bureau	6th Bureau of the Polish General Staff, responsible for communications with Poland and other occupied territories
C-in-C	Commander-in-Chief
Curzon Line	Poland's eastern frontier as proposed by Lord Curzon in 1919
Einsatzgruppe	Special task force of the German Security Police
EU/P	British SOE section dealing with Polish operations outside Poland
FO	British Foreign Office
Gestapo	*Geheime Staatspolizei* (German Secret State Police)
GL	*Gwardia Ludowa* (People's Guard)
IWM	Imperial War Museum
JMU	Jewish Military Union
KB	Security Corps (AK)
Kedyw	*Kierownictwo Dywersji* (Directorate of Diversion). Hence Kedyw partisan units
KPP	*Komunistyczna Partia Polski* (Communist Party of Poland)
KRIPO	*Kriminalpolizei* (Criminal Police)
KRN	*Krajowa rada Narodowa* (Homeland National Council)
Luftwaffe	German Air Force
MI5	British Secret Service
MI(R)	British Military Intelligence (Research)
N Scheme (Action 'N')	Conducted psychological warfare against the Germans in Poland
NA	National Archives
NKVD	Soviet People's Commissariat of Internal Affairs, responsible for security, Intelligence and prisons
NOW	*Narodowe Organisacja Wojsjowa* (National Military Organization)
NSZ	*Narodowe Siły Zbrojne* (National Armed Units)
Obergruppenführer	Senior Group Leader – highest SS rank, inferior only to *Reichsführer-SS* Heinrich Himmler

The Polish Underground 1939–1947

Ordnungspolizei German 'Order police' for general policing
PAL *Polska Armia Ludowa* (Polish People's Army)
Panzer German term for armoured vehicles, especially tanks
PIAT Projector, Infantry, Anti-Tank (British anti-tank weapon)
PKWN *Polski Komitet Wyzwolenia Narodowego* (Polish National Committee of Liberation)
POW Prisoner of War
PPR *Polska Partia Robotnicza* (The Polish Workers' Party)
PPS *Polska Partia Socjalistyczna* (The Polish Socialist Party)
PSL Polish People's Peasant Movement
PUMST Polish Underground Movement Study Trust in Ealing, London
Reichsarbeitsamt Reich Labour Office
Sanacja Polish political movement that came to power after Piłsudski's death
SD *Sichereitsdienst* (German Security Police)
Sejm Polish Parliament
SOE Special Operations Executive (British)
SS Nazi 'Schutzstaffel' or 'defence unit' – its initial role was to protect Hitler's person but by 1939 it controlled the German police and had a paramilitary arm, the *Waffen SS*
SZP *Służba Zwycięstwu Polski* (Service for Poland's Victory)
Todt Organization Organization for civil and military construction projects, founded in 1933 and headed by Fritz Todt – increasingly, from 1940 onwards, it employed POWs and foreign labour
TRJN *Tymczasowy Rzad Jednosci Narodowej* (Provisional Government of National Unity)
V-1 *Vergeltungswaffe* I (flying bomb)
V-2 *Vergeltungswaffe* II (rocket)
Voivodship (*województwa*) Province
Volksdeutsche Ethnic Germans who lived in Poland
Wachlarz ('fan') Diversionary organization of the Home Army in Eastern Poland

Appendices

Waffen SS	Armed SS unit
Wehrmacht	German Army
WiN	*Wolność i Niezawislosc* (Freedom and Independence) Anti-Communist resistance organization in Poland
Żegota	Council for Aid to Jews
ŻOB	*Żydowska Organizacja Bojowa* (Jewish Fighting Organization)
ZPP	Union of Polish Patriots
ZWZ	*Związek Walki Zbrojnej* (Union of Armed Struggle)

Appendix IV: Orders of Battle and Statistics

A. *Polish Intelligence Report Centres in the Reich, August 1942*

1. Group ZN (Region Berlin, Hamburg, Rhineland)
2. Group ZR (Region Berlin, North and East sea coast)
3. Group ZSK (Region Berlin, Special Group)
4. Group ZA (Danzig Area)
5. Group ZB (Coastal region from Gotenhafen to Memel)
6. Group ZSM (Danzig–Gotenhafen area)

[Source: NA, HS4/268]

B. *Mobilization of partisan groups to attack German lines of communication in coordination with* Overlord, *May 1944*

1. Kasia I	controlled by	HQ Warsaw East
2. Kasia II	controlled by	HQ Warsaw West
3. Mania	controlled by	HQ Skarżysko
4. Jaga	controlled by	HQ Lwów
5. Lena	controlled by	HQ Kraków
6. Ola	controlled by	HQ Lublin
7. Stacha I	controlled by	HQ Nowogródek
Stacha II	controlled by	HQ Nowogródek
8. Roma	controlled by	HQ Wilno

[Source: NA, NS4/161]

C. *Summary of air operations in 1944 to Poland by RAF, Commonwealth and Polish flights*

	Successful	Unsuccessful	Aircraft lost	Weight of stores (tons)
January	1	3	1	1.50
February	–	7	–	–
March	1	11	–	1.50
April	65	67	3	76.66
May	76	46	2	96
June	–	–	–	–
July	33	30	3	46.75
August	81	89	26	97.71
September	15	32	10	17.79
October	4	19	2	5.27
November	4	11	–	5.65
December	10	15	1	13.15
Total	290	330	48	361.98

[Source: NA, HS4/177]

D. *Underground members, partisans and 'bandits' captured or killed by the Germans in the Lublin District, May 1943–July 1944*

	Killed	Captured
May	332	93
June	353	121
July	305	142
August	195	101
September	129	56
October	290	323
November	145	103
December	271	159
January	150	91
February	757	142
March	455	35
April	275	10
May	375	112
June	137	284
July	101	86
Total	4,270	1,858

[Source: M.J. Chodakiewicz, *Between the Nazis and the Soviets*, Lexington Books, 2004, p. 368]

Appendices

E. Army, Police and SS personnel stationed in the General Government, 1939–1944

Date	Army	Police/SS	Total
October 1939	550,000	80,000	630,000
April 1940	400,000	70,000	470,000
June 1941	2,000,000	50,000	2,050,000
February 1942	300,000	50,000	350,000
April 1943	450,000	60,000	510,000
November 1943	550,000	70,000	620,000
April 1944	500,000	70,000	570,000
September 1944	1,000,000	80,000	1,080,000

[Source: C. Madajczyk, *Die Okupationspolitik Nazideutschlands in Polen, 1939–1945*, Pahl-Rugenstein, Akademie-Verlag, Cologne, 1988, p. 239]

F. Polish Order of Battle in Warsaw, 1 August 1944

Old Town
* Group Rog, composed of: AK Battalions Boncza, Gustaw-Harnas, Wigry, Dzik, Group PWB/17/5 and 101st Kompania Syndykalistów.
* Group Kuba-Sosna, composed of: AK Battalions Gozdawa, Lukasinski, Chobry, KB (AK Security Corps) Battalion Nalecz and one NSZ platoon.
* Group Lesnik, composed of: 3 AK companies and Battalion Czwartacy (AL).

City Centre
* Western Section: AK Battalions Zaremba-Piorun and Golski.
* Northern Section: AK Battalions Belt, Milośz, Iwo, Ruczaj and KB Battalion Sokol.
* Eastern Section: Group Kryska, composed of: AK Battalions Tur, Tum and Stefan and one AL platoon.

Groups Directly subordinated to Headquarters
* Group Radisław, composed of: AK Battalions Miotla, Parasol, Piesc, Zośka and Broda 53.
* Group Chobry II, composed of: AK Battalions Lech Zelazny and Lech Grzybowski.

225

The Polish Underground 1939–1947

* Group Gurt, composed of: AK Battalion Gurt and WSOP Polish Firefighters (Group IV).
* Group Bartkiewicz (AK).
* Other units: AK Battalions Rum, Kilinski and KB Battalion Jur-Radwari.
* Company Koszta.

Powisle
* Group Krybar, composed of AK Battalions Bicz, Konrad III and Group Elektrowinia.

Mokotów
* Regiment Baszta, composed of: AK Battalions Baltyk, Olza, Karpety.
* Group Grzmaly, composed of: AK Battalions Krawiec and Korwin.
* Other AK Units: 7th Ułan Regiment Jelen, Artillery Group Granat, 1st Squadron Goral, Battalions Odwet, Zygmunt, Oaza and 5th WSOP.

Praga
* AK Battalions: Grunwald, Bolek, Olszyna and Platerowek.

Okecie
* 7th Infantry Regiment Garluch, composed of: AK Battalions 1, 2, 3 and Artillery Company Kuba.

Kampinos Forest
* Group Kampinos, composed of: AK Battalions Korwina, Strzaly, Znicza.

Żoliborz
* AK Groups Zmija, Zubr, Zaglowiec, Zbik, Zniwiarz, Zyrafa and one AL company.

Wola
* Battalion Sowinski and 18 independent platoons.

Ochota
* AK Battalions Wacława and Gustaw plus 12 independent platoons.

Appendices

G. German Order of Battle in Warsaw, 23 August 1944

1. Kampfgruppe (Battle Group) Rohr (commanded by Major-General Rohr).
2. Kampfgruppe Reinefarth (commanded by *SS-Gruppenführer* Heinz Reinefarth.
3. Sturmgruppe (Assault Group) Reck (commanded by Major Reck).
4. Sturmgruppe Schmidt (commanded by Colonel Schmidt).
5. Various support and back-up units.

Manpower total: 289 officers and 16,696 other ranks.

[Sources: Forczyk, pp. 30–32, Davies, pp. 664–667 and List of Military Units in the Warsaw Uprising (http://en.wikipedia.org/wiki/)]

Appendix V: Survivors' Reminiscences

Interview by the Author with Mr Jan Brodzki, 30 August 2011

Jan Brodzki was only sixteen in 1939. At the start of the war he was in Warsaw, but together with all males aged between fifteen and sixty he was ordered on 7 September to move eastwards. He was wounded in the head, but managed to return to Warsaw on 19 October. After he had recovered, he faced a very different world. He was unable to finish his studies at school and had to work for a time in the small transport business his cousin had set up with some illegally retained horses. All sorts of 'dubious cargoes' were carried – most likely part of the thriving black market. However, in 1941 Jan was able to study at a technical college and in 1943 gained his diploma and worked in the laboratories of a pharmaceutical company called 'Motor'. He did not become a member of the AK, but when the Warsaw Uprising broke out he joined its Department of Information and Propaganda in Mokotów. On 25 September he escaped through the sewers and ended up in the city centre after seventeen hours in the sewers. He had lost his way and, although no athlete, had to climb over underground walls some 7 or 8 feet high. He remembers particularly that the junction of the sewers resembled a huge vaulted cathedral. He found his mother, who was running a soup kitchen, and then enrolled in his cousin's unit in the AK. After the surrender on 2 October this unit patrolled Warsaw, together with German troops, to ensure that the evacuation was complete. As he remarked, he was able to observe what was left of Warsaw being burnt down by the Germans. On 17 October he was then sent as a POW to Stalag IVB in Mühlberg,

Germany. When he was liberated by the Russians in the spring of 1945, he managed to avoid being sent back to Poland or, indeed, deportation to the USSR, by claiming – much to the surprise of the Soviet member of the Inter-Allied Commission – that he had been taken prisoner in East Africa and therefore needed to collect his wages before returning home. He was flown to Brussels and then on to Bushy Heath near London where, thanks to the prompting of the officer interviewing him, he stressed that he was a soldier and was thus sent to Kirkcaldy in Scotland to serve under the command of the Polish forces.

Interview by the Author with Hanna Skrzynska, 30 August 2011

Like so many of her contemporaries, the outbreak of war caught Hanna on holiday in Eastern Poland. She managed to return to Warsaw, where she found her mother and family. As the Germans had banned academic secondary education, her Grammar school had metamorphosed into a school for seamstresses. She was a member of the Scouts and learnt first aid, but rapidly became bored and wanted to join the Underground. Her initial contact was with a Communist organization, but through friends she managed to make contact with the Nationalist Party and joined the NOW organization, where she was given the number '143' and became a liaison and messenger girl. At times this could be a difficult task. Once she was stopped and searched by a police patrol when she was carrying important information on rolled up cigarette paper in her gloves. Fortunately, she was not ordered to remove them. Another time, when there was only a short time until the evening curfew on the fateful day of 22 June 1941, she was desperate to get back home on time when her tram was stopped as the street was blocked by interminable columns of German troops passing through to the east. Masses of people were waiting to cross the road. Suddenly there was a brief gap and she attempted to dash through it but was stopped by a German gendarme, who kicked her from behind. To his surprise she knocked him down and then 'ran like a rabbit' and managed to cross the road. Once she reached the other side she remembers being warned by bystanders to slow down, so as not to attract attention to herself.

In many ways Hanna appeared to lead a charmed life. Two years later, in 1943, she remembers a police raid on the block of flats where her parents lived. She was searched by three *Gestapo* officers in the concierge's office, while the other residents were formed up in a large queue awaiting questioning, but she was saved by the possession of her

Appendices

Kennkarte (identity card) and allowed to go. Once freed, she was able to rescue her parents from the queue awaiting questioning, on the grounds that she was now 'frei' and by implication innocent.

She joined the AK in 1942 again as a liaison girl. When the uprising broke out, she was ordered to report to the city centre, but like so many insurgents, was unable to reach her destination. Unknown to her, both her sister and mother were also members of the AK. On her way to the city centre she saw young men building barricades and was told to go to the Red Cross station and stayed the night in a cellar. She eventually made it to the centre, where she reported to the Battalion 'Gustaw'. The Commanding Officer greeted her with the words: 'It's a shame you are not a boy!' She served as both a runner and in a hospital, where she was three times buried by falling masonry. On 30 August she escaped, bent double, through the sludge of the sewers. Through pure chance she was quickly reunited with her mother, who was working in a supply unit and needed a liaison girl.

When the insurgents surrendered, Hanna's mother was advised by a colonel on Bór's staff that it was far safer to leave Warsaw as a POW than as a civilian. The combatants were then gathered together in Ożarów and sent by cattle truck via Fallingbostel and Bergen-Belsen to Oberlangen, where in April Hanna and her sister were liberated by the 1st Polish Armoured Division. Both girls were taken under the wing of this division. Hanna's sister eventually moved to Belgium, while Hanna married a major in the Polish Army and they settled in Britain in 1947. Her father was not so lucky. He was initially sent to Siberia by the Russians but returned in a transport of German POWs to Germany in late 1945. He was arrested again in Poland by the Communist Government in 1951 and only released in 1956.

Interview by the Author with Halina Serafinowicz, 13 September 2011

Halina's memories of the first period of the German occupation are of the acute shortage of food in Warsaw, where she lived. After September 1939 she continued to study for a short time at school but then, in order to help her mother, she had to go out to work at a hairdresser's. The owner was Jewish but it was managed by Halina's eldest brother, whose wife hid the owner in her house. Halina herself did not join the Underground until 1944, as she was simply too busy working and learning her trade as a hairdresser. Her two other brothers were, however, swept up in the war. One brother was sent to Berlin to work in a factory, where he surreptitiously sabotaged production whenever possible. Her other brother, Henry, who had been a Scout and was very interested in military matters, joined the Home Army at an early stage, even though his brother at the hairdresser's thought the whole Underground was a joke. Halina remembers that Henry was often away for months on end, and then would suddenly return home unannounced. He was arrested three times by the *Gestapo* and 'terribly beaten up'. Halina thinks that one reason for this was that he looked Jewish. In 1944 he was taken to Flossenbürg camp and then later to Dachau. He died two weeks after liberation by American troops.

When the uprising broke out, Halina, like so many other people, was caught on the way home. It took her three days to get home from the Old Town to the centre. She wanted just to see her mother and tell her she was all right. After that she returned with a friend to the Old Town to volunteer to fight, and was attached to the 101 Company of Syndicalists, which was a part of Group Rog. Over six decades later Halina's admiration for their fighting prowess and courage remains undimmed: they were, as she said, 'real fighters'. The company had participated in the fighting around the Royal Castle and then, under pressure from the Germans, had retired to defend St John's Cathedral and the Old Town. She served primarily as a messenger and courier, delivering hand grenades concealed in her handbag. She remembers well that, as nothing was given to her in writing, she had to commit the messages to memory by constantly repeating them to herself en route. She was also at times employed as an observer, and from a window on a first floor of the castle, she was able to observe and then inform the company's headquarters about what was happening in the fierce fighting around the Castle Square.

At the end of August she escaped with the company, and, of course, many other insurgents, through the sewers to the centre. She remembers that at times the sludge and water reached their chests. When they emerged safely, they were welcomed, but bombarded with enquiries about whether they knew anything of particular individuals who had gone missing. Amongst these was Halina's own mother, whom she never saw again. Halina herself felt much safer in the centre but continued to act as a messenger and runner for the company, which had become part of Battalion 'Boncza'.

After the capitulation of the insurgents on 2 October, Halina was sent as a POW to Fallingbostel and later to Bergen-Belsen. In the last few months of the war she worked in Hanover, clearing rubble and unloading

Appendices

rations from railway wagons. She was finally liberated by troops of the Polish 1st Armoured Division and returned home briefly to Poland.

Interview by the Author with Maria Karczewska-Schejbal (alias 'Marzenna'), 20 September 2011

Maria's family originally lived in the Warsaw suburb of Praga, but after being bombed out – first by the Germans in 1939 and then by the Russians in 1942 – lived in a fourth-floor flat in the Old Town on Krasinski Square. She remembers vividly the sound of the fighting in the ghetto in April 1943. The flat was a meeting place for one of the Underground groups, but her father specifically warned her not to get involved. Her time would come, he said, when the 'insurrection started'. Sometimes, Jewish fugitives were brought to the flat to shelter overnight before leaving Warsaw for the countryside. One evening, when her parents were out, German police knocked on the door and asked if her family were sheltering Jews. In her surprise and panic Maria was ready to admit them, but fortunately they decided against a search – to the enormous relief of the Jewish lady who was in fact sheltering in the flat! Maria's school closed in September 1939. When it reopened, she was supposed to learn a technical trade but her teachers managed illegally to continue instructing their students in more academic subjects. In case the Germans turned up, the books were hidden beneath the desks. Eventually her *Gimnazjum* (Grammar school) was closed down and Maria received a letter from the *Arbeitsamt* (Labour Office) ordering her to work in Germany. However, her father managed, through contacts with friends, to find her a job at a seed shop in Warsaw.

At the time of 'W' Hour on 1 August 1944 Maria was returning home from the shop. She became caught up in the fighting and had to shelter in a basement until she was able to get home on 3 August. She then joined the Kuba-Sosna group and served in Battalion 'Lukasinski' as a messenger, but one of her major tasks was also to track down medical supplies amidst the rubble of destroyed chemist shops. At the end of August, just before the fall of the Old Town, her platoon was ordered to escape via the sewers, but the main sewers were so full that a scout had to lead them to a manhole, which was very difficult to find, outside the mental asylum on Danietowiezowski Street. When Maria, together with another thirty-eight insurgents, entered the sewer at 8 p.m., they were initially told it would only take three hours to reach safety, but in fact it was not until noon the following day that they emerged from the sewer. At one stage the long column suddenly stopped and was gripped with panic, with some of the young men hysterically shouting that they wanted to kill themselves. According to Maria, it was mainly the girls who managed to calm them down. In the end they realized that it was a swollen corpse that was blocking the tunnel. They were ordered, on the count of three, to form a chain and push like a battering ram. This proved successful and they managed to move forwards. Eventually all of them emerged opposite the Prudential Building on Świętokrzyska Street and, in a reaction to the fresh air, fainted. In the tunnels Maria had cut her head and was already running a temperature. Her main desire, however, was to bathe, and barrels of water were available for this purpose. She climbed into the barrel and fell asleep. Fortunately, she was saved from drowning when her commander realized she was missing. She was rescued, brought out on a stretcher, and her head wound treated with disinfectant. She did not work as a messenger any more but spent her time searching for food.

On 4 October she marched out with the other insurgents as a POW to Ożarów, where they were divided up into groups before being sent to camps in Germany. At Oberlangen Camp she was eventually liberated by the 1st Polish Armoured Division in April 1945. Maria then finished her schooling in one of the Polish schools, which had been specially opened in Germany. She refused to follow the advice of Communist officers who had been sent to persuade the students to return to Poland. Instead, plans were drawn up by the liaison officer and a Polish priest to smuggle the students over the Brenner frontier. Three Polish Army lorries arrived from Anders' II Corps in Italy, allegedly to fetch supplies. Maria and her fellow students were then picked up on a remote forest road leading to the Brenner by these lorries and taken to Trani near Bari, where they studied for three more months in company with other Polish girls who had arrived from Africa and India. Three months later she was sent to a camp in England. She married a Polish officer and was joined by her mother. Her father was 'liberated' in Eastern Germany by the Russians and was sent to work in the coal mines near Leipzig. He was never heard of again.

Sources

Manuscripts in the Imperial War Museum
Baker, C., 87/34/1
Blaichmann, E.F., 02.23/1
Corby, J., 87/44/1
Freund, M., 0/28/1
Goldberg, S., 06/521
Gubbins, C., 04/29/8
Hudson, D., 03/20/1
Krey, W., 94/26/1
Kurylak, S., 78/52/1
Lloyd-Lyne, H., 97/23/1
Manners, G., 95/17/1
Misc 249 Item 3455 (Report on the British Observer Mission, 26 December 1945)
Parker, M. (Pokorney), PPMCR/378
Pomorski, Z.R., 96/55/1
Ślązak, G., 95/13/1
Smorczewski, R., 03/41/1
Stankiewicz, K., 83/10/1
Threlfall, H., 84/10/1
Wilkinson, P., 67/150/1

Oral Testimonies in the Imperial War Museum
Avery, D., 22065
Bibor, T., 17514
Hart-Moxon, K., 16632
Wilkinson, P., 8978/2

The Polish Underground 1939–1947

Photostats of Captured German Documents in the Imperial War Museum
AL 1759
AL 2583/1 and /2
AL 2683
AL 2690
AL 2696

Records at the National Archives, Kew
In its FO371 series the Foreign Office has a considerable amount of material on occupied Poland and Polish affairs during the Second World War. Regular reports from the Embassy in Warsaw were resumed after June 1945. The following files were particularly useful:

> FO371/ 24467–83, 26718–34, 31092–98, 31101–04, 47709–11, 47627–29, 47179, 447648–50, 5645, 56662–72, 56482, 66135, 66149, 66271, 66233, 66238, 66247, 88258

The main sources of information on the Polish Resistance are the SOE archives, Series HS4/6/7/8. The files in HS4/135–328 are a mine of information and were of invaluable assistance to the author, but they are neither chronological nor complete. They were ruthlessly weeded in 1945, and it is possible that a fire in 1946 destroyed even more files.

The following Air Ministry series of files were also very useful for air drops, RAF assistance to SOE, V-1 and V-2 weapons: AIR 8/19/20.23/34/37/40/51.

Polish Underground Study Trust, Ealing, London
Material relating to Polish VI Bureau papers and the *Wildhorn* Operations.

The Polish Institute and Sikorski Museum, Kensington, London
Papers relating to the Polish Government-in-Exile and the II Bureau.

Published Sources: Diaries, Memoirs and Printed Books
Biega, K.C., *Thirteen is my Lucky Number*, Syrena Press, Plainsboro, NJ, 1996
Bines, J., *The Polish Country Section of the Special Operations Executive, 1940–46*, Ph.D thesis for the University of Stirling, 2008 (https://dspace.stir.ac.uk/bitstream/1893/929/1/z%20Thesis.pdf).

Sources

Bór-Komorowski, T., *The Secret Army*, London, Gollancz, 1950.

Borodziej, W., *The Warsaw Uprising of 1944*, University of Wisconsin Press, 2006.

Chodakiewicz, M.J., *Between the Nazis and the Soviets*, Lexington Books, 2004.

Ciechanowski, J., *The Warsaw Uprising of 1944*, CUP, 1974.

Coutouvidis, J. and Reynolds, J., *Poland 1939–1947*, Leicester University Press, 1986.

Davies, N., *God's Playground: A History of Poland, II*, Columbia IP, 1982.

Davies, N., *Rising '44*, Macmillan, 2004.

Dziura-Dziurski, A., *Freedom Fighter*, J.A. Dewer publisher, Portland, 1983.

Forczyk, R., *Warsaw 1944*, Osprey, 2009.

Garliński, J., *Fighting Auschwitz*, Julian Friedman Publishers, 1975.

Garliński, J., *Poland in the Second World War*, Macmillan, 1985.

Graboski, J., *Rescue for Money: Polish Helpers in Poland, 1939–45*, Vad Vashem, 2008.

Gross, J.T., *Polish Society Under German Occupation*, Princeton, 1979.

Hanson, J., *The Civilian Population and the Warsaw Uprising*, Cambridge, 1982.

Hubbard-Hall, C., ' "A Game of Cat and Mouse": The Gestapo Spy Network in Tomaschow Mazowiecki, Poland, 1939–45', in *War in a Twilight World*, ed. Shepherd, B. and Pattinson, J., Palgrave, 2010, pp. 156–77.

Jeffery, R., *Red Runs the Vistula*, Nevron Associates, 1989.

Kahn, L., *No Time to Mourn*, Laurelton Press, Vancouver, 1978.

Kenney, P., *Rebuilding Poland: Workers and Communists 1945–1950*, Cornell University Press, 1997.

Kersten, K., *The Establishment of Communist Rule in Poland*, University of California Press, 1991, Berkeley, Los Angeles, Oxford.

Klukowski, Z., *Diary from the Years of Occupation*, University of Illinois Press, 1993.

Klukowski, Z., *Red Shadow*, ed. Klukowski, A., McFarland and Company, 1997.

Korbonski, S., *The Polish Underground State*, East European Quarterly, Boulder, New York, 1978.

Korbonski, S., *The Jews and the Poles in World War II*, Hippocrene, 1989.

Korbonski, S., *Fighting Warsaw*, Hippocrene, 2004.

The Polish Underground 1939–1947

Krakówski, S., *The War of the Doomed*, Holmes and Meier, 1984.

Latawski, P., 'The Armia Krajowa and Polish Partisan Warfare, 1939–43', in *War in a Twilight World*, ed. Shepherd, B. and Pattinson, J., Palgrave, 2010, pp. 137–55.

Levine, A., *Fugitives of the Forest*, Stoddart, 1998.

Lucas, R., *Forgotten Holocaust*, Hippocrene, 1990.

Madajczyk, C., *Die Okupationspolitik Nazideutschlands in Polen*, Pahl-Rugenstein, 1988.

Masson, M., *Christine: SOE Agent and Churchill's Favourite Spy*, Hamish Hamilton, 1975.

Ney-Krwawicz, M., *The Polish Home Army*, PUMST (1939–1945), London, 1993.

Nowak, J., *Courier from Warsaw*, Collins/Harvill, 1982.

Nowak, J., *Story of a Secret State: My Report to the World*, Penguin, 2011.

Peleg-Marianski, M., and Peleg, M., *Witness, Life in Occupied Krakow*, Routledge, 1991.

Praźmowska, A.J., *Civil War in Poland*, Palgrave, 2004.

Rosenbaum, F., and Pell, J., *Taking Risks: A Jewish Youth in the Soviet Partisans and his Unlikely Life in California*, RDR Books, 2004.

Rowinski, L., *That the Nightingale Return*, McFarland and Co., 1999.

Smorczewski, R., *Bridging the Gap*, Matador, 2007

Sword, K., *Deportation and Exile*, St Martin's Press, 1994.

Szawłowski, Ryszard, 'The Polish–Soviet Wars of 1939', in *The Soviet Takeover of the Polish Eastern Provinces*, ed. Sword, K., pp. 18–43, Macmillan and School of Slavonic and Eastern European Studies, 1991.

Walker, J., *Poland Alone*, History Press, 2008.

Wilkinson, P., *Foreign Fields: The Story of an SOE Operative*, I.B. Taurus, 1997.

Wilkinson, P. and Astley, J., *Gubbins and SOE*, Leo Cooper, 1993.

Williamson, D., *Poland Betrayed*, Pen and Sword, 2009.

Zaloga, S., *The Polish Army, 1939–45*, Osprey, 1982.

Zaloga, S., *V-2 Ballistic Missiles, 1945–52*, Osprey, 2003.

Index

The Polish Underground 1939–1947

Index

Index